Chronicles of ***The Farm Woman***

Chronicles of
The Farm Woman
The Story of Mary Frances McKinney

by

Jean McKay

&

as shared by Kathleen Whitmer

Library of Congress
Control Number: 2007932630

ISBN 978-0-9798068-1-0

First Printing October 2007

Additional copies of this book are available by mail.
Send $20.00 each (includes tax and postage) to:
Whitmer Ranch
12174 SW 90th Avenue
Zenda KS 67159

Printed in the U.S.A. by
Morris Publishing
3212 East Highway 30
Kearney, NE 68847

For the McKinney's
Mac & Mary
and their children
and the grandchildren
And the great-grandchildren and those that come after.

Foreword

What an adventure it has been to try to tell a little of the story of my mother, Mary Frances Evans McKinney.

Mother was born to Tom and Kate Blair Evans, July 29, 1901, at the farm 4 miles northwest of Hartford, Kansas. Dr. Neinstead was the attending physician.

There were many defining moments in mothers life. Early on, in 1907, her brother, John Blair Evans, died of pneumonia. At the age of 12, she spent a year in Montana with her aunt Alice and uncle Ned Snyder. When she was 16, her mother died.

In 1919 she attended the University of Kansas after graduating from Hartford High School. At KU she met a handsome World War I veteran, James Clifford "Mac" McKinney, who would become her love and life partner.

Before graduation from KU, she stopped school for 1 year. She taught at Princeton, KS High School. During that school year, she married "Mac" on March 31, 1923 in Kansas City, Kansas. Their attendants were Pearl and Ike McConnell.

After graduation from KU, they lived in Excelsior Springs, Mo, and Kansas City, Kansas where Mac was a pharmacist. Their son, James Thomas, was born January 12, 1925.

From Kansas City, they moved to Courtland, Kansas, where my father bought a drug store. They left Courtland in 1931 because of the depression.

While they lived in Courtland, I was born, Mary Kathleen on December 14, 1928 and on September 24, 1930 our younger sister, Esther Alice was born. Great friend, Dr. McComas, was their physician.

After moving to the farm in Hartford, mother and dad became active in Extension, conservation, church, school and politics. They were a moving force for good in the community.

Mother's writing career started after she wrote a wail to the Emporia Gazette. William Allen White became a close friend and mentor. He asked her to write about what she knew, and so *The Farm Woman* column was born.

Over the years she typed out many words, on the old Underwood typewriter, in her hunt and peck style. Later, Mother would pound out seven copies of her family letters for children and select friends.

We have memories of her pride in being a KU Alumnus, being a friend and campaigner for Alf Landon, for attending an Associated Country Women of the World Conference, and for being state Republican Vice Chairman.

Most of all, we remember a mother who helped us do the best that we could. A mother who loved us and wrote to us and called us regularly. A grandmother proud of her grandchildren. She was a good woman, content at the end of her life. I have tried to be accurate, but any errors in names, dates, or places are solely mine.

It is with gratitude that I thank Jean McKay for helping me make this book a reality, and more than I dreamed it would be.

Kathleen Whitmer

From the Author

Kathleen and I met at a soap demonstration. You see, I make soap. Sounds kind of like something my great grandmother or even Mary would do, but no, I kid you not, I make soap. Maybe it is my desire to bring back the good ol' days or at least relive them, or maybe capture their essence.

We struck up a friendship and when my first book, *Tillie's Bridge* was published, she wanted to read it. After reading it she contacted me and asked if I would be interested in writing a book about her mother, Mary Frances McKinney. When I read some of *The Farm Woman* articles, I was enamored with the scope and depth of her life on the farm and knew it would be historically worthwhile to have her story published.

It did, however, become exceedingly difficult to whittle away any of the many articles she did over the nearly 30 years of writing. Everything she wrote was extremely pleasant to read, so therein was the difficulty. Since I did not grow up on a farm, I was totally intrigued by everyday country life and the hardships of farm life as well as the joys of living on the land. And, though I do not consider myself particularly interested in politics, I found myself engrossed with her articles about political affairs, mainly because of their historical significance. I was intrigued by her total dedication to so many different concerns. It became apparent to me that the articles that touched my heart would be the those that were kept.

Historically she wrote about the times, that which has changed so drastically. Her life had more significance because she had lived it and written about it, a poignant record of a time past. Her family was all the better for her involvement in that which was going on outside of the home, as well as that which was going on in the home. Women need that perfect balance of kindling the home fires and getting fired up about that which makes the world revolve. It made her all the more interesting, more powerful. She made her children's lives more fascinating, as well.

She was a truly special individual, with so much to offer then, and now. It would have been wonderful to know her, learn from her, and talk to her, but I do feel I have met her. I truly enjoyed the experience. Her articles have stood the test of time, a slice of American History filled with inspiration and joy, witness to her steadfast character, and filled with joy of family. We should all be able to leave behind a precious slice of our lives, just as she has.

We make a life by what we give, and she gave so very much. This is the story of her life, "the life" as she called it.

Table of Content

Illustrations

The Farm Woman

It all started on the fertile banks of the Neosho River in Hartford, Kansas in Lyon County. The land with its rolling hills and grasslands galore, the perfect backdrop for any landscape. The year was 1932.

A young farm wife and mother wrote a letter to the publisher and editor of the *Emporia Gazette.* The article appeared in the Wailing Place. So enamored with her writing, this editor asked her to contribute a column for the paper twice a week. Thus began her journey into the homes of her readers, educating and inspiring the farm families for more than thirty years, with chronicles about life in general, politics and the responsibilities of the farmers and their families.

The editor, publisher and owner of the *Emporia Gazette* was one of the greatest journalists of all time.

William Allen White was known far and wide as the *"Sage of Emporia"*, whose straightforward coverage of controversial issues, combined with often blunt writing style, set him apart from other journalists of his time. He attained national prominence for his writings, interest in politics and dedication to the Emporia Community. Always wanting the best for his community.

He later won the Pulitzer Prize, posthumously, for his autobiography.

But, it was her writing that distinguished her from the ordinary and he saw that, in her, with just one article. She was bright and quick and he could tell she had something to give the readers. Their relationship was a long and endearing one.

Her name was Mary Frances McKinney and she wrote very simply, from her heart, as *The Farm Woman.* It took her beyond the places she expected, but she was in every respect fully at ease with her surroundings. She had a gift and was willing to share it with her neighbors, her friends, her family and anyone who needed it. It was her legacy, her endowment.

Chapter 1

The "Sage of Emporia"

William Allen White was a Pulitzer-prize winning writer, best-selling novelist, and prolific free-lancer who built the *Emporia Gazette* into one of the nation's finest small-town newspapers from 1895 until his death in 1944. He was first and foremost a great liberal who wanted great things for his fellow citizens, and dedicated himself to the people of Emporia and Kansas.

From his articles of political philosophy, he shaped much of the thinking of his readers, working from his littered and battered desk, he became a vital force in Kansas. He influenced great national decisions and taught people to believe in beauty and integrity. His most famous editorial *"What's the Matter With Kansas?"* was written in 1896, a year after he purchased the *Emporia Gazette* for $3,000. The editorial was picked up and reprinted by a Republican Paper in Chicago, then in New

York papers and was later reprinted by thousands of papers distributed nationwide. White catapulted to national prominence as newspaper syndicates sought his comments and *The Saturday Evening Post, Collier's,* and other national publications printed his articles. A poignantly tender editorial, written in 1921 after the accidental death of his daughter, Mary, became a classic.

Men and women read his editorials with great interest, fueling much of Kansan's political interests. From a national perspective, White influenced politics and public opinion. The lasting effect for White was that he established national contacts which kept him in intimate touch with political leaders and affairs. He became an advisor to Presidents and Congressmen, and he visited the White House often. His greatest asset was his ability to express himself in a distinctively clear, blunt and witty writing style with profound wisdom, with biting sarcasm or with gentle tenderness. By remaining in his small town, when his generation was flocking to the city, he eventually became the spokesman, for not just Kansas but, for much of the middle west. He gained great prominence in editorial history, so much so, they called him the "Sage of Emporia."

William Allen White shaped his newspaper into a respectable daily paper. His early years had been spent reading furiously, and he wrote with a passion until his death. He had been born in Emporia, grew up in neighboring El Dorado and loved the simplicity of his upbringing; gathering sand plums, swimming in the Walnut River, swinging on his trapeze bar, a gentle and endearing time. His youth shaped him and made him, however, he never did "spin yarns" of the older days, he was too busy with things that were happening on a daily basis, so much so that he never did finish his autobiography. His son, William Lindsay, edited and published his unfinished autobiography in 1946, for which he received a Pulitzer Prize, posthumously.

The character of the paper developed under the policies of its owner and editor very early. His first editorial stated he had no desire ever to leave Emporia, for more than just a visit. In that editorial he stated "the new editor hopes to live here until he is the old editor, until some of the visions which rise before him as dreams shall have come true. He hopes always to sign 'from Emporia' after his name, when he is abroad, and he trusts that he may so endear himself to the people, that they will be as proud of the first words of the signature as he is of the last words."

In 1903, he wrote an editorial entitled, *A Newspaper's Duty,* so that the town might know what to expect of the *Gazette.*

"The only excuse an editor has for being is that his paper shall print the news," the editorial read. "The question that comes to every man running a newspaper is: What is news? That, he must settle for himself, and having found a rule, must stick as closely to it as possible.

When an editor begins monkeying with his conscience, stretching his rule to shield his friends or to punish his enemies, he is lost. He becomes wobbly and has no anchor and no direction.

Every day matters come up in every community, big or little, that are disagreeable to print. Nasty stories are always afloat. Gossip is always in the air. An editor in a town of one hundred people could fill a six-column daily every night with gossip alone, if he could keep from being lynched. Much of it would be false and all of it would be unfair. And yet often these matters come up in such a shape that they may not be ignored. And, here is where an editor has to set his jaw and go ahead, following his conscience without fear of favor. Such times come to every attorney, to every doctor, to every preacher, to every man in every relation of life. It is a safe rule to follow, that gossip may be ignored, no matter how loudly it buzzes, till it becomes a matter of court record. Then it may not be left out of the paper. If a man has a grievance against his fellow man that he or she is too cowardly to air in public court, it is safe to say that there are two sides to the question and the editor who prints the story prints it at his own peril. But on the other hand, when a man takes his grievance into court, when he spreads it upon the record and gives his opponent a chance to answer in an open, public manner, then the quarrel, no matter whom it involves, is a matter than no editor can overlook. And, after a case gets into court, a newspaper should let the courts try it, printing the claims of each side, not trying to convict or acquit either of the parties.

That, it seems to the Gazette, is the fair way to treat unsavory matters. No honest editor cares to have scandal and improper stories in his paper, and no one should print such stores in such a away that they may not be read aloud in the family circle. It is the way news is handled that counts for or against decency. A vile story may be handled with care the readers be no worse for seeing it."

This principle and another general rule was adopted in the case of divorce and was adhered to religiously. "A divorce means the breaking up of a home and is a sad affair, no matter how just it might be," Mr. White advocated. "Divorce doesn't affect only the man and the woman, but often there are children - innocent victims - and it means the breaking up of a home. Frequently a divorce suit is filed and later dismissed and a happy home is maintained. And so the Gazette prints only the news of divorces being granted, but it always is a short statement of facts. The only reason," explained Mr. White, "is because a divorce changes the legal status of two persons and the public has a right to know."

He had other rules, not common in most newspaper offices, which were more or less flexible but at the same time hold to a pattern and often made decisions border on the hairline. Generally a person not of legal age, or under twenty-one, is protected when he gets into trouble. Mr. White explained that "a juvenile can make a lot of mistakes and still settle down and become a good citizen. But if he is branded publicly, his chances of reforming are hampered by the attitude of the people toward him." Driving under the influence of alcohol, on the other hand, got the works, as far as publicity is concerned. Mr. White felt it was "his duty to inform the general public in order to make the streets a safer place." His readership deserved protection.

Only once did he seek public office. That was in 1924 when, in the midst of a bitter fight against the Ku Klux Klan, which he branded as un-American and cowardly, he ran independently for governor of Kansas.

He wrote crusading editorials attacking the Klan, at a time when it enjoyed the open support of many powerful Americans. While he finished third in the race, the Klan soon died out in Kansas, and he felt he had won his objective.

Ever eager to hire a reporter with a fresh view, or the new kid, fresh out of college, Mr. White hired many reporters for the *Gazette*. Some offered to work for any kind of wage, just to get started, so many so, that some editors had dubbed the paper "The Gazette School of Journalism."

Around the *Gazette* he was affectionately called "The Boss." He, in return, referred to his employees as "The *Gazette* Family." Both Mr. & Mrs. White loved children and celebrated the birth of new babies and held annual Christmas parties and picnics. Much of the success of the paper came from their intimate desire to include this family in their interests.

A young farm wife and mother, Mary Frances McKinney had written an article to the publisher and editor of the *Emporia Gazette* in late 1932. The article appeared in the Wailing Place. So enamored with her writing, Mr. White asked her to contribute a column for the paper twice a week. Thus began her journey into the homes of the *Gazette* readers, educating and inspiring the farm families for nearly thirty years, with chronicles about life in general, politics and the responsibilities of the farmers and their families.

No greater thrill will ever come. My first contribution to the Gazette copied by Justus Timberline in Christian Advocate. He is one of my favorite columnists. MFM

This appeared in the Gazette 9-30-32

"And Thy Neighbor---------

Some of you who glance at my stuff Now and then may think I'm a simple old coot, with hayseed and sandburs stuck all over me.

Well, maybe I am. But the country I know best has more in it than sandburs and jimson weed. There's a sort of instinct for the things that James once described, and Micah before him, as having a lot to do with real religion.

For instance. I've just read a piece in my old friend Will White's Emporia Gazette, by a woman who was chatting a little about the old party-line telephone in the country.

When a small child, I remember hearing a shout in the night. The other details of the episode were told me by my mother.

"Hello," said the voice.

"Hello," my father called.

"I want to use your telephone."

"Walk right in and help yourself," said my father.

The man was heard to enter, ring and soon mount his horse and gallop away.

Before long the telephone rang - our ring!

My mother answered. --------------?

"Hello, Dr. Hughes speaking. Who called me from your house?"

"Why, I don't know, doctor," was mother's reply.

"You don't know? Didn't someone call from there?"

"Yes, but we didn't get up.

"What? Do you permit a stranger to enter your house at night without knowing who it is?"

"No," mother replied, "not strangers -- neighbors."

There you have it. The latch string out, the telephone for anybody's use - quite as a matter of course.

Country people know more of the answer to the lawyer's question, "And who is my neighbor?" than most other people dare to learn.

Chapter 2

Don't ever be afraid to drive!

She was a homemaker and mother, who made bread, canned or froze for later. She rendered lard, gave vitamins, pressed Alfalfa and dispersed Cod Liver Oil to her children. It was customary that, if you were a visitor in her kitchen, you had to help.

She loved to sing but never played an instrument. Her daughters, Kathleen and Esther, took piano lessons. Aunt Hannah paid for these piano lessons. She wanted the girls to play hymns on her pump organ. So, the girls would take the 'doodle bug'[1] to Emporia, 15 miles away, for 11 cents, and then walk the 12 blocks to their Aunt's house were they would play hymns on the pump organ for both Aunt Alice and Aunt Hannah.

When they moved to the farm in 1931, the county home demonstration agent found out that they were

[1] The Doodle Bug was a small local train. It discontinued service in the early 1940's.

going to butcher a steer and some hogs, so they opened their farm up to anyone. Good methods of caring, cutting, curing, rendering and canning were shown to the people who would be interested.

She always stayed close to the women of the community and was especially close with each Cooperative Extension Agent, and was very active in 4-H demonstrations.

As an educated woman & homemaker, wife, mother, and neighbor, it was ingrained in her to be of service to everyone in a way that became second nature to her. She delighted in her homemaking skills and wanted to help her neighbors become better people by teaching them about `the life' and, trusting her nature to `give back,' she wanted more for them. Her writing was another way to teach, it was something she became very comfortable with.

The family was a loyal Kansas University family. Her mother had graduated from KU, received her teaching degree and became a High School Principal. Education was taught to her first by her mother who also worked for Women's Suffrage. Mary attended KU and graduated in 1924 with a Home Economics Degree.

Teaching came naturally to her. She was thankful for her education and was proud of her educated parents, as well. It was from her parents that she had gained the importance of a higher education.

Mary's mother, Kate Blair, had graduated from KU in the spring of 1893. She began teaching at Effingham High School in Lawrence, Kansas that fall. After 5 years she moved to Horton, Kansas for one year. She was engaged in 1898. Her fiancé was teaching in Hartford, Kansas. He was leaving Hartford and got Kate the job at Hartford. When she arrived she discovered that her fiancé had had an affair. The following year Tom Evans took Kate and his niece, Maude Evans, to the first American Royal[2].

It wasn't long after, that Tom and Kate were married in the home of her mother Amanda Blair, in Horton on October 10, 1990. There was an Evans family ruckus. Old bachelor brother Tom, 45 years old, was marrying a college graduate! Only one member of the Evans family had completed high school. Brother Tom wouldn't be living with and taking care of his mother and spinster sisters.

The farm was located 4 miles northwest of Hartford, KS. It had a little three-room house on it, so Kate and Tom added to the house, building on, outward and upward. Tom had not lived on a farm before his marriage.

It was at this farm that Mary Frances Evans was

---

[2] The American Royal began in a tent in 1899 in the Kansas City Stockyards as a national Hereford (cattle) Show. The American Royal remains an annual event of agricultural activities benefiting youth and education.

born on July 29, 1901. Two years later her brother John Blair Evans was born October 14, 1903. Unfortunately, before he reached the age of 4 little John died on April 22, 1907, with pneumonia. Little John's funeral was held in the living room at the farm. He was in a little white casket. Mary Frances was bothered because her little brother had no shoes on in the casket. The family found out later that the aunts, in Emporia, whispered, `that a college graduate didn't know how to care for children and that John died because Kate did not give him proper care'.

Kate Blair Evans & daughter Mary, 1901

Mary Evans, Hartford KS, 14 months, 1902

Kate Blair Evans with children, Mary, 3 years & John Blair, 10 months.

The Fairview school was located across the road from the farm and it was here that Mary Frances started school in 1907. Eunice Meyers was her teacher.

When she graduated in 1913, Kate took Mary to Mrs. Lucy Diamond's home in Leavenworth. Mrs. Diamond had two daughters in Montana and was going out to live with them. Mary's health needed improving so she went with Mrs. Diamond to Montana. Mary lived with Uncle Ned and Aunt Alice Evans Snyder and Aunt Alice brought Mary home at Christmas. Mary had gained weight in Montana and `has been fair ever since' (Mary's own words).

Mary Evans in Montana July 28, 1913

She was taught to drive when she was 13. Her father did not drive, so the car dealership taught young Mary to drive the family car. She later taught her own children `don't ever be afraid to drive,' she rejoiced.

In 1914 she entered Hartford High School. She had missed one year of school. Mamie Moorehead lived in the first house south of the farm so Mary walked to the Moorehead's and Mamie drove the buggy in to school. Later she used the M-K-T[2] train to go back and forth to Hartford.

Mary Evans 1913

[2] The Missouri-Kansas-Texas Railroad known to many as the Katy

After she graduated from Hartford High School, June 3rd,1918, she went to Lawrence and Kansas University with her mother for Kate's 25th commencement anniversary. Kate became terribly ill shortly after their return on June 10th. And later, on June 17th, Kate died. Kate's funeral was in the living room at 406 State Street in Emporia. Ed Rice preached and Ed Lewis sang. Kate was 50 years old.

The following description of Kate's illness and death is from a family letter written by Mary Frances on June 10, 1966.

`Incidentally, it is 48 years ago today that mother became ill. We had been to KU the week before to celebrate her 25th reunion. She rose early on Monday morning to get the wash boiler on to heat. Before she got the washing started she came into the bedroom that is now the den and lay down. She told me that I would have to empty the boiler, that she was too sick to start the washing. The doctor came out. He came again that night and said she would have to go to the hospital. They did an emergency operation in the early morning hours and found a gallstone, the size of a small hen's egg, had ruptured the gall bladder and peritonitis had set in. She died at 6:30am on the 17th and my world fell in. Even then, though I could not wish her back, for she had worked so hard, suffered so much and had not been accepted by the Evans family. I knew she had gone to a golden strand where earthly cares could be left behind. I still feel that way.'

In the fall of 1918 Mary started at KU. Kate's sister Mamie came to the farm to keep house for Tom. Rose Morgan, Alberta Corbin and Mrs. Corman O'Leary, friends of Kate's, took care of Mary that first year. There were 2,000 to 3,000 students at KU at that time. Mary lived at 1124 Mississippi.

The following year Mary was not able to continue at KU because Aunt Mamie did not want to stay on the farm another year. Mary Frances stayed home to keep house for her father. By 1919 she was able to return to school while Tom went back to Emporia to live with his sisters and tenants lived in the farmhouse. Mary lived at 1126 Kentucky with Mrs. Tucker. Mrs. Tucker had been a student of Kate's at Effingham.

Mary went to Richmond, Kansas to teach. There had been a panic (depression) in 1920, stockmen lost money and times were hard. Tom Evans was too poor to afford school for Mary Frances.

In 1921 J.C. `Mac' McKinney went to KU. He lived at 1120 Ohio and ate at a boarding club. Boarding clubs had dances on Saturday nights. Mac and Mary met at one of these "hour dances[1]" and then went on a "line party" to a show after the dance in the fall. Mac would come down on the train on weekends to visit with Mary in Richmond.

---

[1] Hour dances were done in individuals homes where someone would have a dance in the living room for one hour. Line parties were similar in that the dancers would go to another house for another hour.

While teaching in Richmond, Kansas, `Mac' McKinney and Mary were married. He took the train, from school at KU, to get her and Mary's principal, Ira McConnell and his wife Pearl. They all took the train to Kansas City. They were married in the living room of a pastor's home. They spent the night in KC and returned to their own places the next day. The date was March 31, 1923.

Her father had objected to their marriage and sent her a letter begging her not to marry.

KU graduation pictures of J.C. & Mary 1923

Tom Evans 1909

Evans Farmstead early 1900's

Amanda Meeker Blair, Kate Blair Evans
And Mary Frances Evans
1901

Back standing: Margaret Evans, Alice Evans Snyder, Tom Evans, M. & M. Howard Lyons & Child, John Evans
Seated: Hannah Evans, Mrs. Mary Evans, Mary Evans McKinney

Tom Evans & some of his Hereford cattle, early 1900's

Chapter 3

Ordinary people who exercised their extraordinary gifts.

When Mac and Mary returned to Richmond they had a call from Emporia about Tom Evan's having an appendectomy. Since they were married, any schooling they wanted was now not going to be paid for by Tom Evans. They were on their own.

Mac was training for a Pharmaceutical License at KU, so to make a living he worked at R. S. Parker Pharmacy at 10th and Ohio in Kansas City and they lived at 726 Orville in Kansas City, KS for the summer. In the fall they both enrolled at KU and lived at 1332 Tennessee. Of course, her father did not pay any of Mary's expenses.

Mary graduated in 1924 and Mac completed work

for his certificate as Pharmaceutical Chemist. KU never gave Mac the certificate, because he did not have a high school diploma. He had run away to join the army and the war effort when he was 16 and never completed high school. He did, however, pass the necessary tests and was a Kansas registered pharmacist without the certificate from KU. They moved to Kansas City, KS and lived at 1504 Central where Mac worked at OK Leaverage Drug Store at 18th and Minnesota. In the fall Mac went to work in Excelsior Springs and Mary remained in Kansas City awaiting the birth of their first baby.

By 1925 their son James 'Jim' Thomas was born, on January 12th, and they moved to 405 Old Orchard in Excelsior Springs for 8 months then it was back to Kansas City where Mac worked for West Heights Pharmacy.

A year later they moved to the Swedish community of Courtland Kansas were Mac had purchased his own pharmacy. It was here that Mary Kathleen was born, on the kitchen table, December 12th, 1928. And, nearly two years later, Esther Alice was born in the 24th of September, 1930. When the Depression hit in 1931, Mac, swallowed his pride and moved his family from Courtland to the farmhouse 4 miles northwest of Hartford, where Mary had grown up. Later, Mary's father passed away and left the farm to Mary's children, even though he had learned to respect Mac, he didn't want him to get the farm. Old grudges are hard to break.

Mac was 6'2" & weighed 300 pounds, or more. He was big and gruff, but loved his children and they loved him. He was their big `teddy bear', taking care of them when they were hurt or sick. He wore an insignia of two crossed rifles on his wrist. He was proud to have served in the Army of the United States even though he was wounded in the War. He had been 'gassed'[1] and had to go in once a year for checkups at the VA hospital.

He was now wearing the uniform of the farmer, khaki trousers and cotton shirts. It wasn't long before he became a Master Farmer and conservationist and raised Hereford cattle, coveted for their bloodlines. He farmed 260 acres with pastures and a gravel pit for construction of Highway 50, which became a major East-West artery in Kansas. He kept up his pharmacist license even when he was not using it anymore.

Mary was a woman of faith. Her mother had taught her that a relationship with God was a joy. She attended the Methodist Church. Mac didn't go to church, but he always saw to it that his family got to church, no matter the weather or road conditions.

Even though Mary wore a housedress and an apron and was in the kitchen cooking a lot, she found the time to write her articles. She was a good cook and nutrition was important to her. She was also a wonderful baker. At 5'5" she was `pleasingly plump', as a neighbor boy described her. She was not into fancy clothes or jewelry. She loved to sew clothes and made shirts for

---

[1] Mustard Gas as used during World War I affected particularly the skin and mucous membranes of the upper respiratory system putting veterans at risk of frequent complications.

Mac, 6 at a time. She also made Kathleen & Esther beautiful white wool coats for Easter. The girls were well dressed with many outfits their mother sewed for them. In fact, she made most of their clothes until they were out of college. It was during this time that Mary was beginning to write many articles. She hired a neighbor girl for 50 cents a day to help her clean and take care of the children.

Mac and Mary were avid readers. Mac always got up at 5 am and read till light, then went out to do his farm chores. They subscribed to at least 4 newspapers; *The Kansas City Star, Topeka Capitol, Emporia Gazette and Hartford Times Weekly* and 5 or 6 magazines; *Liberty, Collier's, Ladies Home Journal, Life, American Legion Magazine and Saturday Evening Post.*

They became leaders of the community. People came to them for help and counsel. People who needed help came to them because they knew where to send them or who to call to get help. They didn't have money but they did have knowledge. "Ordinary people who exercised their extraordinary gifts".

Once William Allen White recognized her talents as a writer she began to write with fervor. It was clear, to all who read her articles, and Mr. White, that she had a talent not to be wasted.

In 1933 her first letter to the Gazette was $3.00 a column of print. Her children were 9, 5 and 3 when she first started writing. The checklist when the family got in the car to go to Emporia was: Did mother have her teeth, purse and "string"? Her string was her columns cut out and pasted together.

In early 1934 Mary received the following letter from the Department of Home Economics at the University of Kansas. It was from her Home Economics teacher. She wrote:

March 21, 1934

Dear Mary:

In looking over a list of our graduates recently we were quite thrilled to see how many of you have married and are using your training in making homes of your own.

More and more we realize and stress the importance of a successful family life and it seemed to us it would be a wonderful thing and most interesting if we could compile a sort of history of Home Economics graduates who have established their own successful homes. It might be called our "Album of Families"! Won't you please contribute your part?

We should like to have:

1. *A photo of your family group at its best.*
2. *Your name and year of graduation*
3. *Your husbands name and year of graduation (or attendance at school or college), business or profession.*
4. *A picture of your home - especially if owned.*
5. *What are the chief interests of the members of the family?*
   - A. *Personal*
   - B. *Public*

6. *Most important problems in home management which you have experienced?*
7. *In what ways has your college training helped in the organization and administration of your home?*
8. *What has been the most important influence in your success?*

9. & 10. *Any other points which may seem of importance to you.*

We realize that the last years have not been normal for anyone but we trust that they have not affected your progress seriously. If we can get 100% response to this request it should make a wonderful story.

Sincerely,

Elizabeth C. Sprague

Hard times, I know
But there is still the
Family!

was scrawled at the bottom of the letter.

Mary wrote the following letter in December of the same year.

Hartford - December 12

Dear Miss Sprague,

May this letter bear greetings of the season as warm as the gayest card you will receive.

Methinks many of your students are probably as ungrateful as I because we do not tell you how your influence grows with the years. Surely there isn't a day passes that home economics girls do not use their training and breathe a prayer of thanks that they have it.

It is hard enough for any of us in these times but I don't know how we would ever get by without the information we have.

I have been rather active in Farm Bureau the past year. We have a splendid Home Demonstration Agent - a Minnesota girl. Our slogan is `a live at home program for the farm family'. On our Advisory Council of ten women we have two OW. Isn't it a bit unusual?

One of our most interesting projects has been conducting low cost meal schools in our Community. We give printed recipes and samples. It seems to have gone across because the women are using them.

I have intended writing you for some time and tell you how deeply indebted I am to you. When you suggested to me two years ago, that I try to write, I thought I could not. But, I kept the idea in mind and one day I sent in a little contribution to William Allen White. It made the Wailing Place. I sent in something else and it appeared on the editorial page. One day he asked me to come in. For a year now I have sent in two contributions each week under the title of The Plain Farm Woman on the Neosho. The remuneration is small (five or ten dollars a month) but the experience is wonderful. Mr. White is so kind and gives me some of his valuable time each month. I think it is an opportunity that comes to few and it is all due to you. I thank you so much.

May you have a very joyous holiday.

Affectionately,

Mary Frances McKinney

The following articles were among her earliest works, some post-scripted by William Allen White (WAW) before his death in 1944. Her articles centered around farm life, sometimes bleak and always with hope, artfully done reminders of the good and healing life in the country. She wrote about family, with compelling candor, telling it in a way that made everyone proud to be and pleased that she omitted names. And, as a staunch Republican, with a well meaning heart, she wrote about local and national politics. Ever the politicians settler of scores.

She outgrew her first name given to her by Mr. White, *The Plain Farm Woman,* nothing plain about this 'smart' farm woman. Little history lessons included throughout her articles, as times were different, occasionally simpler and sometimes much more complex.

THE FARMERS WIFE REVIEW

A smart farm woman in Lyon County sends The Gazette a brief chronology of the year as it affects the farm woman. It is worth reading:

The year is drawing to its close. Radio crooners, news announcers et al are busy reviewing the high spots of the year. No one will review the farmer's chart. It doesn't seem to be very important, but has been most interesting in 1933.

With the birth of 1933 there was a hush of expectancy in the air. We had voted over-whelmingly for a change and Hoover's days were numbered. The first stroke of the administration, the bank holiday, didn't bother us much.

Then came harvest and 80 and 90 cent wheat. Didn't that make us feel good? Of course we didn't see any wheat money but many debts were eased considerably.

Next came the launching of the NRA[1]*. Every business house*

---

[1] The National Recovery Administration attempted to stabilize prices and wages in 1933. The NRA included a multitude of regulations imposing the pricing and production standards for all sorts of goods and services. Some ridiculed it as the "National Run Around." Most economists were dubious because it was based on fixing prices to reduce competition. In the end, the NRA was struck down by the Supreme Court, and never revived in large part because it was a disaster for the economy.

greeted us with a big Blue Eagle[2] *in its window. We were proud that our town was 100 percent NRA. At the grocery, we were told that beans were up $1 a hundred. In the dry goods store overalls jumped from 59 cents to $1.19 overnight.*

Things began to look serious back in Washington and General Johnson made his good-will tour. Several correspondents also visited us about the same time. A week later reports came back that Johnson's trip was a success, farmers were in much better spirits. Do you suppose they really think it was Johnson? Do they forget our wheat checks were on the way about that time and plans for corn loans were being made in Iowa?

The pulse was steadier for several days.

Harry L. Hopkins contracted to buy 60 million pounds of pork at $6 on the hoof. The packers had no sooner tucked that contract in their vest pocket than hogs catapulted from $5 plus to $3.50. Did that make us see red? Temperatures went up several degrees.

Last week egg and cream prices zoomed down again. The pulse is weak, very weak, but as long as there's life, there's hope.

1-1-34

---

[2] For a while, there was no escaping the bird. Towns all over the country got on the Blue Eagle bandwagon. The oath: "I promise as a good American citizen to do my part for the NRA. I will buy only where the Blue Eagle flies."

THE FARM WOMAN
The Freshman Returns

Vacation is over and college students are bound for alma mater. There was just one question on their lips when they arrived home: "Mom, what y' got to eat?" Was a mother thrilled to sit and watch her offspring eat? She had baked for two days for this homecoming..........all his favorite dishes. She was more than repaid.

The next day it was, "What is there to do?" One wise father took said son out hunting the first day. They tramped 10 miles. That held son for two days. Then they went hunting again. Nothing quiets the bubbling over energy of youth like a hard day's work or a 10-mile hike. Of course, we can't ask kids home on vacation to do a hard day's work.

The freshman longs for Thanksgiving vacation to come. He thoroughly enjoys the first trip home - mothers cooking, sleeping early and late, the entire family waiting on him. He is king again as he was when he was six months old. Christmas vacation is looked forward to as eagerly. The first week is all right. The second week the old burg seems dead and everything so commonplace. Because the students no longer fit into the narrow routine of the hometown we are apt to call them stuck-up. No, these children are not stuck-up. Their interests differ from ours.

We were glad to see them home but the house seems peaceful and quiet tonight.

Father knows his slippers will be right by his chair in the living room and not off upstairs in the cold, where daughter put them. It's fine to have young folks around but it's nice to go to bed and sleep too without being disturbed at all hours of the night.

There was a lonesome pang in the heart as parents saw daughter off to school. Mother and father are most as glad to be alone again as daughter is to get back to the dorm. It's the way of the world.

The stage was all set to listen in to the opening of the 74th congress. The meat was in the oven, potatoes were peeled, the pie on the pantry shelf. The ironing board was set up near the loud speaker. Expectantly we tuned in half an hour early. No juice. Some of the service men must have known that we wanted to listen in on Washington. At 10:57 the lights came on.

We were disillusioned somewhat by listening in today. We always thought congressman put on a cloak of dignity and seriousness and became something more than men and women. The reverberations were not far different from our Aid society.

The clerk pounding for order reminded us of the substitute Sunday school teacher of seventh grade boys. "Now boys be quiet and Donald will read our Scripture. All Right Donald. Oh, boys be quiet. Begin Donald. Oh my, we must be still or we can't hear." 1-8-1934

My Most Embarrassing Moment

THE FARM WOMAN

One young mother in the neighborhood isn't bothered as to how she will answer roll call at club. "My most embarrassing moment," she knows. On a fine warm sunshiny day in January she decided to clean and spray the hen house. She took down the jug of old crank case oil and mixed it with other ingredients and sprayed and sprayed. The mixture burned her hands but she was so anxious to get the job done she paid little attention. She was proud of her afternoon's work.

Of course nothing had been done in the house. Dinner dishes remained on the table, the floor was not swept. The children had taken care of themselves all afternoon. She hurried in to straighten up and get supper. As she was washing her hands a car drove in. There was no time to change her dress so she grabbed a clean apron from behind the door. Of all people, it was the preacher and his wife. Smilingly she tried to apologize for the appearance of her house and children. Suddenly she felt her dress split down the front. It was an old dress, she really didn't care about the dress. She tried to pull the gap together and two splits came, one on either

Chronicles of
The Farm Woman
Embarrassing Moment
(Cont.)

side. What to do? Should she say please excuse me until I change my dress or just sit. She sat. The baby cried. She hated to neglect her child but she could not get up. Her features were smiling but her mind was in torment. Why couldn't that floor open up and swallow her? Somehow time passed and the callers departed.

When friend husband came in to supper she related her tale of woe. He looked at the dress. "Why, you must have got hold of the jug of acid in the garage. Did you take the brown jug? No wonder your dress split."

Probably every farm woman at the club meeting can tell of an embarrassing moment when the pastor called.

We well remember the good neighbor who called and said the preacher was calling out this way. We swept the front room, washed the children's faces and changed our dress. It was one of the most pleasant pastoral calls we ever experienced.

No doubt such experiences are as embarrassing to the minister as they are to us. Now if he announced on Sunday "I plan to call west of town the coming week," every homemaker west of town would keep that living room spotless. But I suppose if he didn't get around to call, the disappointment would be more than we could bear.

We shall go on, glad for callers whenever they come and gladder when the front room is swept and our dress is clean.

1-15-1934

IS INDEPENDENCE FREE?

If you want to know what is going on among the people, get the smart wife of an intelligent farmer to set down what is the talk around the table, and the dining room stove.

Here is a letter that came to the Gazette this week that is most illuminating.

The Smart Farm Woman writes:

We were much interested in your editorial on the Neosho River. "What About Lyon County?" The Lord help us down here below the junction when the next flood comes.

A remark of one of the Lyon county committee seems significant to me. At a meeting which he attended in Iola all the men present were gray haired. The majority of the men on the Lyon county committee are gray haired - if they have any hair! They have grown up with this country and fought inch by inch for every advantage we enjoy today. Theirs is the wisdom of age and experience. Let them head our committee, yes. But let us of the younger generation stand behind them. This is really just one more battle they are fighting for us.

Table talk turned to independence. That word which sends a thrill through every true American. The denial of which will make the same American fight quicker than anything else.

"Do you want to be really independent?" I was asked.

"Of course I do. Doesn't every American cherish independence above almost anything else?"

"Then it is fortunate that you are in the country because you could practically build a fence around you and live. You could dress in skins, live in a sod shanty and raise enough food to supply your needs."

"Is that what independence means? Do I have to give up my easy chair, electricity, radio, telephone, car, mail and all these so-called comforts of civilization? Is this depression making me independent?"

"Our pioneer forbears were about as independent as you could imagine, but they obtained comforts and conveniences for their homes as soon as it was possible."

"Then I do not want to be free and independent. Why, I would raise 500 additional chickens this next year if I could have a water system."

"There you are. You want to enter world trade. But to do that you must be dependent upon someone."

"Who started this talk about freedom anyhow? Please pass the gravy."

1-16-1934

Butchering Week

THE PLAIN FARM WOMAN

That smart farm wife down on the Neosho writes to The Gazette complaining about the word "smart". She doesn't like it. So hereafter when she writes to this paper she will be known as "The Plain Farm Woman" which doesn't refer to her looks. After complaining about the word "smart" she continues:

The past week has been butchering week on the farm. Farmers had been waiting for a right sharp cold spell. Mouths have been watering for backbone, parsnips and potatoes all cooked in the same kettle. Did you ever taste backbone? Folks in town must take theirs with pork chops. On the farm we have long strips of tenderloin and backbone, Roast tenderloin is fit for a king.

Butchering is one of the high spots on the farm calendar. The scalding barrel is set in place. Father is up before day to get the fire going under the kettle in which the water is heated, knives are sharpened on the grindstone, all is hustle and bustle.

No butchering would be complete if the neighbors didn't gather in. Hams and shoulders to put in cure, hearts, tongues and some trimmings in pickle, sausage to grind, lard to cut and render, head cheese, scrapple, souse, liverwurst - all the products of the lowly hog. In the good old days the family soon grew tired of fresh meat because so much had to be eaten immediately, lest it would spoil. Not so now. From the Farm Bureau Meat Utilization program we have learned to can meat and meat products and now all these good things can be enjoyed throughout the year.

1-22-34

Chronicles of
The Farm Woman

THE ALMA MAMMY

The Plain Farm Woman Down on the Neosho, whose comments on local rural life are so illuminating, put on her best bib and tucker and put her hat over one eye and trekked out to commencement last week, and this is her reaction:

We trekked back to commencement last week. Whether the college be large or small nothing is quite so thrilling as commencement at one's own alma mater.

Two vistas are dearer to me than any I have yet seen. One is the view from the highest knob in the far pasture - rolling Kansas prairie. The other, the first glimpse we get of alma mater against the horizon, red roofs, brick chimneys, the tower.

Can it be that any of these 1-eyed creatures were girls we were in school with? We thought as we gazed at the crowd out of our one eye. If any of them chanced to remove their chapeaux we recognized them immediately and decided they had not changed much after all.

Ten years ago we were in the procession and knew exactly what we wanted and how we were going to set about getting it. I was anxious to get back and see if the depression had affected the students as it has us. The trip was very profitable. I have come home with the assurance that the co-eds of today are as carefree, as confident as we were but they are not expecting to step into a $2,000 position. The tender glances betwixt man and maid are just the same as they were 10 years ago.

Somewhere in the throng of graduates from our Kansas colleges this spring may arise one to teach us how to live in the midst of plenty. And, teach us how to do in six hours what it now is done in 12.

6-14-34

Country Kids in Town

The Plain Farm Woman, down on the Neosho, brought her children to town last week. And this is her story of it:

Our school went to Emporia on a tour Friday. I should say about 300 children with parents and teachers gathered at the courthouse. Thence we proceeded to The Gazette office, the Riverside greenhouse, Soden's (Flour) Mill and Poehler Mercantile plant.

Only one child in the group preferred The Gazette - that child was mine! Do you suppose it could be he felt more of an interest in it because his mother is "the Plain Farm Woman on the Neosho?" As a parent I learned more there than at the other stops because I knew nothing about composing and printing a paper. I had visited greenhouses and in my school days we were conducted through a mill and wholesale house. All stops were interesting.

What a splendid thing these tours have been for country children. They are not going to be as green and un-sophisticated as we were when we entered high school. I am sure I voice the sentiment of all parents when I say our thanks to Dr. Munger, Miss Henery and Miss Williams and all the firms cooperating with them. We should like to visit you all again.

As we entered The Gazette office Friday I was impressed with the front

Country Kids in Town (cont.)

entrance and the entrance to the second floor offices. 'W. A White 1900' in a charming, homey, old fashioned way.

Next to it the ultra modern lettering of the Gazette building - swanky, everything up to the minute.

I must be a bit behind the times because I prefer the south entrance. On through the building - rather a clutter everywhere. This modern swank does not allow for cluttering. And in the composing room are roller towels! How many children of this generation have ever seen a roller towel on the back of the bathroom door? You do find them in the country occasionally.

However, when the children need a tonsillectomy, their teeth filled; or something, we shan't hesitate to use the north entrance.

2-21-34

The Plain Farm Woman

"The halo on Lindbergh's brow may be wearing thin on Capitol Hill, as a recent news paragraph stated," writes the Plain Farm Woman down on the Neosho who adds, "but don't let anyone make that remark to us here in the country."

We still think that Lindy and Anne represent the ideals of this generation.

Trail blazing thrills the heart of every pioneer descendant. No only their trail-blazing, their modesty, the way in which they shun society, their strength and fortitude shown in time of greatest sorrow, the manner in which they are carrying on endear us the Lindbergh's. His 'halo' is just as bright out here in Kansas as when he was crowned.

No one abhors graft more than I. As far as political graft goes I have a notion there is little difference in Republican and Democratic varieties.

I know nothing about air mail contracts. But it does seem to me that the lives of three young lieutenants is a rather costly debit for the first few days of army air mail transport. The mail is coming through on schedule, yes, and the army pilots will become seasoned in time regardless of cost - that is the army's way.

As suddenly as air contracts were with-drawn

Lindbergh's (cont.)

from private lines our air thoroughfare was taken away. We hear about two planes going over our farm each day now whereas six or eight used to drone over every 24 hours. We have often dreamed of an air trip - of going to Wichita to board an east-bound plane so we could sail proudly over home. It won't be nearly as much sport, if we can't look down on home folks!

2-26-34

FARM MOVING TIME

March 1 means moving time for farmers in the corn-hog belt. An unusual moving activity or changing around is noted by farm realtors this spring. Mixed joy and pathos seem to arise when a hard hit tenant is "put off" or a horny handed farm owner after a 30-year struggle "signs over" without taking advantage of a moratorium, as illustrated:

"Grandpa, do we have to sell the homestead?"

"No, little Eva, we'll just give the darn thing away."

So hope and despair is carried along in the rural moving van in those makeshift trailers attach-ed to cars which are seen this week on the highways and side roads.

The drought has increased the tension of mutual disagreement between landlords and tenants. Owners through foreclosure do not care to have the unfortunate old owner become a tenant. Those who answered the lure of the city a few years ago want to start up anew on the old quarter section. The AAA[1] *Benefits are*

---

[1] **Agricultural Adjustment Administration** By the time the AAA began its operations, the agricultural season was already under way. In effect, the agency oversaw a large-scale destruction of existing crops and livestock in an attempt to reduce surpluses. For example, six million piglets and 220,000 pregnant sows were slaughtered in the AAA's effort to raise prices.

The AAA was declared *unconstitutional* by the Supreme Court, January 6, 1936 because it taxed one group to pay another.

guaranteeing some cash income. City dwellers without jobs are eager to lease small tracts - own a cow and a few pigs and have a place to raise chickens.

Others who are plumb done and disgusted hold a closeout sale and give place to those with hope for better times ahead and who may operate at a profit for the first time in years. With the year at the spring, movers perpetuate the alliance between man and nature, tote their goods and chattels to a new home and stake out a claim for a fuller share of the bounties of the good earth. 3-1-34

BUSY DAYS ON THE FARM

Here is a good account of what is happening this spring on the Lyon county farms - particularly in the Neosho valley - as The Farm Woman tells it:

Last week was a busy one on the farm. The young cowboy had to be on duty at 6 a.m. to ride in Joneses roundup. The rest of the family were cowhands-a-la-moderne - we trailed to the pasture in the car.

Baked beans never tasted so good as served piping hot from a portable fireless cooker.

After dinner 10 cowboys surrounded the herd and cut and sorted the cattle. Anyone who wonders what horse sense is, should watch a cutting horse work. He is used to nothing else. Each bunch of steers was as even as could be. A train whistled by - all the Herefords put their tails in the air and galloped for the corner of the pasture. We wondered if the bunches would get mixed but the cowhands attended to that. They turned those steers around again.

We had to get up just as early Tuesday morning to get our own cattle out to pasture and go to the May Day celebration. The small calves were hauled out in the trailer. When we let them out one started running like a scared jack-rabbit and he didn't stop until he got home. He was here when we returned. (He had a second car ride that evening.)

We all made lightning changes because we did not want to miss any of the surprises in Peter Pan Park[1]*. How many country children had seen Peter Pan's palace before?*

[1] Peter Pan Park is a 51.7 acre park donated to the city of Emporia, in 1927, by Mr. & Mrs. W. A. White in memory of their daughter, Mary, who died as the result of a riding accident at the age of 16, in 1921.

Young Stock

The Farm Woman, down on the Neosho, contributes this bit of farm philosophy:

Children are about like all other young animals on the farm. How a dozen little white-faced calves delight in getting out of the lot and cavorting around. If they go very far the mother cows bawl anxiously. The calves glance back at their mothers and go merrily on.

The little red pigs cruise around like a gang of small boys. Neither heeds a flower bed. They are out for a good time.

But calves, pigs, boys all show up at meal time.

Our school closed Friday. The big event of the day, as always, was the basket dinner. Three-inch bridge planks were brought in for tables. Anything lighter might not have supported all the good things to eat. Only one difference is noted in the last few years. There is not so much Jello or other store dainties present as formerly. But everything from the farm was there - corned beef and cabbage, fried chicken and corn and peas and tomatoes. Every child ate two pieces of pie and three of cake.

After the dishes were cleared away the children had their last-day program. The girls wore overalls and acted well the parts of boys and in one dialogue the boys appeared in girls clothes. Aside from some giggling, it all went off well. Children are more at ease before folks today than we were. Well do we remember hurrying through "The Barefoot Boy" at a last-day program. Each stanza went a bit faster than the one before and we confess we were breathless at the last line.

All the children are tickled to death that school is out. The teacher can draw a sigh of relief. But what about us poor mothers? We will have a grand vacation with the children for four months, hoeing the garden, canning beans, baking bread as usual, with an occasional game of family baseball. We will draw a sigh of relief and begin packing lunches next September.

5-5-1934

She Visits the City

As a child I used to hear my father talk about the independence of farm life and what slaves clock punchers in cities were. Our household on the farm always rose at 5 a.m. When we went to the city to visit these clock punchers they had lovely homes with hardwood floors, furnace heat, running water and electric lights, things my mother longed for. The man of the house had to punch the clock at 8 a. m. but he prepared his own breakfast and ate lunch downtown.

The rest of the household rose at their leisure and there was nothing special to do until time to prepare dinner to be served at 6:30. It was the daily routine of that household but it seems like a vacation to a little country girl with many home chores and responsibilities?

I am just now beginning to see what my father meant by the independence of farm life.

Last week I went back to the city and visited these friends. The man at one house is gone now. Mrs. B - sits as erect as ever and is as pleasant but Barbara and her husband and babies are there with her now. The babies kiddi-kars have scratched the beautiful rosewood piano and the rug is quite threadbare. And Barbara, with two darling babies, who ought to be bursting with pride and joy, had the most harassed look of any creature I ever saw. I knew Barbara when she had a new fur coat every third winter and took a position as steno just for the fun of it. I wonder if Barbara was hungry.

Mr. H - is not punching the clock now. In fact, I believe he retired about five years ago and planned to live on his investments. They were glad to see me and we had a grand visit. The floors did not seem as highly polished, the toilet was out of order and the overstuffed sofa needed replacing. (Does any piece of household furniture look worse than an overstuffed sofa when the springs have come untied and the stuffing has worn through the cover?)

I have done a deal of thinking since I came home from the city. It was a sad experience but now I know what my father meant about clock punchers. The utter dependence of it all!

One Sure Farm Fact

The farm Woman down on the Neosho turns up one sure, uncontroversial, undisputed, rock-bottom fact about the farm problem.

The question of women working after marriage is arousing a great deal of agitation, Mrs. Roosevelt says. Farm women have always worked after marriage. What would happen to the county and the farms if we didn't? Most of my neighbors make the living for the family from cream and eggs and chickens in addition to the family garden. They dress the girls and send the children to high school. The men work from morning until night to raise crops and pigs and calves to pay taxes and interest and then can't do it. The farm woman's home and career are not controversial. They are one and the same.

Going to the Fair
1934

The annual fair has come and gone. The carnival was bigger and better than ever. As a result, pennies for Sunday school were hard to find the next day. One child who was thrilled with the fair said to her mother, "Now mother you can go on to church and after Sunday school I'll go over and watch the merry-go-round."

One could not help but notice the bored expressions of the carnival troupe. I suppose a carnival day after day for a year would get as monotonous as dish-washing.

You may think this a poor year to exhibit but it was a good time to get in on the prize money in most classes. Its easy enough to place when there are only two entries.

The most interesting part of the fair to us was the 4-H exhibits. Third and fourth year clothing projects were better than most of us mothers could do. And, the boy who constructed the trellises for grapes and pruned them properly will know how to care for grapevines at home.

School Days

Children who were glad to get away from books and desks last spring were just as eager to get back to them this month when the school bells rang. Here's the Plain Farm Woman's experience with here children:

The first day of school! No one had to be called this morning. Do you recall how excited you were the day school began? For days you planned the dress and beads you would wear and the seat you wanted. The children came running and skipping down the road today. They were as glad to enter the old school again as they were to leave it last spring. The little miss who began her school career proudly started out with pencil and tablet and primer. The next stair step at home expanded in her new freedom. She is boss now.

Are the last few weeks of vacation difficult at your house? They are here. The children are tired of their games and toys. In April they can't wait for school to close. They come home and slam their books down with finality. In August they can't wait for it to begin. I confess I am anxious myself. As they swing into school routine there will be less bickering and fewer fistic encounter.

Most of the children in the neighborhood enjoyed vacations this summer. A 3-year-old lass went to the city with her aunt for a 3-week stay. Neither the aunt nor her friends have any children. They dolled the child out like a princess and took her to every-thing they thought she would enjoy in Kansas City. She was a perfect guest, didn't cry once. When she was taken to visit her father's old flame her behavior was A plus.

At the end of three weeks her father went to the city. She clung to him eagerly, would not let him out of her sight. As she was leaving the aunt remarked, "Well, Katherine, have you had a nice time?" "Yes, but I think next year I will take my vacation when my daddy does."

In contrast a 5-year-old, who had never ridden on a train nor seen the bright lights of the city, returned quite sophisticated. It took her about a week to get down to earth again. They go for a nice long ride in the car every evening in the city and have ice cream cones or pop, whichever you want and they have funny telephones and have just a lunch at noon and so forth and so on. Oh, the city is a grand place.

What a really great chasm we cross between three and five years.

9-11-34

The Farmer's Tragedy

The Farm Woman down on the Neosho is witnessing the tragedy of the drought. She writes:

The farmer is a queer critter. He goes down on the corn rows through the dust, corn that is curling, nigh to the burning stage. Why does he do it? Is it because he knows no better or just force of habit? I'll tell you why. He still hopes that rains may come. What is more, his hopes are bolstered by thunderheads out there in the northwest by day and a cloud bank by night.

Right now we are thankful for these symbols of hope.

The smartest picnickers we saw yesterday were perched atop one of the highest knobs in the flint hills. They had put up a canopy square for shade and all the breeze going passed their way. White clouds lazily floating in the azure, which faced steers sleek and fat despite brown curled grass and none of the city's din. This was the environment of the picnic party.

Speaking of picnics, what sort of a picnicker are you? Do you like to take a tablecloth and glasses and silver and have a two course meal in the open? Or are you one of that class which takes a few newspapers, bread and butter sandwiches, fried chicken to eat a la fingers, tomatoes after the same fashion, maybe potato chips, cup cakes and oranges. A jug of aqua pura from the cistern or good cold milk. Have whatever kind you choose but please let me have the latter. The children can gather the papers and chicken bones and collect the tin cups. Mother really feels like she has had an outing.

The family enjoyed a dip in a municipal pool in a neighboring town. It seemed good to have no fence. Johnny Jones was not barred from a swim just because his father had been out of work two years. Fences are often necessary, we suppose, but we are one of those liberty loving souls that crave the open range.

The only requirement was a bathing suit. A boy, tipped son off, that trunks were not allowed. Necessity is the mother of invention. We pinned one corner of father's pocket handkerchief to the front of the trunks and tied two corners around his neck. Son was not banned from the pool.

July is the month of brilliant heavenly displays. Whose heart does not quicken when he sees a blue white meteor shoot across the sky? One after another they darted across last night. But you have to be in the wide open spaces to see them. They can't be seen from the south and east windows of an apartment hotel in the middle of the block.

7-17-1934

The Rain's Symphony

Was man ever roused by sweeter music than the raindrop symphony which wakened us the other day? A gentle tap, tap, and then a chorus of notes in perfect time as the director led his orchestra on the tin roof. There was not a discordant note. The crickets chirped Hooray, Hooray! The thirsty soil drank in the moisture, here and there a tiny rivulet ran down the road. The bluegrass roused, the wheat and rye sprouted and are pushing their green spikes heavenward.

Today the alfalfa is like a silky green carpet. And the sunflowers are queens indeed.

Are we farmers really in the strategic position the press would have us believe? Is a quiet revolution centering around the Midwest farmer as the corn-hog program comes up for discussion. Viewed from the top and from charts of the ups and downs of corn and hogs it looks like the simple and easy thing to do is to control corn alone. Probably in some states it might be all right.

But looking upward from the bottom we see some neighbors who raise considerable corn as a cash crop, others who buy all the corn they feed and some few who raise the amount needed to feed out their pigs. Over here is a man who feeds several carloads of cattle and another fattens sheep on corn. We are in a diversified farming area and justice to more farmers will be brought about by both a corn and hog program. How we do pray that we of the middlewest can agree upon a program. Washington is giving us our chances.

Of one thing we are certain, the new program must be voluntary also. The surest way to blow up the whole program in this section would be to tell us we must do this or that. There is just enough mule in most of us to balk at such a proposition. I have sufficient confidence in farmers to believe that if the control programs are a good thing most of them will enter in.

9-22-34

Four Year Olds Primer

THE FARM WOMAN

Days are getting longer. Hens pick a bit of green bluegrass as they stroll here and there. There is a faint smell of spring in the air. April may be cold and cheerless but a mild day in January warms our hearts. It is the first harbinger that spring will come again.

We have often heard of the tidy housekeeper who mended her children's garments every night. We wonder if by any chance she might have done it for the reason we do these long winter evenings. We could never qualify as a tidy housekeeper.

But we have been darning socks and overalls each night. Young son has only one school outfit. Socks will wait patiently in the mending basket as long as there is a change in the bureau drawer.

A 3 year old, just turned 4 is proud of her new primer. Older sister, who is in the first grade and ready for the first reader, presented it to her.

"Now put it away until you go to school," her mother said.

"No, I can read it now".

And, she can. Perfectly. Each page is identified

by the picture. If another page of type were pasted in she would continue to read the original.

"This same child asks, "What's tomorrow?"

"Saturday."

"What was yesterday?"

"Thursday."

"Well, you said yesterday Friday would be tomorrow."

"Yes, but this is a new day and tomorrow will be Saturday."

"Tomorrow? What is tomorrow? When's it coming?"

Who can answer?

The press makes much of the fact that the farmer's income is much greater. Eight dollar hogs would be mighty nice if we had any hogs.

We are wondering if statisticians have credited us with receiving $5 benefit payments on hogs or $2. Of course I don't suppose the per cent would be much different. As Col. Ruby Garrett said, "9,000 or $90,000---Oh well, what are figures among Democrats?"

Our Farm Account book for 1934 shows a $2 benefit payment. Now if we had the other three dollars, our other income would actually have been greater, the banker and the elevator would have received a bit more money and department store sales would have been a small amount greater. In turn they might have passed the money on ---Just how are comparative statistics compiled anyhow?

We are only wondering.

End of 1934

Chronicles of
The Farm Woman

THE SALESMAN

Fifty years ago the "lightning rod dispenser" and the sewing machine agent used to infest the farms of the Neosho valley. Now the Farm Woman down there writes about the new type of agent who knocks on the farm house door: WAW

A most unusual salesman called on us today. We have been doing mighty little buying in the past three years and perhaps salesmanship has changed. The radio and national weeklies would not lead us to think so.

This man was agent for a nationally advertised product. He said his machine was as good as any on the market, that he was proud of its performance.

He did not say that it would pay for itself, that it would last a lifetime - or that it would not require oiling. We did not buy his product - hogs are still three cents, but the entire family is sold on his machine.

Speaking of agents, why can't I convince patent medicine salesmen that I do not use flavorings? Representatives of no less than six companies have called in the past year. When I say, "No, we do not use lemon or vanilla," they cannot or will not believe it.

We use butter and cream, fruit juices and spices to flavor foods at this house but for more than a decade the family has used no lemon or vanilla, and lived.

Speaking further of agents I cannot buy from a transient, something that my local merchant carries.

I know our local men need what profit there is and they always make anything good, which is not satisfactory. If we should ever need assistance it is the local people who would come to our aid - not the transient salesman.
9-1934

Another article she wrote later mentioned the car salesman:

A car salesman in a shiny new streamlined car drove into a neighbor's yard. The drought was discussed. "Why we'll come out of this all right," the salesman remarked. "We always have. There's no need to get panicky."

"Oh, I'm not panicky," my neighbor replied. "I'm certainly not excited enough to make a down payment on a new car as long as the old one runs."

And then another:

We know nothing of advertising or salesmanship. No doubt the efficient salesman who keeps his ear to the ground has found that is the best way to approach madam, the housewife. We prefer them to say right out that they represent the Everlasting Magazine agency. Especially if they call on wash day.

We are reminded of Dean Blackmer telling us that colleges were teaching students how to sell when what they should be doing was to teach us how to buy. Probably no more important problem faces the homemaker today. How to spend wisely the small change we have. When we do learn how to buy we will demand that labels and advertising contain more information and specifications about their products.
3-15-35

THE FARM WOMAN

The parents as well as the children had a good time when the Rural School Health clubs came to town recently and were entertained at the Granada theater and at the College of Emporia. Here is the Plain Farm Woman's story of the trip after she had returned to her home down on the Neosho. WAW

No doubt you are aware that the country kids were in town last Saturday. All cars from the country were loaded with kids. For the second time within the week no one had to be called. Dishes and separator were soon done and we were on our way. It's great to have a health club in your school and be given such grand trips.

We wonder if any other farm mother saw herself as "Elnora, The Girl of the Limberlost," on the first day of high school along about 1913. The tears that were shed at our house because we had to wear overshoes! Town girls wore rubbers. "But you can't keep rubbers on this gumbo," sensibly argued our mother. Keep them on or not we were adolescent and wanted rubbers like the town girls wore. Now, praise be; town girls and farm girls all wear goulashes.

And were we thrilled when the sounds pealed forth from the pipe organ at C of E? Perhaps we were not the most appreciated audience one has to know something of the subject to really understand and appreciate. It was the first time many of us had seen or heard a pipe organ. We were amazed as the music burst forth. "Look how he moves his feet around," one child remarked to another. "Why, you dumb cluck, he plays with his feet and hands, both!" a more sophisticated sister informed him. Who knows but that the desire for a college education was kindled in the heart of some boy or girl Saturday afternoon?

Chronicles of
The Farm Woman

The Bank Account

THE FARM WOMAN

Thirty-five dollars looked like a lot of money to a small country lad. Probably from the sage advice of his elders he determined to start a bank account. On the way to the bank with his father, they met a prominent cattleman from this section. The father beamingly explained their mission.

"Now son let me tell you something," the cattleman remarked. "You invest that money in a Hereford heifer calf. By the time you are 21, you'll have a string of your own."

Questioningly the boy looked at his father. Father nodded assent. The decision was made to enter the cattle game. Of course, all Hereford lovers are glad to hear this tale. If you love Herefords you delight in sharing that love. It gives us faith in tomorrow to have this cattleman advise a boy to enter the cattle game. To us on the farm a savings account, in a bank in which we have confidence, seems an easy safe way to invest one's capital. We long for such capital to invest. On the other hand there is adventure in the ups and downs in raising Herefords. The banker may experience the same thrill in the investment market.

If this boy will move cautiously and remember the words of wisdom from the district coordinator of the FCA, (Farm Credit Administration) "How much credit can I profitably use rather than how much credit can I get," he may wear diamonds.

The town boy is becoming country broke. He could not understand why we took to our cots soon after dark. After the flies had wakened him at 5 a.m. for a few mornings he began to see why we turn in early.

THE PLAIN FARM WOMAN
Car Keys

The other day in New York in the office of one of American's greatest newspapers, the chief editor asked the writer, "Who is that 'Plain Farm Woman Down on the Neosho' who writes so well for the Gazette?" He added, "I read her stuff whenever it appears. It's good." Another newspaper man in New York, who reads The Gazette daily, made almost the same remark.

Well here is another letter from The Farm Woman Down on The Neosho: WAW

"Father was ready to go to lodge and the car keys could not be found. We searched the house, the car and the path to the garage and decided that the baby had done something with them. (What do folks do when they haven't a baby to blame for every misplaced article?) How we hoped she could remember about them in the morning. Morning came. Father built the fire as usual and as he threw out the ashes a bit of metal caught his eye - the remains of the key case. Now the mystery was solved. Mother dashed home the evening before, picked up a few cobs to start the supper fire and in some way had tossed the keys in too.

The baby, still asleep, was blissfully unconscious of the search and the accusations.

The cattle broke out last night. In making his last round of the night father was just in time to see 30 cows and calves filing out on the oats. The depression corrals around here are like a good many Republican

Car Keys (Continued)

fences in the last campaign. The New Deal in oats looked much better than dry sargo. The pony was in the pasture. There was nothing to do but waken the entire family, except the baby, and round up the cattle. With lanterns in hand we sallied forth and brought home the beefsteak.

This hog-tight fence around the alfalfa was finished this week. How proudly the old sows led their pigs out. Instead of enjoying the delicious alfalfa they explored every inch of the fence to see if there might not be a hole through which they could escape. When none was found they began to eat what was set before them - good green alfalfa.

The family went to the timber the other day. Instead of breaking a few branches of redbud to bring home and put in a vase, we asked our neighbor if we could not get a small tree to plant in the back yard. Now if it grows we will have our own breath of pink to greet the spring.

While in the timber we spaded up several yellow violet plants. Only in the woods do we find yellow violets. Whence came they? Are they natives or did some pioneer mother bring a plant in a covered wagon when she came to these parts a bride? *1934*

THE FARM WOMAN

The Farm Woman, who lives beside the transcontinental air-plane signal beacons, feels that she has a special claim to write a few lines in farewell to Will Rogers. We read:

WAW

There is a pall over the country today. Quietly the word is passed along from farm to farm of the fatal accident to two beloved Americans. There is a solemnity around the supper table. It seems that one of the family is gone. Thus has Will Rogers[1] *won his way into the hearts of every family in America. Above the solemnity rise reminiscences of cowboy humor, of movies in which he has played. The Times will not be the same in the morning without his message. We mourn his passing but thank God that he lived.*

The beacons flash across the heavens - as usual tonight. Transport planes roar overhead, - planes which have carried the humorist over us and beacons which have guided him flash in the night. Wiley Post, ever the pioneer, was not one to follow beaten airways. We are not so sure he flew overhead. Because we are below an air route we somehow feel a part of it. If the evening plane does not roar over on schedule we wonder what the reason. Will this tragedy dampen our enthusiasm for air transportation? Not at all. These two famous Americans would not have it so. 8-1935

[1] Will Rogers, Oklahoma born cowboy, philosophic jester and actor was killed in an airplane crash in Alaska on Aug 15, 1935

THE FARM WOMAN

Harvesting

The Fourth of July was a grand and glorious holiday to you folks in town. It was the finest day for harvesting the farmers have had. You folks arose at 5 a.m. to get to your country cousins by mid-morning. We put our feet on the floor at the same time to get the chickens dressed and the custard for the ice cream made. Ice cream and the first fry of the year were high spots in the celebration on the farm.

The hired man rolled in from the sunrise dance just as the alarm went off. All day the horses enjoyed longer rests than usual at the end of the row while the hired man cat-napped. It seems a long time to the farmer since he could turn in at 2 or 3 a.m. and out again at 4:30.

Is the depression really over or what? Farmers are working hard and long under high pressure this week.

Wheat is ready for the combine, oats are ripe, corn and kafir need cultivating. This is one week that most farmers could use an extra hand. And what is happening? We are using high school boys. The only help available. They are willing and earnest in most cases. Wheat and oats are heavy this year and these boys are soft. Many the story of sunburned arms and stiff, aching muscles they can tell the gang when this harvest is over.

Why is it the farmers cannot get helpers from the relief rolls? Has 30 or 40 cents an hour for six or eight hours spoiled them for farm work? The 82 cent wheat, questionable prospects for corn, broilers at 11 cents a pound do not warrant labor at 30 cents on the farm. 7-1-35

Chronicles of The Farm Woman

THE FARM WOMAN

Spring, that six letter word which means housecleaning is here. And, those housekeepers that rushed the season will have it all to do over again. The dust has been no respecter of persons or houses, - or chickens or cows for that matter. The chickens stood around on one foot, glancing up at the sky occasionally. They did not go out and scratch industriously. The cows were sad-eyed and gray. It will take a warm spring rain to make them clean again.

Many folks know now what is meant by a dust storm.

Spring Oats are sprouting. Peach buds are pink and swelling. Easter lilies, probably you call them dog tooth violets, dot the pastures. The blossoms of the cottonwoods are falling to the ground. Boys at school make the girls believe those blossoms are red worms. Of course, any girl will scream at the sight of a worm.

Potatoes and early gardens are planted. Will the certified seed give a better yield of good potatoes? We believe so. Every farm woman is planning to can more vegetables than ever before. Hopes are high as we leaf through seed catalogs and make a garden budget. Farm Bureau women are studying tree fruits this month. They go home from the meetings all enthused and suggest to friend husband that they try to set out a small orchard. Perhaps a dozen trees and a few grapes. One enthusiast remarked that she wished her husband might have heard the extension specialist. As she continued that the trees must have good care and be sprayed said husband decided it all sounded like too much work. If the men don't take hold the women will have to. They are determined to have some home fruits.

Those skirts flapping in the old apple tree as you passed by was not a scarecrow. It was a farm woman trying out her newly acquired information on pruning of trees. If you noticed as you passed by again that the tree looked much better than its neighbors. The scarecrow had done her laboratory work and climbed down.

THE FARM WOMAN

The farm census taker called today. We all received sample copies two weeks ago. Some folks sat down right then and filled in the answers. Most of us glanced at it, thought we would read it carefully when we had more time. That time never comes. The census taker found us with a blank sample copy. It wasn't as bad as we thought it would be.

We wonder how great the back to the land movement has been. There aren't nearly as many houses in the country as there were a generation ago.

Have you ever noticed a group of trees as you drive along a country road? Perhaps there is a cedar among them and maybe a gnarled old apple. A yellow rose bush to blossom first in spring and possibly a lilac and a clump of asparagus. If you drive more slowly you will see a pile of stones and the ruins of a cave - the remains of a Kansas homestead. As I sit on my front porch I can see six such groups of trees. A generation ago those houses were teeming with life. Three or six or eight children. The boys slept in the loft and girls in the front room.

As the boys grew up they turned their backs on the farm. The girls married and left it. The old folks passed on. Fire and time have brought the houses to ruins - a clump of trees, a few stones and a yellow rose.

No doubt some of those sons and daughters are on relief. And they must remain there. They cannot return to the land. Their ancestral home has been destroyed. 2-13-35

THE FARM WOMAN
Scrap Iron

Barn courtyards are being cleaned up. The old cultivator and mowing machine and the clutter in the corner have been cleaned out and some of the relics go. For instance, three pairs of perfectly good wheels from rakes and cultivators, and the third from the last old chassis. Never know where he may need some part from the old car for repairs.

The Farm Bureau units have a 5-year landscaping program under way. But it is not this project alone that is bringing about the clean up. It seems that scrap iron is in demand. Boys with trucks are around in the county buying this discarded machinery and paying real money for it. The depression must be over when farmers can exchange these eyesores, which are no earthly good to anyone, for cold cash.

Yet we wonder.

What is this scrap iron for?

Have our supplies of iron ore diminished to the point where it is more economical for manufacturers to melt and process discarded machinery? Or is it possible that the old plow frame will go to some maker of munitions? We seem to hear the faint rumble of war clouds far beyond the horizon. Can it be that these crisp one dollar bills which I hold in my hand will be a boomerang? Will ridding these Lyon county farms of needless junk one day draw my boy and the lad across the way into a terrible, futile war?

Mars is a master of subtlety. Lest we are on our guard we may be innocently drawn into the cauldron. As unwittingly as by selling worthless scrap iron instead of hauling it to the draw in the back pasture.

THE PLAIN FARM WOMAN

Precious Water

The farmer's side of the drouth and the water shortage is a sad one. Hauling water to thirsty stock in the rain is only one of the jobs of the farmer this summer. Here is the Plain farm Woman's story of the drouth down on the Neosho: WAW

Water! Water is the all important thing now. Will we of this generation ever cease to be water conscious? Will we forget the drouth the next time a flood comes sweeping over the valley?

It seems ironical to haul water in the rain. But at that it isn't as bad as hauling in the dead of winter when snow and sleet spit in your face and water freezes on your mittens.

The farmers are grateful to Uncle Sam who has provided all the government pumps over the county. We have heard of Uncle's helping the bankers and the railroads when they needed assistance. This is our first direct contact. How a little needed assistance helps. Imagine if you will, dipping four tank loads of water from the river and a hard pull up the bank each time. Now the government has a man there who pumps the water right into our wagons on the bank. The children can haul the water now.

Have you ever passed by a pasture when the cattle were around the tank waiting for water? Cattle follow an exact routine every day. They drink and eat and sleep with clocklike regularity in normal times. They mill around the tank waiting for water. You may see a cloud of dust rise.

A calf gets lost in the

shuffle and bawls for its mother. Ah! There is the sound of the tank wagon. Heads are thrown up, the bosses of the herd, the sleek fat cows, walk a few steps to fall in behind the wagon. It is backed up to the tank and water, precious fluid, gushes forth. The leaders will not let any other critters come near until they get their fill. Nor will they drink and leave the tank. They sip and meditate and take several more sips before leaving.

The tank wagon is soon emptied and on its way for another load. After a time the ringleaders do move away and others crowd in. They drink their fill and move on. The timid ones go up but the tank is empty. They look down the road, into the tank again and move away. A calf goes up and tries to get a drink but he can't reach the few drops of water in the very bottom. The calves will have to wait until perhaps the third load before they can get a drink.

As we read of Emporia's water conservation program and the test wells we wonder why there is not more agitation for the dam on the Neosho above Council Grove. It has been spoken of as a flood control measure but it would be even more effective as a water conservation aid. If there were several thousand acre feet of water impounded above Council Grove you would have no water worries in Emporia today.

The army engineers have recommended this project and if all the voters in the Neosho Valley demanded it no doubt the dam would be constructed. But, I don't believe the government will ever make the appropriation until we, the folks who would benefit from it, show more interest in the project.

9-6-1934

THE FARM WOMAN

Circus & Fair

The first week of school was severely disrupted. A circus on Wednesday and the local fair on Friday. We didn't know there were as many children in Lyon county as lined the streets to watch the circus parade. We thought until we saw the circus that Tom Mix himself led the parade. (That probably reveals the fact that farm folks do not attend many movies.) The elephant may have been old and decrepit but if it was the first elephant you had seen you thought it pretty grand. We are glad now that the muddy roads kept us at home from the first circus that came to town.

Our annual fair may not seem much to you except a carnival. But it is the time each year when old timers plan to return. You will see small groups huddled together on the benches. Likely they have not visited for a year. If you did not take time to embroider a pair of pillow cases or bake a cake or lift a jar of beans off the cellar shelf you may have thought the exhibits did not amount to much. If you had even one small jar in the exhibition it seemed like a pretty good fair. Ask any 4-H boy or girl. They had a fine display. Twenty potatoes of uniform size and shape sound like a simple exhibit but after selecting 20 potatoes from 20 bushels one boy says it's not so easy as it sounds. We venture that the peaches and the fancy work will not be excelled at the Topeka or Hutchinson fairs.

Two Aid societies beam with satisfaction as they tuck receipts from the fair

Circus & Fair (cont.)

dinner in their bank accounts. Aiders have learned how to work and visit at the same time. Donations keep the members up on their toes. If the time ever comes that the Aids turn their time and attention to other activities than fair dinners and frequent suppers. We fear a decadence in good cooking. As it is now one member will not let another outdo her. There is enough of the contest spirit that it keeps us in constant trim.

We are glad that so many Emporia folks found that these fine all weather roads which lead into Emporia also lead out to country towns. Your presence and your friendliness helps us more than you know. We may have a better fair next year as a consequence.

KANSAS FARM CHRISTMAS

This, says it all from the farm woman on the Neosho: WAW

Christmas carols on the air have cast a spell of peace and good will over us. Christmas eve and the program at the church. It carries us back to our childhood when mother hitched "Goldie" to the buggy and took us to the Christmas tree and Santa. Of all childhood memories this stands out as perhaps the pleasantest.

There was snow on the ground. It was cold, bitter cold. We didn't mind, we had warm bricks at our feet. Never was a Christmas tree more beautiful, the candle light and little folks singing carols. Oh how we wished we were a town girl so that we could be in that program. The bricks weren't so warm going home. We were cold and sleepy. We whimpered. Mother carried us in by the fire while she went out to unhitch in the cold.

Then came the motorcar.

As we looked over the audience it didn't seem as if there were as many country folks there this year as in horse and buggy days. We wonder why. Isn't the sack of candy and nuts as enticing in these days? What will stand out in the memories of today's children comparable to the Christmas program of our childhood?

We are also thinking tonight of the many greetings and gifts we would like to send. To the neighbor who have kept the children on numberless occasions. To those same neighbors who came in to help when we have thrashers or silo fillers, illness or any time they are needed. To the mail carrier who comes every day regardless of weather. Always he wears a smile. He has as many admirers as there are children on his route. To the telephone girl who is always there to answer our ring. To the school teacher who apparently does more for the children in six hours than we do in 18. To our pastor and church school workers who nurture our spirits and help and inspire us. To the county health officer and nurse who help keep us in good health. To our family doctor who comes any hour day or night and makes us feel better by his presence as well as his prescriptions. To the home town merchants who know us and are really interested in our welfare. To the county agent and home demonstration agent for their help. To the radio for the parade it brings. To the press for the many good things we can read. To the friends and acquaintances who do so much for us. The list goes on and on.

12-24-34

THE FARM WOMAN'S QUAIL

Down on the Neosho the farm Woman considers the quail season from a widely different angle from that which the town woman sees it. The Farm Woman writes:

Quail season is here. The season the whole family looks forward to. Not that we want quail exterminated - our sympathy is always with the birds, but because of friends we know will come. Every time we hear guns boom we wonder how many birds are victims. The check up at night shows not many. Dogs and men come in weary but smiling, ready to eat anything. One thing about a quail hunter, he relishes food and sleeps soundly. The way to a man's heart may be via his stomach but the way to keep the cook in a good humor is to praise her bean soup. The children sit wide eyed while tall tales are swapped around the supper table.

The old timer who has hunted up and down the valley for years has many a good yarn to spin. His steps are 3 inches shorter than those of tall young hunters. Figure out for yourself how far he is behind the group after a 10 mile tramp.

Who could fail to get a thrill from watching the dogs work? One goes along with his nose to the ground. Suddenly he stops with right front paw lifted in a beautiful pose. The old dog holds her head up and moves it gracefully from side to side until she gets the wind. Then like a statue she stands. The dogs pointed one covey and the quail ran along the ground. Of course, no sportsman worthy of the name will shoot a bird on the ground. They trailed those birds for a half mile. Finally one of the flock flew and sacrificed himself for the others. The rest scattered and hid. Men and dogs moved on the next hedge row.

The old collie is jealous of the bird dogs. The visitors eat fancy dog food out of tin cans. He looks on with mixed feelings of desire and contempt. He prefers fresh rabbit. He goes along with the crowd until the first gun sounds then back to the house and under the kitchen table. The soft hearted cook lets him stay under the circumstances.

Nimrods from a sandy country were tired from carrying so much gumbo. "Why," said the old timer, "we used to have four pairs of rubbers in Emporia. One pair where we slept, one where we ate, one where we worked and one at our best girl's house. Now I've been in Arkansas City 40 years and have forgotten what rubbers are."

Soaked with rain, weighed down with gumbo are minor discomforts in comparison with perfect retrieves the dogs made.

12-5-34

THE COUNTRY FIRE

Here is a picture of a country fire down on the Neosho. Read it as the Farm Woman tells it - a pathetic story:

Town was especially crowded Saturday night. There was as much double parking in our one block as in a block on Commercial Street. The picture show was over. The week's bartering was done and folks were beginning to leave town. A mile out we saw a blaze on the prairie.

"Can anyone be burning a straw stack in this drought?" we exclaimed. "Why, wheat straw and cotton cake may possibly bring the cattle through the winter."

"That's no straw stack," father remarked, "That's a building." It was our neighbor's house.

The family rushed around to get to town. The boys left their wagon by the back step when they went in from play. Four little tikes were scrubbed and dressed. The family bath tub hung on its nail on the back porch. Saturday's baking for Sunday dinner was on the pantry shelf. They traded their cream and eggs as we had. And they noticed the fire too. Two miles from home they realized it was their house. Everything they possessed.

The father left the mother and babies with a neighbor while he went on. Three hours before this spot had been home. Simple furnishings battered by the children's toys, the trunk containing the mother's wedding ring and family keepsakes. All these were going up in bright yellow flames fanned by a stiff south breeze. In 80 minutes all was gone. Mattresses smoldered. A few blazing studding continued to stand upright for a time. They, too, toppled and fell. Not a dish, not a pan, not one bit of clothing was saved. The wash tub and the boiler burned.

And the little red wagon! There it stood. The tongue drooped on the step. The pretty, bright red paint was gone and the rubber tires were melted.

Flood, drought, fire and pestilence all are tragic. Today our minds dwell on the fire.

Chronicles of
The Farm Woman

The Farm Woman Answers

The Farm Woman down on the Neosho heard our beloved President asking America to take stock of itself and see if it wasn't better off than it was last year. Here is her reply:

We haven't yet lost faith in the New Deal. In his speech the other night, the President asked each of us five questions. "The simplest way for each of you to judge recovery lies in the plain facts of your own individual situation," he said.

1. Are farmers better off than we were last year? Personally we must answer no. Last winter's feed bill is not yet all paid for. Putting corn that was pegged at 45 cents into 3 cent hogs did not make both ends meet. Prospects for the coming winter's feed look rather dim at the present writing.

2. Are farmers' debts less burdensome? Perhaps, but we are unable to get a federal loan at cheaper interest than we are now paying.

3. Is your bank account more secure? Our bank account was nil a year ago - still is.

4. Are your working conditions better? How are they bettered on the farm? Should say little changed.

5. Is the farmer's faith in his individual future more firmly grounded? No. Would that, we could say yes. A year ago new blue eagles were everywhere. We were as enthusiastic as anyone. Industry was taking on new life. Prices of many things we had to buy jumped overnight. Our turn will soon come, we thought We have waited patiently this year. We turned in our corn hog evidence to the best of our ability. Now the county committee is sweating blood trying to squeeze out 21 per cent. Our faith in the future is not stronger because we cannot see anything better ahead. Did we expect too much?

Another question: Have you lost any of your rights or liberty.....? Yes, we should say farmers have given up rights and liberty. From the old order of raising kinds and quantities desired we have relinquished some of our liberty for what we think will eventually be the greatest good for the greatest number. We hope to see agriculture so planned that at weaning time we will have some idea what those pigs will bring when they weigh 200 pounds. Or when we put steers on feed how much we can expect to get for them in 180 or 250 days. We have not lost faith because we think the New Deal has helped others. For ourselves we must answer thus.

But isn't America a great country led by a great man? If everyone will answer these questions the administration can measure the success of the NRA.

In Germany one wouldn't dare put such a letter in the mail. 7-6-34

THE FARM WOMAN

Wimpy, the neighborhood pooch is dead. He was killed by a motorist passing along a country lane. It wasn't the motorist's fault that Wimpy was killed. He was standing in the road with his attention centered on one of his canine friends, and made no move to get out of the car's path. However there is a lump in the throat when we speak of him today.

No doubt Wimpy could boast of ancestry in the canine blue book but the breeds were a bit mixed. There was collie and rat terrier and fox terrier that we know of. He inherited from his terrier mother the ability to sniff a rat and kill it. He learned to keep the chickens out of the yard. If an old hen didn't heed his warning to get out, it was the end of the old hen. Wimpy was determined to see a task through to the end.

The milk cows paid little attention to him. Nevertheless he trailed them to the pasture and home again. Often across the fields in late evening - when a stillness settles over the countryside, Wimpy's shrill bark could be heard. This was his way of warning that all was not well. Nothing serious, perhaps, but he had discovered something amiss.

Wimpy was a diplomat. He never quarreled with the big dog on the farm. No use starting a fight one can't win, and he knew it. But he became a master hand at attracting or distracting the big dog's attention. If he wanted the nice warm corner by the fire and the big dog was there, he didn't whine and beg for the corner. Oh no. Instead he found an old bone and began to gnaw on it so enticingly that the big dog roused himself and came to see if that bone was as good as advertised. Wimpy gave it to him without a single growl and dashed for heart's desire. One couldn't decide where the old dog's curiosity was merely satisfied or if his sense of humor came to the rescue. He sniffed the bone, then hunted another spot to lie. This bit of comedy was enacted repeatedly.

Coupled with the tragedy of losing Wimpy is the regret that the driver did not stop. Likely he thought it just another mongrel. Which is quite true. However, one may become as attached to a mongrel as to a pedigreed Scottie. Had the driver stopped he would feel better and so would we. It would have been such a little thing to do, yet aren't the little things in life the most important? The two words "I'm sorry" smooth out many situations in this world that might otherwise become intolerable.

Those two words, if spoken, would ease the hurt of Wimpy's passing.

THE FARM WOMAN

TB Tests

Last week a good many country children in Lyon county were given a simple skin test for tuberculosis. It was purely voluntary on the part of pupils and parents.

About 25 years ago, if memory serves us correctly, the first tests for TB in cattle were given free to farmers who wished to co-operate. Today no breeding cattle may be shipped into the state without a health certificate certifying freedom from TB and most buyers require a Bangs' test also. This is really an accommodation to breeders because a healthy herd of cows is more profitable any day.

Condemned cows, those which are reactors, must be sent to market. But never fear, no such plans are on the minds of the State Board of Health for Kansas children. It is a comfort to the entire family if all tests showed negative. Those who had a positive reaction do not necessarily have tuberculosis but they should have further examination. Tuberculosis need not be the great white plague any longer if treatment is begun in the early stages. By giving this simple test we can ofttimes discover it in the earliest stages.

Let us rejoice that we have not waited longer than 25 years to test our children than to test our cattle.
1936

THE FARM WOMAN

Country girls down this way are not waiting for June, the month of roses. They are choosing this balmy March as their wedding month. The air is filled with news of weddings. Grapevine calls for charivaris[1] *are relayed nearly every day. Neighbor boys are overcome from smoking too many wedding cigars. A cigar once in awhile doesn't bother, but three or four in a row prove too much. A few days after the charivari comes the bridal shower. Wise homemakers keep a reserve of kitchen gadgets for shower gifts. Most of us raid the notion store hurriedly on our way to the party. If you have never been to a neighborhood shower in the country you have missed something. Whole families go. The big moment of course, comes when the bride and groom together undo the gifts and display them. Simple, useful gifts. But no bride could ever be more thrilled over Towle sterling or imported linens than these girls are with their shower presents. A heap of good wishes accompany these little remembrances.*

These young folks are starting out simply and sensibly. The girls have hope chests filled with quilts and dish towels and pillow cases. The boys have a team and a milk cow. They expect to found a family and stay married. We have not statistics at hand but from observation, we would say that divorces are fewer among farm folk. Verily, they are the salt of the earth.

---

[1] A shiveree or charivari is a noisy serenade (made by banging pans and kettles) to a newly married couple who is expected to furnish refreshments to silence the noisemakers

THE FARM WOMAN

Every farm in the community is overrun with rats and mice Abundant feed crops and rodents seem to go together. In the drouth years these pests did not bother.

Mice are sleek and saucy and bold. Homemakers complain of them. Local dealers report record sales of mouse traps. Cats seem too lax in their hunts. The hired man has caught several mice and fed them to the cats, thinking to shame them. They ate the preferred tidbits with never a blink of shame. However a life of luxury and ease, with food handed to them without any effort whatever on their part, is contrary to something in cat nature.

The cats have all died. The mice gather in groups and squeal in triumph and multiply. Today we long for rugged individualistic cats who are mouse hungry.

Selected in-part from an article dated 6-24-39

The McKinney Family 1934

Chapter 4

Threads of Hope

She was always active and aware of women's needs and rights - because her mother was a suffragist and used to take her in the buggy to county schools at night to work for Women's Suffrage[1]. Her father was a sheriff in the 1800's, so the family was always active in the community. Mary was an exceptional person, successful, in part, because her husband supported her efforts, and her efforts were usually politically oriented.

The Country Women of the World met in Washington, D. C. and the Lyon county women elected Mary and June Gardner to go and represent them in 1936.

[1] Women's suffrage (long called woman suffrage) represents the first stage in the demand for political equality. Women's organizations in many countries made the fight for suffrage their most fundamental demand because they saw the right to vote as the defining feature of full citizenship.

While they were in the East they visited Ella Griffin in Tarrytown, N.Y. It was always special to see her childhood friend, who grew up in Hartford, married an attorney and lived in Tarrytown, New York. Known to the family as Aunt Ella, she always sent unique gifts to Mary's children. She had no children of her own, so Mary's children were very special to her.

Mary had met Alf Landon in the grocery store in Hartford in 1932, and by 1934 Landon was the only Republican Party governor elected. He was then nominated by the GOP to run for President during Mary and June Gardner's visit in Washington D.C. After the nomination the GOP wanted someone on a national radio program and Landon suggested Mary Frances. Mary went to Chicago with Evadna Claybaugh and was on the Vic & Sade Show[2] sponsored by Proctor and Gamble. Later, Proctor and Gamble sent Mary a record of the program, but it was broken in the mail.

While she was in Chicago, Mary Frances was asked to go on a speaking tour for Mr. Landon. She and `Mac'

---

[2] **Vic and Sade**, created and written by Paul Rhymer, had a 14-year run and was the most popular radio series of its kind, reaching 7,000,000 listeners by1943, according to *Time*. For the majority of its span on the air, *Vic and Sade* was heard in 15-minute episodes without a continuing storyline. The central characters, known as "radio's home folks," were accountant Victor Rodney Gook (Art Van Harvey), his wife Sade (Bernadine Flynn) and their adopted son Rush (Bill Idelson). The three lived on Virginia Avenue in "the small house halfway up in the next block." The program was presented with a low-key ease and naturalness, and Rhymer's humorous dialogue was delivered with a subtleness that made even the most outrageous events seem commonplace and normal.

spent the next 4-6 weeks campaigning for Alf Landon in Kansas, Minnesota, Ohio, and Indianapolis to Milwaukee along lake shore. She gave talks in rural areas. She later said that every precinct she `stumped' went for Landon.

Alf Landon was defeated, in a landslide, by Franklin D. Roosevelt in the 1936 presidential election.

Kansas Club celebrates the birth of this great state once a year the last of January, and noted speakers and individuals, with conviction, are asked to speak. Mary gave the following speech in Topeka.

Mary Frances McKinney
Kansas Day Club
January 29, 1940

Mr. Chairman, Distinguished Guests, Fellow Kansans: We are gathered here tonight to celebrate the 79th birthday anniversary of our state. This great state of ours was conceived in turbulent times four score years ago. Her birth was not easy. No twilight was used on that occasion.

Your grandparents or your great grandparents and mine came to make this the kind of state they desired, whether that was slave or free. It was not a place of neutrals. Every man had decided beliefs and the courage to stand by those convictions.

My maternal grandmother was a young school teacher in Atchison seventy nine years ago. A young girl in Ohio she felt the romantic call of the west and the urge to do her part to help make Kansas free. A year after she came her parents followed with that same desire in their hearts. The pioneers of this state did not come to amass great wealth. They came because they believed in a principle of government. Thus what a noble heritage is ours.

I am so thankful to be a farm homemaker in this era. I like the perspective we get in looking out from the farm. There is a joy and satisfaction in producing two thirds or three fourths of the food we eat. Electricity has brought the conveniences of the city to us with none of the city's soot and grime and crowded living. Our neighbors in the country are sitting by their radios tonight to listen to the distinguished speaker of the evening. The RFD brings us the daily papers. While folk in town may read only the headlines, the farmer reads the paper from cover to cover including the want ads. Good roads enable him to get about over the country and see what it is like. Our children have the opportunity of elementary schools and attractive extra curricular activities.

All of these things which make for more abundant living on the land have been introduced since Kansas had its birth. My grandmother saw each of these miracles come to pass. Our children take them for granted.

Now in spite of all these blessings here in Kansas we are want to look toward Washington and ask the government to help us. How can the government or anyone else help us when we do not avail ourselves of the helps now at our command? Experiment and experience have shown the value of crop rotation, summer fallow, terracing and other conservation practices. Conservation is merely obedience to natural law. Yet what a small percentage of our farmers follow these proven practices. The successful farmer loves his land, he loves the crops that grow upon it. He loves the livestock that he raises. What is true of the farm is also true of business and the professions. The successful merchant puts love into his business.

As pioneer women came with their men folk to establish our state and build its heritages, so we, the women of this decade have much to do. It is our task to assist in the preservation of these heritages. This task requires courage and a vast capacity for work. There is much mistrust and hatred abroad in the world. Tonight I see challenge to this state, in fact to the entire nation to supplant suspicion, mistrust, and hatred with faith, faith in the land, faith in our neighbors, faith in God. "Faith", says the Scripture, "can move mountains."

Here then is our challenge. It is a challenge to the Republican party. Let us choose leaders in whom we can have faith and elect those leaders.

Throughout her lifetime she remained an active member of the GOP and held many posts from 1938-1952, elected as Precinct Committee Woman and served as County Vice-chairman and State Vice-Chairman for many of those years. Her concerns were many and she displayed her anxieties in her writings and articles.

The following article was written March 16, 1940 by Mary Frances McKinney as a University of Oklahoma writing assignment:

World Peace

One may wonder what good we as farm homemakers can do in discussing peace - world peace at this time.

Conditions in the world look dark and discouraging. As this is being written the headlines carry the story of peace in Finland. Our sympathy is all with Finland, the little country who desired to go her way, paying her debts, trading with world neighbors and instilling a great warm patriotism in her people. With absolutely no choice on her part, Finland was overrun by the great Russian bear. Perhaps this sentence from a war correspondent may have some significance for us, "The fact that the Finns calmly chose to sign peace now on harsh Russian terms means only to some of these observers that Finland is willing to sacrifice greatly for a breathing spell in which she can reorganize defense of her independence on a modern basis, particularly as concerns defense against enemy bombing fleets. Finnish air force and anti aircraft bodies were almost nonexistent. Finns say they won't let that happen again." From all the news stories one gathers that the spirit of Finland still lives on. They have agreed to peace because they must. No doubt the remaining remnant and their descendants will cling to the ideals of peace and freedom. We are reminded that the body may be destroyed but the spirit lives on.

This then is the significant fact, the thread of hope to which we can cling in these dark days. Our task is to radiate the spirit of freedom in our democracy. To instill a devotion in the hearts of our children, that come what will, they will stand out for freedom.

How may we radiate this spirit of freedom? Ours is not the voice of the orator, the wisdom of the statesman, or the power of a member of Congress. Yet we can implant the leaven of love of freedom in our communities and permit it to work quietly and unseen.

First of all, we can rejoice in our hearts that we are citizens of the United States. There is no other country like it in the world today. It is a great heritage. The preservation of it will require faith, courage, determination and a vast capacity for work. Secondly we have a great opportunity. Womankind in America has more privileges than in any other country. We enjoy opportunities in education, in church work and social services, in the business and professional world and in politics and government. These opportunities impose responsibilities upon us. If we would preserve the heritage that is ours we must inform ourselves on current community, national and international happenings. This information may be gleaned from the printed page, the radio and contacts with people. After we have this knowledge let each one do her own thinking and form her own opinions. In a democracy one does not dare entrust her thinking to another.

As for instilling love of country in our youth, the pattern of our love and fidelity will be the guide they are most apt to follow. In fact, both home and school have responsibilities here. At the present time there is a trend among publishers of supplemementary readers to emphasize citizenship in our democracy. A number of publishers are bringing new series of readers on the market which are well written, attractively illustrated and children enjoy them. What children read is important. We can ask our teachers and school boards to supply these readers. However, greatest of all will be the attitude of mind and heart of parents and friends towards freedom.

No one knows exactly what the next day or the next year may bring about in world conditions. We do know that dictatorships cannot bring world peace. The foundation of world peace lies in the very foundation of our democracy. If we rejoice in our hearts, embrace our opportunities and accept our responsibilities as citizens in a democracy, and impart these attributes to our children, we shall be doing our bit. That little bit that we can do may point to world peace. *MFMcK*

If life and everyday displays of political consequence were not stressed enough she continued to write articles about the importance of everyday life on the farm, with family. Her readers were in the same situation, they understood fully what she was writing about. At one point in her writing William Allen White wrote: *The other day in New York in the office of one of America's greatest newspapers, the chief editor asked the writer, "Who is that 'Plain Farm Woman Down on the Neosho' who writes so well for the Gazette? He added, "I read her stuff whenever it appears. It's good." Another newspaper man in New York, who reads The Gazette daily made almost the same remark.*

In an article she wrote in September of 1936 she pretty much summed up how she felt about writing, government and her feelings for the farm homestead. She wrote:

I am grateful to a government that permits me to say or to write what I choose. I am grateful for a heritage of small landowners for 150 years. I am grateful for a government that promotes scientific research from which I may profit if I choose. I crave protection from my government from all things big.

I want to work with my hands, use my intellect and initiative to solve problems which may arise. I want to survive as a result of industry and intellect rather than a regimented homesteader of a beneficent government.

And thus, she became a voice for the farmers, and the homemakers, and all who came after. She had metal, forged of steel, and the conviction, that she was somehow going to make changes occur. If it was by pen, so be it. Like a warm brick in the buggy, she was the warmth, and moral fiber of her community, stimulating the neighbors to action and always maintaining her reasonably 'fluffed' perfection. I'm quite sure she would enjoy this analogy of herself.

THE FARM WOMAN

Young chickens seem to be eating their heads off these days. Old hens steal their nests under the mangers and feed bunks. Hens with baby chicks insist on leading them across the road. Chickens are one of the trials of the farm homemaker. But it is chickens that are sending two farm women to the conference of Associated Country Women of the World in Washington, D.C.

A committee of women in this county was appointed to plan how to finance a delegate. They asked each farm Bureau member to donate a chicken to the fund. Some chickens were dressed and sold. Others were marketed undressed. Those who did not have Chickens, sold eggs or cream and gave a cash donation. The nest egg grew and rates were lower than expected. The advisor council and executive board decided to send two delegates. Hence two farm women are preening their feathers and giving last minute instructions to the families who will remain at home. The writer of these lines is one of the chosen. With the thrill of election comes a deep sense of humility. Most of our members sacrificed something in order to donate a chicken.

The campaign just closed is one proof that democracy still exists. Seventeen women were nominated by their respective units. Any one would have been an able delegate. No electioneering was done. Ballots were mailed. Several of those nominated have confessed they did not vote for them-

selves. What a contrast to political campaigns now getting under way. There it seems that we expect a good man to get up and brag on himself and prove to us that he is the best candidate. Is there no room for humility in a campaign for elective office?

Of course it is because the farm woman is expected to write letters home that she was one of those elected. I have never been east of Excelsior Springs. Consequently all points of interest will be brand new and I will endeavor to bring the trip through these eyes. There is some risk on placing such responsibility on a novice.

It means something to represent the 400 up-and-coming Farm Bureau women in this county.

5-3-36

FARM WOMAN'S HIKE

For three years Mrs. Mary Frances McKinney, who lives down on the Neosho, has been writing for the editorial page, of the farm, the farm woman's view-point. Her articles have been widely quoted. This spring she was elected as a delegate from Lyon county to the Farm Woman's National Convention in Washington. She will write about her experiences for the Gazette while she is away. Here is her first story.

On the train,
May 30, 1936,
Going to Washington

We are on the train. Some 200 Kansas farm women hung there kitchen aprons on the hook after an extra early breakfast. For 10 days the kitchen apron will hang on the nail, unused. These carefree mothers are on a holiday - a holiday from the farm in June. June is the month when peas are ready to can, beans are blooming, men folks are making hay and weeds are growing in the corn and the garden. These mothers would never have left home had not families urged and insisted. For once boys and girls could say, "Now mother, behave yourself," "Mother, watch your step."

Every day for the past week letters of instruction have been arriving. Each one to be tucked in the new purse. A farm homemaker with a new purse and an old one is worse off than the farmer with two pairs of trousers. Instructions came to wear comfortable shoes - 99 percent of the feet which have passed down the aisle are encased in new shoes. Neighbors front and back have confessed that the new corset isn't broken in yet. Mother is all decked out to go to Washington D.C.

Sunflower badges were a welcome greeting in the Kansas City Union Station. Many Kansas women climbed the steps to the Liberty memorial and spent an hour in the museum. It seemed especially fitting on Memorial Day. There stood the memorial war bell. The bell which was rung at noon each day from September 13, 1918, until Armistice. It called the people to five minutes of silent prayer for victory and protection of our soldiers on land and sea. Undoubtedly there is power in concerted prayer. Concerted prayer in harmony with Omnipotent will. As we read the inscription we wondered why not have a memorial peace bell. A bell to call all citizens each day to silent meditation for peace. Sincere concerted prayer for peace would certainly be heard on High. How badly do American citizens want peace?

The coach we are in is air conditioned. But the thermostat was set for winter temperatures rather than summer. That has been remedied now and we are as cool as cucumbers before sunrise. Farmsteads in this section of Missouri are in much the same condition as those in Lyon county. Some terracing is seen. Much more needs to be done. Red clover in full bloom is seen all along the way. At each station not one or two Missouri women board the train but seven or 10 or a dozen. It begins to look as if Kansas would be outnumbered.

The porter has issued the first call for supper.

Chronicles of
The Farm Woman

THE FARM WOMAN

Cincinnati, June 1 - The union station in Cincinnati will be one of the high spots of the tour to be remembered. The architectural uniqueness of the dome, the color harmony and contrast, the soothing yet stimulating lighting effect. Murals surround the dome - murals of the pioneers of the 18th and 19th centuries. Down the lobby are murals of the 20th century industrialist. His clothes are tailored in the modern manner. He is suave and conceited. But he does not have the picturequeness or the courage of the pioneers. We supposed that these pictures, so outstanding in light and shadow, were painted. The train secretary explained that they were built up of pieces no larger than one's thumb nail. Surely they are the work of genius. As we were oh-ing and ah-ing one of our women who has been to Washington cautioned us to save some of our adjectives for the Congressional library. All too soon we returned to the train. We do want to get to Washington.

About 9:30 the lights in one car were turned low for the night. But not car 28. They staged a parade. They played hide the pillow instead of hide the thimble. It was most as exciting as going to grandma's on the train a generation ago. Of course, quiet little country kids of that day would not have thought of playing a game on the train. It was fun to parade to the water faucet to use the new folding cup. One of our group, in car 28, has a folding cup. She maintains the water tastes better in it than in a dainty sanitary paper cup.

Confidences of evening are being exchanged. From the moment they heard of this tour these women have planned ways and means. One member, from the dust bowl, sold water. Another one sold 750 chicks when three weeks old. Turkeys are sending a delegate.

Sometime in the night we crossed the Ohio into Parkersburg, W. Va. Those who were asleep were awakened to see this just as the baby is roused at a country social to eat ice cream for fear he may cry the next day when he finds out what he has missed.

We did not turn over more than twice before the farm women began to stir. The steward had told us that breakfast would be served at 5 o'clock. Some of the lazy ones dozed again, but there was no more sleep. Scenery is beautiful this morning. Wooded hills, clear streams that sparkle in the morning sun. But where is the livestock? We have seen only two herds of Hereford cattle since we left Illinois - one in Indiana, one in Ohio, and one herd of eight Jersey cows. On the journey thus far from St. Louis we have noted just one farm well improved and in repair. Paint is needed everywhere and hammer, and not a few boards. Or better still replacement. Again one of our women tells us we pass through the poorest sections of Indiana and Ohio.

We are rounding curves and it is fun to see the engine puffing ahead of us. My equilibrium or sense of direction fails to function and the sun appears to be first in the east, now in the west or north or south. The train stops at Harper's Ferry where three states and two rivers meet. The photographers and hotel managers are to meet us in Harper's Ferry. We are clicking along not far from Washington, D. C. One of the party is suffering from eye strain. 6-1-36

THE FARM WOMAN

The farm women are speeding across Maryland now - my knowledge is increasing. We see orchards on the hillsides, an occasional well improved farm. For the most part farms are not as well improved as in Lyon county. A man is cutting alfalfa. He is driving a scrub team.

The railroad skirts the Chesapeake and Ohio canal - a ditch which reminds me of the one north of the Ewing ranch in east Lyon county. The canal parallels the Potomac River. We begin to see dairy herds. Farmers here have a market in Washington.

We have received final instructions. A blue tag has been placed on our bags. We have pooled our tips. In Washington we are to tip no one. Our manager will see to that for us. The word has come over the grapevine to dress on the train for a garden party at the White House. How can I put on my fine feathers here? For days I have been planning to go to the White House as a queen. Wearing my new dress, white gloves and all. Are we to dress without a bath?

We are pulling into the station. This heart always beats three jumps faster when the alma mater's skyline first comes into view. The same reaction was felt when the Washington monument appeared in the distance. We are not dressed for the garden party.

Washington is booming, new construction to the right and left. Our cab driver pointed out the senate and house office buildings all those on the triangle. Do you know that we the people have 110,000 government employees here in Washington?

The first glimpse of the Washington I expected to find was the little girl at the registration desk who typed our badges. The roll upon when she typed our names ran out. She did not have a reserve roll in her desk. She rose, took four steps and told a man she needed another roll. He in turn told a man at the desk. The man at the desk telephoned. "Can't we write our names long hand?" was asked. "No," the girl replied. The crowd is wondering why we do not move on. The congestion is so noticeable that a supervisor comes over. He says to write them long hand. We are registered. We now have the coveted invitation.

The sun is hot as we wait outside the gates. A tennis court is near us. Perhaps the very court where Calvin Coolidge, Jr., bruised his heel. The gates are opened. We are pushed through with the throng, 100 feet inside the gates stand three plain clothes me. Many chairs are scattered over the lawn. We do not see a chair. Suddenly there is a mad stampede. Every woman with a chair picks it up and dashes as near the White House entrance as possible. We didn't stampede because we did not have chairs. Whereas the chairs were in the shade they are now in the boiling sun.

Mrs. Roosevelt appears. There is an attractiveness of strength of character which is more impressive upon seeing her. After the President's address she mingled through the crowd. She must needs be surrounded by three attendants who encircle her. Otherwise the crowd would crush her. This crowd reminds one of that at the exhibit of the whale in Emporia. I did think there would be more dignity and decorum at a White House party.

Chronicles of
The Farm Woman

By the Gazette's Farm Woman

Washington, D. C., June 5

It is interesting to watch the evolution of these Kansas women. They arrived here Monday a group of shy country girls few of whom had ever been east before. Today, three days later, each one is flitting here and there about the capital city. She has found something of particular interest to her which does not appeal to the rest of the group. Perhaps it is something about which she has read. Perhaps it is a dinner out with a cousin or friend. We have also learned that it isn't so terribly far from Capitol Hill to our hotel. It is a delightful walk in early morning.

Taxi fare is the item which is unbalancing the budget. But these Kansas women are beginning to use their heads and their heels as funds run low. Those new shoes are rubbing blisters on heels and under toes and on top of toes. Many a delegate longs for her dilapidated work shoes at home. The next time they come to Washington they will bring their old shoes and a supply of 1-cent postage stamps. It gripes one to pay five cents for four stamps when you are sending greetings to all the folks back home. They tell us there is a post office here in town where 1-cent stamps can be purchased at a window for one cent each.

One of our women engaged a young man in conversation who admitted he was a communist. He wanted to tear down the new buildings. If that is the definition of a communist it might be applied in this case, I want to tear down some of the centralization here and take it back to the states. Every Farm Bureau member in Lyon county should read 'The Fall of Rome Recreated," Washington is booming even as Rome was.

It is difficult to get the Washington atmosphere in large sightseeing parties. When one talks to the bell hop, the casual stroller through the Smithsonian, the cab drive, as well as the sincere crusader for the new deal one begins to get a glimpse of the cross section of Washington.

The farm women of the east have such a different viewpoint from European country women that are here, they think much more in International terms. It is good to get this exchange.

But thanks be, we can go back to the prairies and the wide open spaces to digest it all 6-8-36

THE FARM WOMAN

Washington, D. C. June 6 - We are speeding out of Washington. The redcap told us that he had never seen such traffic in the station there. Two sections of the presidential train to Tennessee, the regular traffic, the week-end traffic and all those country women going home. Not all farm women are leaving today, however. The ticket limit is midnight Saturday, and some of our women will be leaving one hour before midnight. Others thought they would remain until Saturday but they are broke and weary and headed home.

I am leaving my crowd here to go to Chester, Pa. The League of Women Voters there has invited the Plain Farm Woman to a Monday tea. The president of the league will show me historic Philadelphia. In all it was an invitation highly acceptable.

What are we taking back from the country women's conference? It will take weeks to classify and digest it all, if ever. As good a summary of the conference as I know was brought at a small informal luncheon. Delegates from Germany, Sweden, Norway, England and the United States attended. In all of these countries the problem has been to teach farmers to eat spinach! The people on the land wanted meat, preferably pork in many instances, and potatoes. Handcrafts are taught in all countries. Such things are hooked rugs and wall plaques which our Lyon country women do. Handcrafts of the primitives have come down to us in the beautiful tapestries which we saw in the Corcoran Art Gallery. Something of the personality of the artist is woven into the tapestry. If the artist is genius his work is apt to live on. The director pointed out so clearly that often the primitive rugs and tapestries far surpassed those of several hundred years later. The Corcoran art collection is a gift of the late Senator Clark of Montana. A collection of tapestries, rugs and paintings. Perugino, who was Raphael's teacher, used egg white and the whole egg as a medium in "Madonna and Child, Saints and Angels," This medium is being used in some of the classes of the women's institutes in England.

The return to the luncheon, the English delegate present is chairman of the committee on hand-crafts, lectures on the League of Nations and demonstrates making of salads. Every woman at the table nodded in assent when she said that we could not talk in terms of over production when there was one hungry in the world. We cannot think in terms of nationalism. It may require generations or centuries to bring this about but it is a goal to work toward. How often that thought has come to us as we sit at home on the farm. The practical hard-boiled statesmen will tell you it cannot be. However, many impossible things have been brought about. If this is sound in principle, which it is, and we work for it, we will some day achieve it. 6-9-36

THE FARM WOMAN

Washington, D. C. June 7. The Library of Congress was one of the high spots of Washington. There one can make out a blank from the index file for the one book in the 65 acres of books, which he desires. The slip is deposited in a pneumatic tube; such as Poole's use in their store, and sent to that part of the library where the book is to be found. Here an attendant gets the book from the stacks, places it on a dumb-waiter, presses a button and sends it back to the main desk.

I believe the guide told us that the library is the greatest architectural achievement in America. It does surpass the Union Station in Cincinnati in many ways but not in simplicity. There is an elegance of adornment - gingerbread on marble columns, which to my simple mind overdoes the thing. When one puts the gingerbread behind him and gazes at the mosaic of Minerva and symbolic murals he cannot help being lifted up. All the adjectives at one's command are brought out. The mosaic was done by Elihu Veder. He also has six murals of government which should be reproduced in the school books for every child in America.

Good Administration sits before an arch which symbolizes strength and unity of 48 states supporting her. She holds the book of law in her lap. In one hand are the scales of justice and the other supports a shield signifying our 2-party political system. To her left is the ballot box. A youth comes to drop in his ballot. Under his arms are books of knowledge signifying that we must have an informed electorate. On the right of Good Administration kneels Public Opinion winnowing the wheat from the chaff. A fig tree and wheat fields in the background signify domestic peace and tranquility.

Opposite Good Administration is the mural of Corrupt Legislation. The corruptionist sits at the left of Government. He holds the book of laws in his lap. He places gold on the scales of justice. The ballot urn is overturned. The factories are belching out black smoke. On the other side of Administration stands Honest Industry, pleading. Her factories are closed. The leaves of the fig tree are falling, presaging decay.

These two murals are one of the outstanding, if not the most outstanding, impression I am bringing home.

6-10-36

Chronicles of
The Farm Woman

THE FARM WOMAN

Home again! We are reminded of the farm boy who reported after his first trip, "If the world's as big the other way as the way I been, she's a whopper."

Is courage or audacity shown when a farm woman leaves home at the busiest season of the year? My neighbor tells me that if she left home for two weeks there would not be a chicken or a calf alive when she returned and the house would be unrecognizable. Speaking from experience the chickens, the pigs, the lambs, the children have all grown in two weeks' time. Even the row of canned vegetables on the cellar shelf doubled in size.

No spot on the entire trip looked so good or was more inspiring than the knob in the far pasture. That horizon bounded by the trees along eagle creek on the south. The flint hills on the west. Smoke from Emporia and Santa Fe trains to the north. Hedges and fields in neat cross sections, green and gold and black. Sleek, fat steers grazing. I am a child of the prairies.

Have you ever engineered an aid society social? Or taken a group of high school students on a day's trip? Or, have you planned dinner for 10 and had 20 guests arrive? Each requires organization and ofttimes quick adaptation. Our hat is off to Miss Freysinger, the general chairman in charge of the conference of Associated Country women of the world. Some 3,000 women were looked for. Seven thousand arrived. As far as we could tell everything went off as scheduled. We congratulate Miss Freysinger and her helpers. Theirs was a Herculean task.

We may think the farmer has a hard lot. He has. What with dry hot weather, chinch bugs, grasshoppers, etc. but *consider the managers of the Baltimore and Ohio tour for farm women. Five hundred farm women were on the special train from Kansas city to Washington, D.C. We had to be checked in. Each woman was given her ticket, checked again. Since the group was larger than expected, there was a refund of $1.40. Rechecked. As we neared Washington, hotel reserva-tions and baggage markers were given out. Double check. In between checking's, there were questions. Every woman on the train had at least one question.*

The management of a tour is no picnic. Nor is it our idea of a pleasure trip. We prefer to cook for thrashers on a Kansas farm.

Neighbors are mentioned frequently in this column. They are one of the blessings of the farm. One can pass block after block of apartment houses in the city. Numbers of families live under the same roof without knowing each other or caring. How can they exist without neighbors? Neighbors to drop in, in case of illness. Neighbors who can help to can peas or peaches. Neighbors who invite the children to spend the night at convenient times. Above all their smile of welcome upon one's returning home. And when this welcoming smile is accompanied by a neighbor-hood ice cream sociable.

My neighbors are the best in the world. More priceless than rubies.

6-17-36

THE FARM WOMAN

About a year ago some 3,000 Midwest farmers marched on Washington. Farm Bureaus in the state advanced $35. One delegate was sent from each three counties. His expense account was $105. Nothing like it had ever been done before. There were threats of investigations because executive boards had dared take $35 out of the contingent fund and send a man to Washington. Membership dues are budgeted in the contingent fund.

This year 7,000 farm women marched on the nation's capital. They were financed in various ways. Chickens were the means of sending the two delegates from Lyon county. Perhaps some of the readers of this column may be interested in a farm woman's expense account:

Tickets from Kansas City $40.30

May 30

Gas to Kansas City.........$2
Dinner...................... .35
Red cap..................... .35
Taxi......................... .35

May 31

Hotel, St. Louis...........$1.00
Breakfast .... .25
Bellhop, red cap............ .40
Sightseeing tour..........$1.00
Tips, entire tour..........$1.00
Lunch...................... .95

June 1

Taxi, 40c, 20c,25c........ .95

June 2

Taxi......................... .20
Telephone................. .20

June 3

Taxi, 30c, 50c........... .80

June 4

Taxi....................... .20

June 5

Taxi, Mt. Vernon........ $1.50
Taxi, red cap............. .50

Total $52.20

Each delegate was allowed $50.30. There was a refund of $1.40 on the ticket which leaves an o. d. of 50 cents in *the budget. The excursion ticket included transportation, hotel and morning and evening meal. You will note that I preferred taxiing around to eating lunch at noon. Many Kansas women did the same. However luncheon invitations were accepted.*

When the men went to Washington they went for a purpose - to save the nation's agriculture. The women had no specific motive. Something difficult for many folks to understand. We shan't forget the brilliant young writer for the North American Review. A two sentence quotation in the press from the report of the Norwegian delegate bothered him so much that he took the first train for Washington. He was quite convinced before his interview that this was a European feminist movement endeavoring to invade America. We hope he learned, as we did, from the lips of this delegate that she is against feminism. The Associated Country Women of the world stand for improved home-making. They probably will not meet on these shores again in a generation.

Then, too, the men started something a year ago. There were a number of women in our party whose husbands were on last year's tour. Father could not say no to mother when he himself had gone. We wonder if the women did not see as much or more for $50 as the men did for $105

6-29-1936

THE FARM WOMAN

Loss of trust or confidence is surely one of the saddest things in this world. It may be absolute faith of a child in his mother is shattered by the mother fibbing to him and then slipping away to a party. Children know us perhaps even better than we know ourselves. The mother who continues to fib to her child is sowing seeds of distrust.

Or the growing child may feel his world crash at his feet as he finds his hero, the idol that he worshipped and tried to emulate, is not true blue. That scar may never be erased. Or the adult who has found a friend, the one man in a thousand so he thinks. When he loses faith in his friend he loses faith in humanity. Thus the aches and disappointments and the misery are caused in this world by disillusionment.

As with individuals, so with government. A government which does not have the faith of the people behind it cannot long endure. We feel very close to our school district, our township and county government. We know the folks who administer it. They are our neighbors. We feel that our vote counts more in these elections than in the state and national ticket. From the headlines and from whispers on the street we gather that we have a mess in our courthouse. The assistant to the attorney general is wise to make a thorough investigation before giving the story to the press. When the facts are found it seems to us that the tax payers and the voters of the county should be given them. We dislike street whispers and gossip. Undoubtedly there are wild rumors. Especially do we dislike the rumor that this thing will be hushed up, that nothing will be done about it. Right there is where seeds of mistrust spring in our breast. We know there was a scandal in the office of the county clerk which was never cleared up. The truth may hurt. It may involve our friends. But for the sake of good government for the preservation of the faith of Lyon county people and for our children's sake let us hear the truth.

THE FARM WOMAN

A new word has been added to the household vocabulary here on the farm; the word homogenized. Homogenized milk was sketched in frosted letters on the mirror behind the fountain in the drug store.

Now farmers have heard of raw milk, pasteurized milk, irradiated milk, Grade A or AA from tuberculin tested and Bangs free herds. Most animals on the farm get their start in life from the milk of the mother that bore them. But what was homogenized milk?

The soda clerk pleasantly explained that milk is homogenized to keep the cream from rising. It is done in a machine under pressure of steam. A home economist seated alongside was surprised that anyone wouldn't know the meaning of homogenized milk. It is a process which has been used in cities and ice cream factories for years.

It was amazing to learn that some had invented a machine to keep cream from rising. We on the farm do everything we can to get more cream to rise. Old Bossy is a temperamental soul. She is wheedled and petted, never hurried in from the pasture in the evening, and she is fed on choicest bits of alfalfa, cotton cake, corn chop and bran. Always we strive for more butterfat. The milk is cooled to the proper temperature in order that we may see and skim the thick yellow cream. What is the use of all this time and effort if butterfat is to be kept in colloidal solution? It may be all right to have homogenized milk in town in order that the last spoonful of milk shall contain as much cream as the first one poured from the bottle. But if the jersey cow hears anything about homogenized milk she will either kick over the bucket or refuse to give down her milk.

Homogenized milk is definitely a town word and does not belong in the farm vocabulary after all. 10-23-39

THE FARM WOMAN

Farmers note the interest being shown in attempting to secure an armory or a town hall for Emporia. It was described as a building of plain finish, rough walls, with room for drill, room for farm gatherings and perhaps an indoor fair. Does that appeal to farm folks in this county? Already corn-fed farm women have visions of not having to puff up the stairs at the Teachers College gymnasium carrying a basket dinner or materials for a booth. We have read nowhere of a proposed kitchen. We sincerely trust that the specifications will call for a gas or electric plate in some corner. Then the vision will be complete. No boilers of coffee to be carried up the stairs. No imposing on the power company to install a stove for the occasion. If the proposed building will be opened for farm gatherings we suggest that Earl DeLong or some equally well-known farmer be appointed on this committee. Let the farmers have a hand in planning and boosting for the town hall. 1936

THE FARM WOMAN

Farm women in this county are becoming water system conscious. For years they have longed for running water, but with drouth, flood and low prices they have dismissed the longing as impossible of fulfillment. They have continued to trudge in and out with the water pail and the slop bucket. It seems there was no money for a pump and sink.

The farm which has a Dunn and Bradstreet rating as being the best equipped in Kansas does not have running water in the house. There is running water in the barn and every lot. Adequate machinery for every farming need is housed in well built sheds. Fences and swinging gates are a joy to see and use. A group of women in discussing this situation, question such a classification. They feel that the home is an integral part of the farm plant. No farm should be given such a rating unless the home is comparably equipped to the rest of the farm.

One of the projects in Farm Bureau units this year is a household water supply survey. Women are counting the gallons of water they carry into the house and the distance they carry it. Forty-two gallons per day for seven days of the week, an extra 40 gallons on wash day and 12 gallons more on Saturday night - all of this carried from the well at the barn, a distance of 125 feet. The round trip therefore is 250 feet, probably seven gallons are carried each time. This means 2 ½ miles are spent each week in walking to and fro to satisfy an ever gaping water bucket.

As a result of this survey one family in the neighborhood has water in the house. All through the years they have continued to use the old oaken bucket just off the back porch. Friend husband was requested to price pitcher pumps in town. There was some pipe in the barn lot which at one time led from the well to a tank there. It was a Sunday morning's task to unearth the buried pipe. Another Sunday morning was required to dig the trench from the well to the foundation and install the pump in the house. The total cash outlay was $2 plus two Sunday mornings of labor. My neighbor insists that many other farm homes could have water in the house as simply as this plan was executed.

At least this survey is making us water conscious. And when women make up their minds that they want water in the house, why there will be a pitcher in every kitchen. 5-29-39

THE FARM WOMAN

A 4-inch rain on the upland last night. This morning the bottom is flooded. So quickly do well graded roads and open roadside ditches carry the water down upon us. It was a relief when central told us there was nothing to fear from the hills in Morris and Chase. At daybreak the silver sheen of water was everywhere. It requires distance and perspective to get the effect of the silver sheen - say from the highest knob in the neighborhood. If you are right down to it you see a dirty black wall, seething, swirling, selfish, destructive. The reaction is one of fear and hate.

Today we wonder why the district office of the army engineer in Memphis reported that flood control on the Neosho is economically unfeasible. Wheat, whose bright green spikes filled our hearts with hope yesterday cannot be seen today. Is the bottom farmer in Lyon county a simple fool? Shall he abandon this rich black land?

There is a better way. We try to teach our children they must finish anything they begin - that one thing calls for another. The same thing applies to the problem of water conservation. We want good roads for the farmer. But if we are going to have well drained roads and open ditches on the upland shouldn't something be done to impound the water or to care for it in the river? Is it all right to dump this water upon us? These streams can be harnessed. The gray-haired men who have labored for years on this problem may not live to see that day. A new generation will take up the fight. Farmers and townspeople all up and down the valley must form a united front and with one voice demand water conservation. Water conservation will include erosion control, ponds and dams, channel clearing and rectification and dikes where needed. (But no dikes for the towns of Hartford and Neosho Rapids please).

THE FARM WOMAN

What is the greatest need in Lyon county? Our needs are many and varied. Yet above everything else the greatest need here is for the preservation and care of our rolling prairie acres and rich black bottom lands.

There can be found in Emporia, folk who have never been on a farm, who know little about the farmers' problems. It seems unbelievable. Yet it is true. The clerk in the dime store or in the railroad offices may not realize it, but agriculture is basic in Lyon county. The land has been entrusted to us. It is the land that has built up the farmsteads and the towns. Now the virginity of the land has faded and still more in the form of taxes and payments on farm machinery is required.

In some regions of the United States a crop may be expected every year. In this region we must farm by decades rather than by years. Yes, we have geared our outgo to the level of a bumper crop each season. The old adages and fables were debunked vociferously in the gay twenties. Nevertheless it is coming home to us that they were based on the facts and experiences of our forebears. The men who slew the goose that laid the golden eggs had only disillusions as a reward. Thirty-seven per cent of the soil in Kansas is ruined or badly in need of restoration. Seventy per cent suffers from erosion. Sheet erosion on comparatively flat land causes as much damage as gullies and ditches. If the land is poor then poor people, poor homes, poor towns are to be found also.

The basis of agricultural extension work has been to assist the farmer to be a better steward of the land. The late Fred Newman realized this when he spent so much time and trouble in his endeavor to establish a Farm Bureau in

Continued

this county. Our present county agent is an alarmist on the subject of soil conservation. If we do not wake up and do something to keep Lyon county soil in place, civilization will one day pass us by. Conservation measures are those common sense practices which the pioneer learned from experience. Burning of wheat stubble makes plowing easier and may increase the wheat yield for the year immediately following. But burning the straw and stubble robs the soil of organic matter. Organic matter in turn, makes for water penetration and reten-tion. Wheat in this section of Kansas should only be a part of a crop rotation program.

When the smoke is cleared away and we glimpse the New Deal in perspective it will surprise some of us to see how many good things there are mingled with undesirable features. It is possible to establish a soil conservation district on the upper reaches of the Neosho and Cottonwood rivers. Soil conservation should include crops, terraces, ponds and small dams for flood control. The establishment of such a district depends upon the consent of 75 per cent of farmers and landowners. Is not such a district worth working for? It would not mean waiting for Uncle Sam to come out and save our land for us. It would mean some one to lay out terraces, ponds and approved conservation measures. Technical advice for the farmer by trained technicians. It is really the same type of work that county agents have been advocating for 25 years. The duties of the county agent have multiplied to the extent that he cannot assist everyone who wants assistance with terraces and other personal services. Hence the need for a soil conservation district. After the district is established, participation in the program is purely voluntary. There is no regimentation or compulsion.

The opportunity is ours if we will accept it. 12-8-37

THE FARM WOMAN

A rural electric survey has been made in Lyon county under the auspices of the REA[1]*. The large majority of farmers, whether tenants or land-owners, have signed, signifying their desire to use electricity. Fifteen years ago farmers had no such desire. Today the picture is changed. Every farmer may not be able to afford it but the desire is there.*

On the other hand the attitude of the utilities has changed also. There was a time when the power companies did not court farm users. The farmer could build his own line at a cost of a thousand dollars or more per mile and there were other prohibitive features. Today in contrast the local company will build to any farm or group of farms in their territory, which will guarantee a fixed minimum per mile. This minimum is based on interest, taxes, construction and other overhead costs as approved for the Public Service commission. The only thing the farmer has to do is to wire his own house and buildings and agree to pay his bill each month. A young engineering student tells me that it is not the production of electricity that is its greatest cost but its transmission. There are line losses and transformer losses et cetera. When there are large numbers of families using current off one master switch in an apartment, hotel, the utility magnate beams because the profits come rolling in. However when isolated

[1] Rural Electrification Administration

farmers, who would not use as much energy as one family in the hotel, want electricity a question arises. Will electricity pay on the farm? Will a mutual or cooperative line owned by the framers themselves, be more satisfactory than a company owned line?

The average family spends less than 50 cents per month for kerosene or gasoline lighting, exclusive of the time and energy required for cleaning, trimming, and refueling. If electricity then is to be used for lights only, there is no economy. At prevailing rates on the farm lights alone cost in the neighborhood of one dollar and a half or two dollars. By thrift the small family can have lights, radio, washer and iron for three dollars per month, but some planning is necessary to get by on this amount. If the farmer has livestock and can use power for grinding, etc. then it begins to earn on the farm. If poultry houses are lighted on these short wintry days a healthy, vigorous flock will more than pay the entire light bill in increased egg production. As farmers learn the uses and economy of electrical energy on the farm their desire for it increases. The fulfillment of this desire becomes a matter of farm management. Rural electrification cannot be a widespread success unless it pays in dollars and cents.

1937

THE FARM WOMAN

Gravel is being hauled by the door today. Hooray, Hooray! In quick succession awesome trucks dump hummocks of yellow hill gravel at one side of the road. Becker's corner pales into insignificance. It is no longer the end of all weather roads. As our grandfathers must have rejoiced when the railroad was extended from Lawrence to Emporia, making the tedious journey with teams unnecessary, so we shout in merry glee today. To our township board, the country engineer, the county commissioner, the WPA set-up. The men who are shoveling the gravel and glad for an honest day's work, the truck drivers, the man who sets the stakes and directs the drivers when to dump their loads. To one and all, who have had any part in getting the job done we give a hearty vote of thanks.

Within our memory the mud was never worse than during the winter just past. For days no one passed this way but the mail carrier. Today the carrier wears a broad grin. No longer will the neighborhood have to meet the milk truck at Becker's corner. Nor will our county commissioner have to abandon his car on this stretch of road again. We will have to find a new alibi to give the preacher. Mud can no longer be an excuse for remaining away from church. We are out of the mud!

School children run up and down the mountains as they play follow-the-leader on the way to and from school. The school ma'am will not have to remain in the district over the week-end. Everyone is smiling down this way today.

We wish all of our neighbors could have all weather roads to their lanes. That time is coming. The farmer deserves no less. Not a fancy or a wide road. But a strip of gravel or crushed rock that will enable him to get out in any kind of weather. 3-6-36

Mary Frances McKinney in 1944

Chapter 5

It's The Life!

Editorial written in 1940
By Mary Frances McKinney

At the turn of the century I was born on the farm where we now live. Farmers here in Kansas were struggling then. They are struggling today. But the outlook and the struggle has changed in these forty years.

A generation ago every farmer in the school district was a landowner. For the most part the farms were free from encumbrance. Some of them had small mortgages. Land was a more or less fluid investment. The farmer who wanted to sell could do so at any time and get more than his equity. Older residents sold out and moved to town to retire.

Little or no land is changing hands today. 1929 is the year associated with the stock market crash and the onset of the depression, but the farmer in this region has suffered since 1920. For in 1919 we had a great land boom. Land skyrocketed from fifty or sixty dollars an acre to one hundred and twenty five dollars. Only one of the many families who came into the community at that time remains on its farm. The others were foreclosed long ago. And incidentally, the only resident landowners remaining in the community, aside from this one family, are those that became established before 1919. That land boom changed our community, and many others in the Midwest, from landowners to tenant farmers. Hence the struggle today is that of the tenant farmer rather than that of the free and independent resident landowner.

My father gloried in the independence of the farmer. The farmer was his own boss and did not have to punch a clock. I used to question that. For the alarm clock rang at five o'clock every morning of the year. Chores were done with precise regularity. My mother did the milking and ofttimes the hired man would be waiting for supper while she did it. Looking back now I know she enjoyed the milking and didn't want any hired man ruining her good Jersey cows. But my mother worked too hard and shortened her life thereby.

We would go to the city occasionally and all the folk we visited had shiny hardwood floors, gas or electric lights and running water. They always seemed to have abundance of leisure,--time for the theater, for lectures and dinner parties. The head of the household likely prepared his own breakfast on the gas stove and was off to work an hour or two before anyone else wakened. There did not seem to be the bustle and tension that we knew on the farm. At home every member of the family knew the day's program and had a part in it. In the city the family did not know or care what went on at the office. Punching the clock did not seem so bad, I thought, especially when life was so delightful.

It was not that I minded life on the farm, for I am a child of the soil. I longed for the comforts and conveniences the city offered. "You cannot have your cake and eat it too", my father commented sternly. In many ways it seems that we are eating our cake today.

We may have polished floors and running water, and electricity from the high lines, the gas engine or the wind---all these we may have if we can afford them. The trouble is too many cannot afford them. The daily paper from the city is tossed on our doorstep on a country side road as soon as it is delivered in the suburban areas. The RFD brings the day's mail. The telephone on the wall can summon the preacher, the doctor or the undertaker, or tell of the postponement of the Ladies Aid. The radio brings world wide events and Metropolitan opera right into our living room.

Most country children still attend the one room country school. Twelve children are enrolled in the school across the way. The teacher has had two years at the State Teachers College. Once each week a music supervisor comes and spends an hour with the children. Of all the changes that have come about in the rural school in the past quarter century, I would put public school music at the head of the list. Children finish the country school and attend the nearby high school. They make the glee club and the sextet[1] now. In my day, only the town children were included. No one had taught us to sing. Some country boys and girls attend college after finishing high school. And, often they carry off the honors in their Senior year. The whole community is proud of such achievements.

New vistas for farm women have been opened by Extension in home economics with its emphasis on a live-at-home program coupled with consumer education. A home demonstration agent directs the program in the county. We have local clubs or units to carry on the work. Each unit has leaders in nutrition, clothing, home management, home furnishings, garden etc. The local leaders go to the county seat to attend training schools conducted by specialists from the staff of our State College. In turn the local leaders bring the lessons back to our local unit. No longer do we look or feel like hayseeds when we go to town. We have had lessons in clothing, its construction and design, color harmony and

---

[1] A formation containing exactly six members. It is commonly associated with musical groups, but can be applied to any situation where six similar or related objects are considered a single unit.

accessories. This has given us poise and confidence which our mothers lacked.

Public health studies have shown that health of rural children is below that of urban groups. Our nutrition leaders have given many demonstrations of adequate diets, meat utilization, cereals and fruits in the diet, a home canning budget etc. At the Triennial Conference of Associated Country Women of the World held in Washington D.C. in 1936, it was brought out that the diets of farmers in Germany, Norway and the United States consisted generally of meat and potatoes. Certainly that was true of Kansas farmers. Studies in nutrition show dietary needs and it is necessary to show these needs to the people.

Every school child needs a quart of milk each day. Rural children, on farms where milk is produced, were not drinking milk. Why? The chief reason for low milk consumption, is lack of refrigeration. Children do not like milk unless it is cold. Today an ice route follows the rural mail routes. REA lines through-out the country are bringing mechanical refrigeration. Farm families are drinking milk and moreover the farm homemaker does not have to start from scratch to get supper. She can plan some cold dishes from the refrigerator thus saving time, labor and fuel.

Our extension groups follow a home canning budget. Thirty one quarts of vegetables per person in the family for the thirty weeks when gardens do not furnish fresh produce. However if we ever have a surplus in Kansas, we preserve it, for some years gardens are failures. This year has been bountiful. Every jar and container in the neighborhood has been filled. We have learned that certain varieties are better adapted to our region than others. Most any vegetable looks good as pictures in the catalog. The expected normal yield of adapted varieties is important also.

A generation ago, butchering meant the slaughter of five or six hogs along in January or February. The family gorged on fresh meat in order to eat it up before it spoiled. Hams and shoulders were cured with salt and brown sugar as were the sides of bacon. All meat that could not be eaten fresh was ground into sausage and the sausage fried down. The last ham was usually used about the Fourth of July, as even cured meat because strong and rancid in hot weather. Fried chicken season commenced on the Fourth of July and chicken was the chief fare until cold weather and butchering season again.

When the home demonstration agent came to the county she conducted meat utilization meetings and taught us how to can fresh meat. This tended to increase meat consumption, especially of beef, in the diet of farm families. With the county agent she taught us how to cut pork chops, we had always had backbone previously. She also taught us to make and can liverwurst, souse, headcheese[2] and a variety of meats, which formerly had

[2] Not a cheese at all, also called souse and brawn, but a sausage made from the meaty bits of the head of a calf or pig that are seasoned, combined with a gelatinous meat broth and cooked in a mold. When cool, the sausage is unmolded and thinly sliced, Mary fried headcheese.

to be eaten fresh. She introduced canning of meats with a pressure cooker. At first we took turns and borrowed the agent's cooker to do our canning. Now every member of our unit owns a pressure cooker. We use it to can non-acid vegetables, as well as meats.

Within the last few years freezer lockers have been introduced. For a small fee we rent a locker in town, which will hold two hundred and fifty pounds of meat when it is packaged and wrapped. Now, instead of canning fresh pork or beef or lamb we cut it in family size roasts, steaks and stews, wrap it in parchment paper, label it and stow it away to freeze until we wish to use it. Thus we can butcher one animal as needed and have fresh meats throughout the year. At the present time we have beef, pork, lamb and chicken in our locker. It is simply a matter of opening the door and choosing what we will have for dinner. We slaughter a number of chickens at culling time in the fall because at that time they are in prime condition and it saves feed. Vegetables and fruits may also be frozen and stored in the locker. For vegetables a quick freeze device is necessary and our local operator has not installed it, as yet.

A farm homemaker probably receives more compliments on homemade bread, spread with homemade butter than any other thing she serves her guests. There is a thrill and satisfaction in whicking a bit of butter over the top of a golden brown loaf as it comes from the oven. We drill the seed that produces the wheat, we combine the wheat and haul it to town to the mill to exchange for flour. Then we mix that flour into bread dough and bake it. It is a delightful chore.

At our last unit meeting we were told to count all the steps we take in our kitchen to make a simple spice cake. Then we are to try grouping ingredients and utensils to take less steps and thus improve our kitchen arrangement. It is surprising how many helpful hints our leader had to improve each kitchen. We become so accustomed to our unhandy kitchen arrangement we see no way to improve it until it is pointed out to us.

Through the years we have had lessons in home care of the sick, bandages, first aid and child welfare. In cooperation with the county health officer we have stressed immunization against diphtheria, smallpox and typhoid and skin tests for tuberculosis. This year it is dental inspection with particular stress on the six year molars.

The past year we have taken up speech education. We are told at our meetings, that we are studying as a group the same things Mrs. Roosevelt studies with a private instructor. Major Bowes says Kansans have the most unattractive speaking voices in America and we propose to do something about it. Some of the finest things about the Extension program are the county, state and national events at which we meet other farm women. Simply getting away from home widens our horizons. To find that other folk have problems much the same as ours is interesting.

Nearly all members read the Ladies Home Journal or the Woman's Home Companion and various farm papers. The library leader stresses book reviews, and the past year each member reviewed at least one book. Willa Cather, Dorothy Canfield Fisher, Bess Streeter Aldrich, Stuart Chase, James Truslow Adams and our own William Allen White were listed as favorite authors. Farm families read the daily paper from cover to cover including the want ads. As the farmer rides his tractor or drives his team back and forth across the fields, he reflects upon what he has read or perhaps heard over the radio. In his meditation much of the dross is sieved out leaving nuggets of information and wisdom. Working the soil with one's hands is a veritable mental cathartic.

On the day that the hired man and his pal drove to town to register for conscription, one commented to the other, "If the President is as smart as he should be, and if things are as bad as he says they are, why didn't he call for conscription a year ago, right after this war started.

All he would have had to do was call for conscription and Congress would have passed it. They do everything he wants them to." "Yes", his companion replied, "then we would be better prepared and other countries would be a darned sight more afraid of us than they are today."

This written on the eve of election. No one knows what the outcome will be but to all appearances Kansas farmers will vote for Wilkie. Farm women agree with their husbands more often than not but the husbands do not make up their minds for them. More than one woman quietly goes into the election booth and there, alone with her maker, kills her husband's vote.

There has been a great deal of confusion in the farmer's thinking in the past few years. The way millions and millions are spent when we do not have them, startle us. The great burden of farm debt and farm tenancy coupled with two of the worst droughts in the history of the region, has sapped considerable of the independence which the founding fathers possessed. However it has not altered his philosophy. We accepted many of the agricultural experiments with our fingers crossed. We have learned that the law of supply and demand is a natural law. Soil conservation is fundamentally sound. Crop insurance is an interesting experiment which we hope will continue to work out successfully.

Kansas farm women pay scant attention to Karl Browder[3]. His name is seldom mentioned in conversation. Instead, Kansas farm women are ready and eager for information on birth control. A young public health nurse came into the country a few years ago. In her graduate work she had studied the subject of birth control. I asked her if she would come to my home and

---

[3] Karl Browder was Secretary of the Communist Party of the US from 1930 to 1945. He was therefore at the head of the party during the period of the wartime alliance of the US and the Soviet Union when CP policy veered to the extreme right. After the war he became the scapegoat for this policy which was dubbed "Browderism" although it was imposed by the Kremlin on every Communist party in the world.

talk on the subject to a group of neighbors who might be interested. She consented, explaining that as a nurse she would talk to them and send each one of them to her own family doctor for information. Quietly I contacted those whom I thought might be interested. Without exception each one was eager to come. They had heard that the doctor might give some information, but they did not know how to go to him and ask for it. That was what they wanted the nurse to tell them. A week later the nurse came to see me explaining that the public health doctor, her superior, had requested her not to discuss the subject of birth control. Each neighbor had to be informed that the meeting would not be held.

Since that time, three of these mothers have had children, one her ninth child, one her sixth and one her second. The two former families are on relief. The case worker asked one mother why they did not stop having children. The family with two children are young folk and wanted to get better established before their family increased. The thing that concerns me, especially, is the health of these mothers. Our country cemeteries are dotted with the graves of mothers and babies, and too often they need not have died. It seems too bad that methods of contraception must be whispered. Although farm women have undergone a metamorphosis in the last generation, they are yet too shy and timid to ask their doctor for information on birth control.

As one drives over the countryside here in autumn, the sunflower and the goldenrod, gay feather and snow on the mountain background of native bluestem, is a picture that thrills the heart of every lover of the plains. Too often the farms do not add to this picture. Here and there one sees a farmstead neatly kept, painted and in good repair. More frequently paint and repairs are badly needed and a general cleanup campaign, as well.

Here in our school district we have two extremes in farming. We have a counterpart of the Jode family[4] and also one of the best farmers in the state. The land in both farms was originally the same virgin prairie. The good farmer works harder than the one who has failed. He loves his land and takes good care of it. His buildings have a fresh gleaming coat of paint. His records show a small net income. The other neighbor has never hauled a load of manure, he does not add phosphate and lime where needed, he does not terrace his fields nor does he practice crop rotation. He does not take as good care of his livestock or machinery. Many simple minor repairs are neglected, as are the grounds and lots. He does not keep records. We have too many such farmers on the land. It is one of the serious ills of agriculture.

I have come to have the same tenacious love for the land that my father possessed. The city stifles me. One cannot turn around without spending a nickel. The farm is not the place to come if one would get rich quick, but it is a grand place to live. By hard work and careful management we have the conveniences of the city with

[4] In reference to the poor family in the movie "The Grapes of Wrath"

none of its smoke and grime and crowded living. Farm mothers can shoo the children from underfoot after the breakfast dishes are done and see little of them until noon. There is no fear of traffic and no need to entertain the children. They can entertain themselves. They learn the ways of the birds and the wild life along the creek. They learn many of the facts of life in a natural way. Calves and pigs and colts are born, crops are planted and harvested in season.

What greater delight is there than to sit down with congenial company to a home produced, home prepared meal? A broiled sirloin steak garnished with French fried potatoes, a salad of head lettuce with vine ripened tomatoes, hot rolls, butter and wild plum jelly, with apple pie a la mode for dessert.

It's the life.

The McKinney Farm Home
Hartford, Kansas

Chapter 6

Life on the Farm

"Children are the most important crop out here on the farm."
-MFMcK

Farm life is not for the weak at heart, or the timid. It's a challenge to be repeated year after year, an act of faith, and Mary sums it up in these excerpts from her many articles:

By and large the farmer who has succeeded in the past has learned to work with nature. He is a philosopher. He studies the clouds and the weather. He may plant by the moon and foretell seasons by the signs. He knows he may not get a crop every year. He keeps corn in the crib until he gathers corn again. He likely has few of the comforts of life. He is largely self sustaining. He has weathered storms of adversity.

The sophisticated may laugh at this type of farmer. But

his counterpart has not been found in the machine age. We stand at the crossroads. We want bath tubs and tractors, radios and streamlined cars. Is the farmer wise to cut loose from old moorings, old customs and accept the technological age? Or should he first learn something of markets and marketing, reserves, working capital, depreciation, replacements etc.?

We have learned that expensive farm machinery does not pay for itself. What dumb clucks we were to fall for that line. However labor problems tend to force the farmer to mechanize. The New Deal is zealous in defense of high wages. Which is all very well. But how can the farmer, who rakes and scrapes to pay taxes and payments on his government loan, pay relief wages? Farming is needful. Thus far chemists have not been able to devise food supplies form sources other than the land. When one sees thousands in crowded cities that are dependent upon some one to grow their food, it makes the producer seem fully as important as the distributor or the processor.

Some years ago farm women were easily distinguished by their dress. Today that distinction cannot be made. But if you observe a group of farm women you likely can identify them by their hands. They wear gloves or otherwise try to obscure their wrinkled hands with finger nails broken or chipped short.

It has always been regretted that my mother could not have enjoyed a 'chore boy.' The inventor of that metal sponge to scrape the bottom of our pots and pans has saved many a homemaker broken nails and bruised quick's. Someday a monument should be erected in his honor.

A generation ago father hustled around early, hitched the bays to the surrey or the lumber wagon and the family was off to spend the day with grandma. There was bustling in that household, much as there is today to get every member scrubbed and combed and into his Sunday best. Grandma in those days lived 12 or 15 miles away. At that it was a 2 ½ or three hour journey. If there was mud-hole along the way travelers drove the inside wheels at the edge of it, eating out the bog, making it a little larger with each succeeding tire tread.

Do you stop to think as you speed along today that it is improvement in roads as well as in cars that makes this homecoming possible? Grandfather tells of driving across the prairie at will. There were no roads. Then roads were laid out on section lines but nothing was done to them. Next they were graded and dragged. What a forward step that was. Now we are looking forward to the time when every farm home will have an all weather path to its garage.

A professional man in town has an appointment with my neighbor in the near future. He is coming to the farm to get his fill of home made bread. His request is that she not fix such a bountiful dinner that he will have no room for bread. It will be all right to have bread and milk, bread and gravy, bread and honey or any of a dozen complements of bread which will make a full meal.

Probably good homemade bread gets more attention and compliments than anything else a farm homemaker serves for guests from town. At a recent gathering at the schoolhouse down this way, one of the men was scrutinizing the heaping pile of sandwiches. "Isn't there any home made bread amongst all them?" he asked. Not a single slice could be found. Farm homemakers are either slipping in this warm weather or else they did not want to stay home from town on Saturday and bake bread, (the basket dinner being on Sunday).

Another neighbor has not had a failure with her yeast bread since the home demonstration agent in the county conducted a class in bread making in the church basement. She sat on the front row and took many mental notes on technique. Orphaned when a child and married young, she had never known the proper technique of good bread making. Her husband is proud and says that one lesson is easily worth five years dues in the Farm Bureau.

Yes, homemade bread is one of the high spots of the farm meal. City cousins delight in bread and cream and fried chicken with ice cream and all the trimmings. They talk often about reducing and dieting when they get back home; never while they are still on the farm.

Who remembers the old town pump with its rusty cup on the Hook? Water never tasted better than from the old pump on the Fourth of July, Fair time and Saturday afternoons.

A boy lay ill of fever. For days he tossed in delirium. Half rousing, he said, "Mother, I believe if I had a drink from the town pump I could go to sleep." It was midnight. The streets were dark. But the mother hurried through the blackness. She wondered if this might be the last thing she could ever do for her boy. He drank half a glass eagerly, all his mother would let him have. He turned over and went to sleep. The next morning he was better, much better. The crisis had passed.

We thought so much of the old town pump that we built a canopy over it and planted shrubs around it. Now the handle is broken, the shrubs are overgrown and untrimmed. The old town pump went out with the horse and buggy.

We gather 'round the soda fountain today as we once did around the old town pump. 3-17-34

Mud Ruts

There is a trite expression about getting in a rut. Farm folks on muddy roads have had much experience with ruts this fall. Ruts may be crooked and bumpy but if you stay in the rut you will get to your destination. As the roads get drier some soul with the pioneer instinct pulls to one side and forms a nice straight track down the road. We like to follow that track but the urge that brought our forebears westward is not strong enough that we want to lay out that trail.

It rains again. One driver decides to make a new rut rather than follow the deep one. He plows along for a quarter mile. Then he decides to cross over to the old rut. That brings real trouble. The moral of the story seems to be, "Don't try to get from one rut to another."

The mud with its joys and sorrows and disgust bordering on the profane, nevertheless brings a smile to the farmer. Old timers know from experience that snow and mud in winter bid fair for a crop next season.

Farming is a gamble. There is no doubt about it. Yet today with the smell of spring in the air, with the hope of another crop the dirt farmer wouldn't exchange places with the bank president.

Farmers as a class are law abiding citizens. They want to comply with the laws of the land. They also believe in safety measures. Everyone of them would like to drive a shiny new car with the black and white OK sticker on the windshield. They would junk these derelicts tomorrow if they could afford a trade. Yet the farmer must have a means of transportation. The spring wagon and the buckboard are museum pieces. The one remaining buggy in the neighborhood should be placed alongside them. We are in the machine age. The only car the farmer can afford is the third or fourth hand auto you see on the township roads and the local trading centers. Most of these cars do not get more than 25 miles away from home at any time. Oftener only five or six. The radiators leak, they sputter and spit. They have scarce any brakes. But they get the family there and home again more often than not. If there is a way to get to town without getting on the main highway, that way is chosen.

The manager of a 3-ring circus has nothing on farmers these busy spring days. The last of the treated oats is no sooner planted than corn planting and grass seeding dogs his footsteps. And since cattle are gone to the pasture there are the feedlots to clean. For the homemaker there is garden and chickens and sewing for high school commencement. It's a great time to be alive on the farm. Daylight comes two hours earlier, than it did a few weeks ago.

And still the days are not long enough to crowd into them all that should be done.

We saw the meanest man last Sunday. He was driving a Lyon county car. The car stopped momentarily and a dog was boosted out - a small dog. We imagined that the small boy in the back seat was wiping the tears with the back of his fist. The dog, poor thing, was bewildered and confused. He went yipping across the pasture, frightened the yearling heifers and one of them jumped the fence. She could not be induced to jump back in again. She had to be driven to the gate. Did you ever try to drive a calf to the gate when the rest of the heard is drifting in the opposite direction? It tries the patience.

If you folks in town have a dog you do not want, we read that there is a dog pound. If you live in the country or a small town in the county don't try to deliberately lose them on a lonely country road. Such a deed is done only by a low down, contemptible ....(words fail us.)

We know that spring is on the way. Seed catalogs are arriving this week. Farm Bureau women are planning 1937 gardens. The plans call for the largest seedlings ever to be planted. These farm women are so weary of bare cellar shelves that if a good garden year ever comes again they will fill every jar they can lay hands on.

From spinach to tomatoes and squash, everything is perfect. No bugs, no diseases, even the labor doesn't show up in today's plan. Few artists can vie with those in the seed catalog for realism, unless it is those in the women's magazines which display food dishes in such attractive settings.

The garden derby is on. Lettuce, radishes and onions are a common-place. One neighbor had new peas from her garden for Sunday dinner. They are the next on the calendar to can. Beans are blooming as are tomatoes. Mouths water for a fresh picked garden ripe tomato.

But something is the matter. These gardens are not exact replicas of those portrayed in the favorite seed catalogs. Thousands of tiny weed seedlings glisten in the sun as the hoe stirs moist loose earth. And then the aphids! Have you seen millions of New Deal aphids on the onions? Often one finds the green parasites on kale or spinach. This year they have chosen onions and left the leafy vegetables scot free. Something is stripping the tomato vines and eating holes in the cabbage. The first generation of potato bugs are laying eggs on the underneath side of potato leaves. The skirmish with insects is on. One thing to be grateful for is that ladybugs in great numbers are present. May they eat and be filled.

The conversation turned to hair and hair styles. The father of a 10 year old lad pondered the beautiful waves so many youths seem to have today. According to each boy the wave is perfectly natural, all he does is comb it. Father, whose locks are thinning, remarks it is strange that none of the boys had waves like that when he was young.

Another father and son had a round-up regarding hair oil. The parent insisted that son used entirely too much. Which is true in nearly every case. "Now when I was your age," the father stormed. "I didn't use a bit of oil on my hair." In a quiet aside mother, who has a keen memory and a sense of humor, remarked, "Just ask him if he ever slicked it down with soap?" Son being a fairly good diplomat, knew that was not the moment to pop such a question. Has dad forgotten that he used to rub the cake of soap over his hair to keep his locks in place? Soap was the formula used by country boys 25 or 30 years ago to get a slick, stiff pompadour. Perhaps soft finger wave could not be fashioned with this soap application.

What a snow this has been. Teen age youngsters have seen few to compare with it. Sleighing parties can no longer be, because there isn't a sleigh in the neighborhood. Sled parties are the vogue instead. Home made sleds, little brothers' sleds, any-thing with runners, all are taken to the top of Chicago Mound. The end of the run is a spill in a snowdrift. Each one comes up smiling, to puff up the incline and come down again. What glorious sport. No wonder youth in the northern states longs for the winter season to set in.

The drifts this time were deep enough to build snow houses in. As school children play hide and seek they can drop out of sight in a drift, and likely have to call for help to get out. Snowballs fly though the air. Eyes are bright, cheeks rosy and overalls damp as urchins come in to sit by the fire.

Farmers and children are smiling over the big snow.

Our grandmothers always saved everything - bits of string, wrapping paper, boxes, etc. Today practically every advertiser wants us to save labels, box tops or cartons. It is housecleaning time and as we cleaned the pantry cupboard we found five oatmeal boxes, a half dozen coffee containers, tea and spice cartons, used tooth paste and shaving cream tubes. If the manufacturer wants these, we will gladly send same if they will forward postage. We do not like to have an announcer tell us that he will send something absolutely free if we will mail a box top to him. That isn't absolutely free. It is an exchange. One farm boy wrote down three cans of evaporated milk on the grocery list. And we milk three Jersey cows night and morning.

Did it rain the other night? Can't you tell by the farmer's step, by his thrown back shoulders and by the glint of hope in his eye? His steps were slow the week before, his shoulders drooped and his eyes were troubled. Of course this inch of rain hasn't made the corn but now that it has rained we think it will again. Farmers are whistling today.

Sixty-five little calves had clean white faces today. The rain gave many of them their first water bath. Their mothers give them a spit bath every day and slick them up but how much whiter the white looked today.

Harvest is over. Enough wheat in the bin for seed and flour. Father saved enough out of the wheat check for shoes all around. Shoes for the baby, shoes for the car, shoes for the rest of us. If you see us parading down street looking at our toes, smile with us. It's the first pair of new shoes we've had for a long time.

The big and the little dog are a great farm pair. From the ancestry written on the face of the big dog, one would say he is part bull dog, coon dog, shepherd, et cetera, mostly et cetera. The little dog is fox terrier plus. Every day the dogs hunt together. Farm dogs must hunt a good share of their living. The little dog goes in a hole and chases out the rabbit or the opossum. The big dog is there to nab them. Yesterday from the yips in the pasture - one knew a chase was on. A cocky jack rabbit bounded across the road and into the alfalfa. One miscalculation that jack rabbit made. The yon side of the alfalfa is fenced hog tight. As he leaped against the wire again and again the dogs bore down hard upon him. He half turned as if to flee from the fence and there was the little dog. An instant's hesitation and the big dog leaped for the catch.

The great dog carried off the prize while the small dog trotted alongside. Across the pasture, under the railroad trestle they carried their trophy. There they feasted.

We saw a calculator the other day for the first time - a machine that can do long division and discount problems in the wink of an eye. And get the right answer every time. An engineer can probably calculate as rapidly on his slide rule but a slide rule is beyond our ken. Why do children have to struggle with the multiplication table and percentage if they can work it all out on a machine? What boon this would be to math teachers.

We learned that the calculator cost several hundred dollars. As long as the state printing department furnishes arithmetic for 40 cents each it is probably best for the children to exercise their gray mater on fractions and decimals.

Weather is always good conversation in Kansas.

Perhaps one of the greatest thrills of the farm is enjoying the fruits of one's labor. The clerk in the department store must handle articles some one else will eventually use, the worker in industry must make things for others, the beauty operator must bake the head of another. The poet or artist has the thrill of seeing his verse or canvas but we plant the seeds, and with the help of the Creator, nurse and tend them. We not only see the results but taste, as well. 6-9-34

A good many Farm Bureau women are taking time to go to the Gazette cooking school. Did you ever notice how well fed a group of farm women appear? Of course there are always one or two slender ones but mostly they represent the stylish stouts. We enjoy our cream and mashed potatoes and home made bread. Miss Dixon encouraged us immensely. She concocted a tempting banana milk shake and announced she intended drinking it herself. From her clear skin and rounded curves one could easily believe she enjoyed her banana milk shakes. New recipes, new hints and short cuts along with contagious enthusiasm have inspired us all. How many families in Lyon county had ham loaf and pineapple sweet potatoes yesterday? If we will set out a grand meal as that the family would like us to attend cooking school every day!

What did you pay for pork chops today? Was it any less than you paid last week? As consumers you may know little about the hog market. The market is down this week. We know because we have a truck load of porkers ready for the packers. Our pessimistic neighbor says the reason hogs went down is because we have some ready to go. Out of idle curiosity we asked our butcher the price of pork chops. They are the same today as last week for loin. A 200 pound hog is bringing two dollars less on the market this week. What we would like to know is where has that two dollars gone? Button, button, who's got the two bucks? The farmer hasn't them. The grocer hasn't them. The consumer doesn't have them. Who has?

What do you do when you wait? Do you twiddle your thumbs or do you cool your heels? We confess waiting is out of our line. By the time we are ready to go the whole family is waiting on us. There are only two classes of people in the world, those who wait and those who are waited on. One man at the Topeka fair fooled his wife. They agreed to meet at 4 o'clock but he did not appear until 5. At 5:05 said wife came hurrying up with an elaborate alibi. Friend husband is enjoying his little joke immensely. He has not explained that he waited only five minutes. He is apt to get in bad if such becomes a practice. Some day this wife may have to wait on him and there won't be any joke at all.

"I have read," remarked the old timer, "that if you drive a car 35 miles an hour it will last four times as long as if you drive it 65."

"Yes," replied the youth, "that's true, but who's going to do it?"

I imagine the old timer seldom exceeds 35 miles. He followed a yoke of oxen across the prairies when he was a boy and 35 miles seems plenty fast to him. He doesn't cover as many miles as the youth. He starts out a bit sooner, goes in fewer circles, has a more definite idea of where he wants to go and gets there on time.

It was explained to me that manufacturers constantly increase the top speed of an engine to lengthen its life. I supposed the car that could travel the fastest in this day of speed was the car with the record sales.

Most highways have speed limits. Why doesn't the state or the manufacturer put governors on these cars of perhaps 45 miles an hour?

You see, I am betwixt youth and the old timer.

Far too many accidents occur on the farm and in the home. As sure as the summer passes there is an accident in the neighborhood. As we think back over the past few years, each of the accidents here could have been avoided. Had the tractor been shut off when the combine clogged down, a broken and mangled foot might have been prevented. When a brake on the tractor failed to hold, the tractor rolled back and a painfully injured hand resulted. Another time an injured back might have been spared by the use of a jack. A stop sign at the county road might have saved a farm family from serious injury.......

Time was when our fear of accidents was runaway horses or the mowing machine or the hay rake. With today's intricate farm equipment, the farmer who is careless runs a great risk. After a recent accident in this community a farmer visited around among his neighbors and noted accident hazards. He was amazed at the number of needless risks he found.

In this machine age, farm families must think safety and constantly check and remove accident hazards. Good safety practices for business and industry are also good for the farm.

8-4-56

Times must be improving somewhere along the line. The old car littered the back yard while we waited for a free day to take it to the gulch in the pasture. Some enterprising lads came along and bought the old car and hauled it away for us. With this coin in hand we feel very much as we do when we visit the dentist. Instead of paying him for extraction we think he should pay us. Thus instead of those boys paying us for the old car it looks as if we should have paid them. Maybe this is one way to get even with our dentist. 12-22-34

Have you ever been on a farm in October? Indian summer haze hangs around the horizon, dust rises from the feedlots as the men cut and sort the cattle for winter feeding. Calves that arrived in the pasture must have their shots of blackleg, hemorrhagic septicemia and a tattoo in the ear. We must have 9-point calves as well as children. The cows bawl and run up to the fence anxiously watching it all. The constant bawling for two nights after weaning.

If you have ever lived on a farm surely these things come back to you in October - the best time of the year.

Friends were out from the city last week-end. Kansas mud was a real treat to the children. Old clothes were hunted up and we watched a 4-reel comedy. Don't you remember how you liked to "squish" mud between your toes after a summer rain? A real slippery slide was constructed on the bank of the creek. No one could go down without soiling the seat of his pants. We put the family bath tub on the back porch and each child had to pass through it before coming in. I suppose that is one advantage of a portable tub, otherwise there would have been muddy tracks from the back door to the bathroom.

Always with the swelling of buds and the return of the birds come many farm babies. The kittens are in the hay mow. We haven't found them yet. They will be a Sunday afternoon excursion. The little pup should have his eyes open Friday, if he doesn't pass out from too much handling before then. The orphan pig, sole survivor of the family that arrived in zero weather, has been boosted out of the parlor. She doesn't like it and comes squealing to the door. Little calves cuddle down in the straw and sunshine and sleep the day through. The neighbors baby chicks boast tail and wing feathers. New life, new hope comes to the farm every-year with the spring season.

The old white rooster struts very proudly. His spurs are long and pointed. Occasionally he comes in the yard. If small children turn and run he chases them and flies at them. But the old rooster has met his match. His feathers are drooping. He circled the orphan lamb. The lamb galloped after him and chased him all over the yard. The cock became weary and would have called king's-ex. The lamb was having great fun. Right willingly did the rooster return to the poultry yard when the gate was opened. He has not been seen in the yard since.

Farm sleeping quarters have been moved outdoors. Beds in the back yard may not add to the aesthetic atmosphere of the landscape. But snoozing is grand. Flies serve as an alarm clock. Along toward sunrise they begin to stir and attack any enemy in sight. The only thing for the farmer to do is to go to bed when the flies do. 5-5-36

Farmers hurried in the house last week when a few rain drops spat in their faces. Mattresses and summer bedding were hastily placed on the front porch. Upstairs beds were spread for occupancy. For three nights we approached the civilized state again. We decided the summer heat wave had disappeared. Come Sunday. The hottest, stickiest day of the year. Beds and cots were all set up in the back yard again.

No sooner had the family quieted down for the night than a blinding flash of light appeared in the northeast. The first reaction was the hired man was flashing his headlights upon us or that it was the moon. Fully awake we realized there was fire at the neighbor's It was not the farmhouse because it was silhouetted against the night sky by the blaze. Likewise the silo. It was the barn! The barn chuck full of oats straw and baled hay. With oats in the bin and seed corn hanging from the rafters. With harness and binder canvas and any amount of small tools and equipment.

In five minutes all the near neighbors had arrived. The Emporia fire department reached the scene in an unbelievably short time. Then came a stream of headlights. Folks curious, anxious, interested, eager to help.

When a car drives in the back yard these hot days we know it is apt to be a politician or a peddler. Children are dispatched to the door to greet the caller while mother scrambles into shoes and a clean bungalow apron.

Grandmother had it over us today. Visitors coming in the buggy had to get out at the road and open and close the gate. Then they would come jogging down the lane. After visitors were sighted there was time to wash the baby's face, change his clothes, put on a clean bib apron and brush up the kitchen floor. Today these new cars steal in quietly and catch us unawares.

The other day we heard a charming woman lecture on charm. It was her suggestion that we have a department of charm in our college curricula. We gather that is one of the goals of finishing schools. Heaven help us, if charm or personality is taught in our colleges. No doubt there would be a cut and dried recipe for charm comparable to the recipe for salesmanship which the house-to-house canvasser memorizes.

THE FARM WOMAN'S DAY

We have been asked to outline the activities of a farm woman's day. Just which day shall we describe? Shall it be wash-day, the one day of the week when everything must click if the day is run smoothly? Or shall it be a day that we wish to go somewhere? Perhaps then is seen family cooperation at its best. Children do their tasks swiftly and well and ask what is next. Or, those days when we putter around all day and have nothing to show for our day's work when night comes? Washing, ironing, mending, cleaning, canning in season, sewing and gadding, all are included in the week's schedule. Many tasks not finished today will wait patiently until we get at them. A farm homemaker has only to visit a town club to find out how busy your schedules are and to realize how little we do on the farm.

On the surface it might appear that there is a drab monotony about life on the farm. The monotony comes from working hard year after year and then not having sufficient income to pay taxes and interest. Monotony, it seems to us, is to be found in the city. The worker, if he is fortunate enough to have a job, punches the clock at the same time every morning, does the same routine task for 50 weeks in the year. He comes and goes over the same beaten path through the same street canyons. He lives in a street in which all houses in the block are exactly alike. He probably does not see one green thing growing or get a glimpse of the sunset.

Each day brings a new dawn on the farm. The alarm rings at 5:30 now. In well ordered households the whole family, washed and brushed sits down to breakfast en masse. In other homes, not so well ordered, perhaps, each member rises and prepares his own repast. If it is bread baking day the bread must be mixed first thing. The chickens must be tended. Frequently breakfast dishes are pushed back and before the table is cleared the day's correspondence is taken care of. The mail comes and we peek at the headlines and the Starbeams. Before we know it, it is 10:30. The bread must be made into loaves, potatoes peeled, carrots and cabbage gathered for dinner. Breakfast dishes are whisked away in time to set out again for dinner. If company drops in after noon we may wish we had dusted the living room and mopped the kitchen floor, but we are glad to see them and we forget mussed up surroundings. The next thing school is out and the youngsters come home half starved. Eggs must be gathered, wood and kindling carried in and supper set out.

Sunsets, pale salmon, rich red orange and warm violet all beautifully blended, all harmonious, crown the day's efforts.

9-6-35

THE FARM WOMAN

It was a treat to representatives of the Women's advisory council of the Farm Bureau to be invited to the mothers' recreational camp in Leavenworth county. Ninety-eight farm women left family cares behind them last Sunday and hied to the annual camp at Lake Tonganoxie. The Farm Bureau in that county owns 20 acres adjoining the state lake. Two cottages have been erected by the men and boys. Here it is that 4-H clubs, vocational agricultural groups and farm women go annually for an outing. Grandmothers and stylish stouts climbed agilely to double-deck beds. We rejoiced they had assigned us a lower berth.

Not once did we hear mention of the work or the folks at home. One grandmother did boast a little of her wonderful granddaughter. Another grandmother, 87, has attended camp regularly for five years. When asked whether she was at farm and home week in '34 or '35 she replied, "I was there both years." A mother of 14 children was there. She shared some of her reminiscences with us. Each one learned a new bit of handwork at camp. Some beginners learned to swim. Along with fun and recreation went some rather meaty discussions. And did those mothers put on the feed bags! Nine meals which they had no hand in preparation or serving.

The central states supervisor from the Washington office was there to listen and to inspire us.

She told us that camp discussions give us fundamental things to think about. The most important expression of art in the home is a smiling face. That we must learn "what are your rights are my obligations and what are my rights are your obligations."

The group agreed that all phases of the extension program have been helpful. Above all the work in clothing, in color and design has done more to eradicated the inferiority complex, to give the farm woman poise and confidence and place her on a par with urban woman.

In the background were the home demonstration agents. The trained home economists who did all the groundwork and planning for the camp and kept it running smoothly. They made each mother feel that she was a special guest. Much of the advance of farm women is due to home demonstration agents.

All had a splendid good time. Lake Tonganoxie is one of the beauty spots of Kansas. All the time we wished that Lyon county could have similar camp. A place for farmers to congregate that they could call their own. Then the county agents would not have to hunt around as they do now to find a place for us to meet. Surely we do not want to admit that Leavenworth county folks are any better or more progressive than we are. The material cost of the cottages is small. Wouldn't this be a good project for WPA why not make the effort among ourselves?

THE FARM WOMAN

The Royal

For the first time that anyone in the group is aware a group of farm women writers were invited to be guests of the American Royal in Kansas City this year. They came from the farms of Missouri, Kansas and Oklahoma.

Each one present was modest in response to her introduction about her writing activities. As soon as introductions were finished, though the room began to buzz. One was able to meet the girls she had read in the exchanges and others she had not heard of before.

Do you live on a farm? How many children do you have? How did you begin writing? These were the questions one heard on every hand. Everyone does live on a farm - that was one condition of the invitation. So far as one could gather each one has a family and a family of three or more children. Most of them began their careers by accident or incidence. Each one had some kind of problem about getting to the luncheon - such as a drive through flood. Each one left bread baked at home and enough food for the folks to get along. Each one, too, was grateful to a family that brought her or urged her to attend.

Five hundred farm women were guests of the Royal for the Thursday matinee. There they saw the finest collections of horseflesh to be found in the world. It was a deeply appreciative section - this group of farm women. This show was an event in the lives of each one present. In the first place farm women aren't used to passes. And believe me it is a thrill to hand a guest ticket to the gatekeeper.

These groups have been guests of the Royal over a number of years. So far as the writer knows it is the only show which gives recognition to farm women. At the women's headquarters one can sit down or meet her family or telephone her aunt or get an aspirin or a needle and thread. They meet others interested in home demonstration work and each one resolves that next year the rest of the family must see the show. The attendance this year is greater than ever before and one wonders if those good resolves are not bearing fruit.

After the show the crowd spreads out through the exhibits. The draft horse may be disappearing from the farms but he is at the Royal in all his glory. The Grand Champion Clydesdale is one of the finest animals the writer has ever seen. (We used to raise Clydesdales and I may be prejudiced.) These horse's tails receive as much care as does milady at the beauty shop.

Sleek, square Herefords with perfect marcels and smooth black Angus and Shorthorns all are there. Hogs with all their swiny odor and sheep and crowing cocks - all these things one sees between shows.

10-27-41

THE FARM WOMAN

Every Farm Bureau woman has a tear in her eye and a tightening of the throat today. Letters have come telling us that our home demonstration agent is going to leave. Our first reaction is that she cannot go. We cannot get along without her. When we stop to reason that she is going to college again for advanced work we know that wider vistas will open for her and we must not hold her here. Our hearts would keep her, reason would bid her Godspeed.

For more than six years Miss Gertrude Allen has worked long and faithfully in this county. She has brought farm women together so that today women for Hartford know the women from Bushong and Olpe and Americus. She has interested us in a live-at-home program. Today farm bureau women follow a nutrition budget, fruit every day, potatoes and at least one other vegetable, meat, milk and cereal. We know that we should can 31 quarts of vegetables for each member of the family. We have had meat utilization meetings in every neighborhood and now have a variety of meats throughout the year. Before we had these lessons we ate our fill of ribs and tenderloin and head cheese right after butchering and lived on ham and side and fried down sausage the rest of the time. We take our wheat to the mill and exchange it for a variety of products. We have been shown the romance of bread making. It is no longer a twice-a-week chore.

Farm Bureau units have studied foot care and today farm women want well fitting, straight line shoes. Shower baths seem a simple thing after they are constructed but extension service gave the idea to us. Old walnut chairs and tables have been brought from the hay mow, refinished, glued and re-caned. One learns to appreciate a family heirloom by the time all the layers of varnish are removed and it glows with several coats of wax. Tours have brought us closer together and shown us what our neighbors have done to their homes at little expense.

These thoughts come crowding in as we think on the things Miss Allen has taught us. We should like to have a party and a grand send off. It was her request that she be permitted to slip quietly away. Partings from those we love tug at the heart.

THE FARM WOMAN

Each day a new straw stack appears in the neighborhood as the thrashing outfit completes one job and moves on to the next. Time wasn't even taken out for the Fourth of July. The appearance of this golden yellow mound in the feedlot means that there is oats in the bin and likely a warehouse receipt for wheat in the farmer's pocket.

Many farmers in the county had intended to seal wheat in bins on their farms. However, the moisture content was too high, the wheat began to heat and to the elevator it went. My neighbor estimates that a little more than half of the wheat is being sold outright. For the remainder, warehouse receipts are accepted. A little, but very little, is being placed under government loan.

Warehouse receipt is a new word in the household. It means to us that our wheat has been sealed in one of the huge terminal elevators in Kansas City. There it can be moved by the simple touch of a button. It can be moved or dried or cooled or deweeviled. One wonders if there are any mice or rats around the terminals or do they get rid of them by electricity too?

This slip of paper - the warehouse receipt - gives a feeling of comfort. Here is insurance against next year's crop. We have wheat in the bin, although we cannot see it.

However this same slip of paper is a negotiable instrument. It can be taken to the bank and exchanged for coin of the realm. Or one can get a government loan which in turn is negotiable and can also be converted into cold cash. With part of the cash one can take out government insurance on next year's crop. All of which seems as if the farmer is having his cake and eating it too. Only it is the farm equipment people who are eating the cake. Their finance men are here to take it before the farmer even gets a good smell.

Warehouse receipts, government idle acres, government crop insurance, government loans - all these phrases have been added to the farm vocabulary in the past few years. There is considerable skepticism about accepting these new words whole-heartedly. But it's a great time to be on the land.

7-7-39

THE FARM WOMAN

Pea Green Hats

With the approach of Easter the farm homemaker scrutinizes the market page and the egg crate, wondering if there will be enough left over to get a new spring bonnet. Groceries must be paid for and new shoes for the children out of the egg money. If the price will only stay where it is, it looks as if things would work out. The biddies are co-operating. They have laid more eggs the past week than any time yet. Thus does the homemaker dream as she kneads the bread or brushes down cobwebs.

As she rides to town the rich green of the wheat fields, bluegrass peeping out from its brown winter covering and the trees ready to burst into bloom, all these things exalt her spirit, these and the anticipation of that new Easter hat, probably no doctor's prescription serves as quite the tonic to a farm woman as does a bright new hat. It lifts her out of her depression, banishes inferiority and brings poise and satisfaction.

The eggs are sold. Groceries and shoes are paid for. Alone the farm woman sets out to window shop for hats. And what is this that greets her eye? Every window is filled with bilious yellow-green hats and accessories. Was the color designer affected by a week-end hangover when he brought out that color? Or is that the color that green appears in the distorted light of canyon-like streets in a smoke filled city. That is the color of onion tops which have sprouted in the warm damp cellar away from the sun. Now who could wear that color in the light of day? The homemaker looked again at the window. There were other hats there, of course. But they were all affected by the sickly green. She fingered the change in her purse and decided if that nauseating color was the style leader this spring she would wait another year to blossom out in an Easter bonnet. A new hat is an event in the farm household.

That pallid pea green color is an affront to the women of Lyon county and to Mother nature as well. Just get Nature aroused and she may send us a hail, flood or tornado. For the sake of the poor farmers down here on the bottom a plea is made to box those bilious colored hats and duds up and send them back to Chicago or New York or Pittsburgh, where they will not stand in sad comparison to the green of April wheat fields or prairie bluestem.

4-3-39

THE FARM WOMAN

The weather is the most common topic of conversation these days. All last week eyes hopefully and prayerfully scanned the sky for signs of rain. This week there is a calmer acceptance of the fact that it will rain when it gets ready. There is nothing we can do about it. Much corn is gone now.

There may be a few nubbins in the fields here and there or a protected spot that will give a fair yield, but in the main the Lyon county corn crop is gone. And with it the dreams of the farm family. That water system or the new rug will have to wait. We cannot expect a corn crop every year and this is one of those years. However do not think for one minute that the revised estimate of the Kansas corn crop will alter the national or international situation. Vacationists traveling home through Iowa and Illinois tell of the tall corn there. Our short crop will never be missed.

Some weeks ago when the wheat kernels were entering the dough and corn prospects were as good as any one had ever seen, the old timer shook his head and said it was mighty seldom that we got both a wheat harvest and a corn crop in this county. It was his observation that the county actually fared better in the years when they had a corn crop At the present writing one tends to agree.

All rejoiced over the wheat harvest. The crop over the county was a good average yield. When the farmer fished his stub pencil out of his vest pocket and began to figure on the back

of an envelope the list ran something like this:
20 bushels an acre at 53 cents $10.80
Plowing $1.25
Disking........... .40
Drilling........... .40
Seed 1 ¼ bushels.. .75
Phosphate......... 1.40
Combining....... 2.00
Total.................. 6.20
Profit................. 4.40

If he had 40 acres, his profit was $175. Did he get to pocket this? The chances are that an alert, ambitious young finance man, who has his eyes fixed on a promotion to a nice office berth with his farm machinery equipment company, was right there to take all that wheat money as payment on the tractor for both this year and last. The grocer and other local merchants waited until the farmer got to town to press their claims. The finance man waited in the field. The local men will have to wait. The idealist might think that a more equitable way would be to prorate payments on all accounts, thereby letting each creditor have something. But the idealist would never become vice president of a machinery equipment company.

8-2-39

THE FARM WOMAN

A neighbor has a government loan. It required much time and red tape to acquire. It is an amortization mortgage. The interest rate is lower and as it is written for 33 years there will not be the cost of renewal every five years.

She read in the Kansas City Star about the Tugwell colony of 146 families that is to be established in 14 northeastern Kansas counties. The average cost of the land is $80 an acre and cost of modernization and improvements averages $70 an acre in addition. The families who are being established in this colony haven't a dime with which to make a down payment. In 40 years they will have enjoyed their cake all the while and it is all down on paper to prove that the farms will belong to them.

"Humph," my neighbor remarked after reading this article. "If Tugwell will just show me how to pay off the $3,200 load we have on our 160, I'll not ask for any bathroom, electricity or modern home. Of course, I'd like to have all that but what we want to do is to get our land paid for. We aren't as young as we used to be. We have put our inheritance and the best of years of our lives in on this farm. What we want most of all is to be free of that debt."

My neighbor represents the attitude of many farm folk. Kansas is dotted with farms where a lot of money was spent on modernizing and improving the farm home that the family might live in comfort. A little lien was placed on the land to finish the job. Ere long the land was foreclosed and land, home, all was lost. I wish Dr. Tugwell would point out how these folks might have retained their farms.

Would it not seem more logical to assist farmers who have an interest, a nest egg, in their farms than to put families without anything upon land on which the cost of the improvements is almost equal to the cost of the land itself. Most farmers think this cannot possibly work out. Some of us may live 40 years to see.

Is the experience, the wisdom of old timers to be entirely ignored? One sage of the village says that land must be emancipated. Our scale of living is geared to a bumper crop every year. That isn't done in Kansas. This man is a well-to-do retired farmer. He succeeded because he followed a pay as you go policy. Because he paid only $3 an acre for rich bottom land. He lived in a log house until he had the money to build a good home. He never could have made it had he had a high initial outlay.

8-15-36

THE FARM WOMAN

The men were working past 8 o'clock bailing straw. The sun had beat down all afternoon. The wind was hot but farmers are always thankful for any breeze. One neighbor was cleaning up straw around the baler, then they would quit for the day. Suddenly one of the boys noticed a gray smudge rising out of the straw at his feet. In a flash he jerked off his unbuttoned blue chambray shirt and beat frantically. In a few seconds smoke could be seen all the way to the top of what remained of the straw stack. Flames leaped out. The men knew they were in for it. They tried to pull the baler away, but the heat was too intense.

The water wagon at the house, 200 yards way, was loaded. It had been filled for the evening's haul to the pasture. The wagon was brought near. Great chunks of blazing straw were carried across the road by the hot south wind. Fear clutched the hearts of those men. A neighbor's straw stack was right in line with the burning mass. Pastures were veritable tinder boxes. If flames ever started across the road, could the fire be checked before it reached the river?

The river was two miles away. Two farmsteads lay along the dry creek bed between the burning mass and the river. Mercifully the fire did not spread.

In 30 minutes the blaze died down. Ten tons of bright yellow oat straw had risen in smoke. A serious loss in this year of the drought, 1936. The cause of the conflagration is thought to have been a spark from the exhaust of the tractor. Wild animals fear fire. Fire has been man's protection and means of self preservation, but in this dry season farmers are on the defensive.

We fear fire even as the slinking prairie coyote.

THE FARM WOMAN

When we were a high school sophomore, life's most embarrassing moment was the bringing of a little half-frozen calf in the house. We had company from town that night. That girl had electric lights, an electric curling iron and a warm bedroom to undress in. Out here we had to heat the curling iron in the lamp chimney and our pride and modesty compelled us to undress and dress in the cold. That point of pride pricked us only when we had company. Other times we dressed by the stove as the rest of the family. These inconveniences were bad enough. To have a white-faced calf brought into the house was more than we could bear.

But last week when father brought a tiny incubator calf into the house not a murmur was heard. That calf was as tenderly watched over as the neighbor's new baby. The children wanted to feed her every time she cried. We have named the calf Prima. She is a genuine blue blood. Her ancestors have been recorded in Hereford aristocracy for generations.

Prima is a week old today and frolicking in the sunshine. Her bed and box have been moved to the granary. The dining room has been aired and scrubbed. The young, enthusiastic extension specialist would no doubt frown on such improper use of a dining room. He took great pains to explain that each room in the house was designed for a specific purpose and should be used as designed. The kitchen for preparation of food, the bedroom for personal room, etc. That would be grand. But even under the New Deal we continued to use the kitchen for bath, laundry, canning and an occasional harbor for calves, chicks and pups.

2-22-35

Chronicles of The Farm Woman

THE FARM WOMAN

We visited friends in town the other day. It was pay day. We fear we looked longingly at the four crisp bills friend husband handed the wife. The bills were of larger denomination than farmers ever see. Immediately we accompanied the homemaker downstairs to give the manager one of these crisp bills. The rent included garage, heat, light, water, gas and telephone. It is a thrifty city homemaker that gets all those service for 25 per cent of the family income.

We continued on down town to look at shoes - there was a shoe sale on. Sales seem to be another thing thrifty town women watch. From the shoe store we drove to the market. The vegetable counter intrigued us. Have you seen the sprinklers that constantly spray the lettuce, spinach, carrots, etc? When visitors from the farm come, the larder must be well stocked. Farmers do have appetites. T-bone steaks, mushrooms, two tomatoes, one cucumber, one avocado, one head of lettuce, prepared salad dressing, 10 pounds of potatoes, one pound butter, two loaves bread, a can of peas, an extra bottle of milk and cream, a chocolate cake and a can of peaches completed the order there. We went farther down the street where there was a special on lard that day. Next door was a sugar sale.

On the way home we stopped for a gasoline coupon book. At the apartment again, the high school sophomore was handed her carfare and lunch allowance for the week. It was an exciting afternoon for a farm homemaker. Any longing for those four crisp bills had vanished. We began to wonder how we could make the remainder stretch to the first of the following month.

Imagine buying ten pounds of potatoes when we have twenty bushels stored in the cellar. Or two pounds of lard when we have 15 gallons on the cellar shelf. Milk and cream and butter are on the back porch. Fruits, vegetables and meat in the cellar cupboard. The bread box is filled with a baking of home-made bread. There are no avocadoes, or cucumbers or tomatoes out of season. No mushrooms and broiled T-bone only at butchering time. No wonder town folks feel that we are rich when they come to the farm. We need to go to town once in a while to realize the blessings of home products. What city consumers often do not realize is that the producer gets less than 40 percent of the consumer dollar. There's the rub.

THE FARM WOMAN

Scarlet fever is rampant in this end of the country again. Just when mothers were beginning to breathe easy and decide that children could go to town again, comes a new outbreak. Whence the germs come authorities do not seem to know. Scarlet fever germs, invisible, long lived, hiding and lurking one knows not where, are a scourge to the community.

And when it snatches one of our neighbors - a good neighbor - then is the vicinity gripped with fear. Immediate harm to children may not be apparent but in 10 or 20 years, eye, ear, kidney or heart complications may develop, traceable to scarlet fever in childhood.

Some folks have had such light cases that they are innocent carriers of the disease. Others, not realizing (surely they would care if they knew) the danger of spreading contagion, do not summon a doctor at the first sign of a cold or sore throat. Also, there is the matter of fumigation. The amateur feels there is much he does not know about the destruction of germs. Conscientiously most farm women have scrubbed these old houses with diluted formalin solution. They have sprayed the concentrated solution until they could stand it in the room no longer. But is there one germ somewhere that they did not get? That is what the conscientious homemaker wonders.

Sad to say, there are some farmers, and perhaps some town dwellers, too, who do not believe in fumigation.

We doubt if they would believe if they were shown slides and stains of before and after. How can these people who do not believe in fumigation be expected to do a thorough job of it. We are told of the house in Emporia which some folks used to say was haunted. Every family which moved into it seemed to sicken and die. It was discovered that the cause of deaths was scarlet fever. Eventually the haunted house was torn down. There are today houses in Lyon county in which families had scarlet fever in past years. Tenants changed and the new occupants developed the disease. We would welcome fumigation by the county health department. A thorough knowledge of germs of contagion, which all public health officials must have, should aid in their eradication. Conscientious citizens would welcome such a plan. Unbelievers would not then contaminate the entire community. But the cost, you say! Would the cost be prohibitive or would it be a saving to the county?

Sure our epidemics would not reach the widespread proportions which they do. Such a plan would result in a net saving of cold cash and human lives.

Think this over!

THE FARM WOMAN

The White Rock pullet must have been reading the headlines or listening to news dispatches, via the radio, regarding child marriages. The pullet was hatched on the eighth day of April and today she brought forth a brood of six baby chicks. At silo filling time she was discovered, high in the haymow, sitting on 10 diminutive pullet eggs. A daily pilgrimage was rewarded by hearing the cheep cheep of baby chicks. Part little fluff balls, scarce larger than a day old quail peered out from under their mother's wing.

They are housed in a small coop in the yard tonight. The mother clucks to the babies and tells them that she was reared in the big brooder house close by, beneath a great electric brooder. She was pampered by having prepared feed and treated water kept before her at all times. She knows her offspring will never have such luxuries. Never mind, she is strong and she learned to catch grass-hoppers out on the range. There is food aplenty this year. Although they may not have the comforts and luxuries, her baby chicks will have a mother's care and attention. Something the young pullet never knew.

The family is divided over the young mother hen and her brood. Children have visions of fried chicken at Christmas time. Mother wonders if she will have to knit shoes for them. Father proclaims that as soon as the chicks are weaned this gay young pullet will go into the noodle pot; that she is a bad example for the rest of the flock. Is that the answer? Is that the price the young pullet should pay for her indiscretion? Or isn't there danger in persecuting the young mother that she may become a martyr? May not all the other pullets become crusaders and set in defense of their sister? What to do with the unorthodox young hens?

Grandmother shakes her head and declares it all lies within the electric brooder. The young pullet would never have conceived such notions had she been brought up properly by a mother hen.

It is front page news when farm income is 9 million dollars. However as you read those glaring headlines just remember that is the estimated gross income of six million farm families. When one reads the income of industry one is reading about net income. This has been a a good year for farmers. As fast as we can we are buying cars, tractors, radios and gew gaws. 10-37

THE FARM WOMAN

Another red letter day on the farm calendar is here. The last day of school. Girls have new dresses and new white shoes for the occasion. For 30 years the basket dinner has been the feature of the day.

One teacher confided that her brood were like wild savages the last week. All was riot and confusion, reviews and tests. Practicing for the program. Cleaning out desks and carrying home books and papers. Washing the windows and slicking up the schoolhouse for parents and patrons. The eighth graders crammed for county examinations. Seventh graders are jubilant because the state let them off this year.

Farm mothers, as they chat, admit that they think their offspring just as smart as town kids. But town youngsters do not have to go to a strange place among strangers to take eighth grade exams. College professors teach prospective teachers not to cram their students for examinations. Yet what are these young teachers to do? They firmly believe they are training for character and citizenship and build to that end. However, if they do not drill on the two or three hundred review questions their pupils will not do well in the quizzes. Regardless of how the teacher of the individual would score him in citizenship, honesty, industry, thrift, neighborly-ness, et cetera, both teacher and child are scored by examination grades.

Occasionally we think there is not enough drill in

the 3 R's today. Any child should be able to learn the multiplication tables. Perhaps teachers are too lenient and do not require as much as they should. Then we go to the grocery store with our crate of eggs. After candling them the clerk gets down the chart to see instantly what eleven dozen eleven should bring. If we purchase a number of items they are totaled on the adding machine. We go to the bank for a small loan. Does the banker figure interest in his head? No, he reaches for a chart. It is similar in appearance to the key in the grocery store except that it is not so soiled and is bound in leather. Probably it does not see as much use. The engineer keeps a slide rule in his pocket and does his arithmetic upon it. One wonders why there must be so many tears over eighth grade problems if out in the world all calculating is done by tables and machines.

THE FARM WOMAN

The little house stands sad and forlorn. Even the casual passerby notes it as he whizzes past. To one who, since childhood, has known the little house its neglect pierces the heart. Tall weeds reach the eaves. The garden and chicken pen and orchard are overgrown. Cedar trees which were always neatly shaped and trimmed are ragged and frowzy.

One remembers that the farmer who owned this land was one of the first in the community to invest in a manure spreader and to grow alfalfa. The old canes were cut out of the blackberry patch every year. The strawberry bed was one of the best. Products from the orchard and small fruits were sold every year. The earliest fries of the season were to be found in the chicken pen. We may not care for cedars trimmed in fancy shapes today but in childhood they were an object of envy.

Time passed. The farmer and his good wife grew in years. Probably high pressure salesmen persuaded them to buy things which they could have done without. Demoralized agriculture made it successively harder to meet interest payments. Ill health descended. The doctor prescribed no manual labor. Gradually the farm slipped away. One day it was repossessed by the mortgage holder and the occupants forced off the land.

There are too many such instances in Lyon county.

Perhaps one farmer can make a success where another fails. Many com-

plexities enter into every problem. To a sentimental farm woman there is a sense of needless tragedy when an old couple who have tended the land faithfully for years are forced off it only for the house to remain staring and vacant. Let a hustling young farmer tend the land if it must be repossessed. In many cases would it not be as well for the old farmer and his good wife to live in the house, mow the lawn, trim the hedge as for the farmstead to become a jungle and the house a specter of desolation?

7-28-37

THE FARM WOMAN

A farm woman stood in the grocery store one evening last week and heard the customer ahead of her ask for a peck of potatoes, a quart of milk, a dozen eggs and a loaf of bread. Quickly her mind darted over the inventory at home. Her family had stored 50 bushels of potatoes in the cellar, they would soon be doing the evening milking, the eggs would be gathered and there were four loaves of fresh, homemade bread on the kitchen table when she left home. All of the items that the town customer asked for, this neighbor had at home. All those things and more. She had butter and sweet rendered lard and row after row of canned foods on the cellar shelves. The garden still furnishes tomatoes, cabbage, peppers, turnips and green beans. She would stop at the freezer locker on her way home to get several days supply of meat and at the mill for a sack of custom ground flour, breakfast food and wheat germ.

This farm woman was so absorbed in all the foods she had at home she could not remember what she had come to the store to buy. She fumbled a moment and discovered that she held the grocery list in her hand - sugar, coffee, matches, tobacco. A curious thing about this grocery order is that sugar, coffee and tobacco are all processed farm products from another clime or community. The grocery store is closely linked with products of the land.

The groceries were paid for with proceeds from eggs

and cream which my neighbor took to town. Another part of the produce check went for shoes and stockings. Graveled roads are fine in wet weather but they are hard on children's shoes. Thus proving that there are advantages and disadvantages in all things.

The leftovers from the cream check have been hoarded for a new coat and hat this season. However, there are so many demands on the cash account that it looks as if mother would have to wait. Retail merchants would have a boom in business if farm families could stretch the cream check farther. The window decorator and the advertising page have succeeded in planting the desire. If someone will point the way to greater returns, the planted desires will be fulfilled.

At any rate the family larder is well stocked as we go into this winter of 1940-41.

10-25-40

THE FARM WOMAN

Pastures in this region are filling rapidly. For six months the cattle will actually live on the fat of the land - verdant bluestem. Turning out to grass is one of the high spots of the year. Old cows knew what was coming the morning they were driven to the pasture, for old cows are weather-wise and they have learned through the years what to expect.

When the calves were run through the chute to be vaccinated against blackleg and pink eye the younger heifers were nervous and flighty. They bawled and paced along the fence trying to get to their offspring. Older cows were more complacent. None-the-less they licked their offspring eagerly when they were restored to them. They gazed off toward the rolling prairie and knew this meant they would soon get to the bluestem again.

When the day arrived the cows were not fed ensilage topped with cake as usual. Instead the barn doors were closed and the gate to the water lot as well. The 2-year-old heifers who had not been with the herd since they were baby calves were brought into the main lot. The herd bull was led down. Two or three saddle horses nosed the gate. And the old cows knew. The minute the gate to the lower lot was opened they galloped through and cavorted about. The enthusiasm was contagious and the entire herd frisked and frolicked. When the main gate was opened they all surged out as children troop out of school for the noon recess. It was a disorganized mass at first. However by the time they came to the first culvert Princess Rose was leading the herd as she has done for several years now, ever since Miss Blanc reacted to the Bangs test and was sent to market. Princess Rose sets a comparatively fast pace but if any of the younger females try to supersede her she rolls her eyes or her head as if to inform them that she is of true bluebloods. Her ancestry can be traced back to Herefordshire in England. Of course the blood of the younger cows is just as aristocratic. Either they do not realize it or they do not care to lock horns with the Princess.

There may be some cows who choose to have chopped and prepared food served them twice daily, who like to stay in a cool dark barn away from the sun and the flies. But not the Herefords Now that they are turned on grass they can eat where they please, when they please and take their ease on the warm sweet smelling earth. They can drink at the pond when they choose. For six months their life will be one of freedom. True they must live out in sunshine and rain, and the lightning often gets in at least one fatal lick during the season and flies sometimes get pretty bad. Yet given their choice between security and the wide open spaces there isn't any hesitancy. The Herefords choose the blue stem, God's gift to Kansas.

THE FARM WOMAN

The first cold spell of the season always brings a demand for golden brown doughnuts. Grandmother preferred to wait until right after butchering to fry doughnuts in fresh sweet lard. Now grandmother could not explain the underlying scientific reason for her preference but as was often the case, experience guided grandmother down a sound scientific path. Fresh lard probably does make better doughnuts.

You may not know it but hog prices to the farmer have been distressingly low this year. Commission men tell us that large stocks of lard in storage are one of the depressing factors in low hog prices. It seems that town cooks in the corn Belt no longer use lard in cooking. Southern cooks still prefer and use lard.

However one large packing house proposes to do something about lard. The grocer handed me a can of a new lard product. This product is a result of a nationwide survey. A large number of city consumers were asked if they used lard. If they answered no, they were asked why not. Some did not like the color, the odor, the texture, the low melting point, the carton, and so on. This new lard which the grocer handed me was packed in a vacuum sealed can. It had been deodorized, whitened, hardened, so that it will not melt at room temperature even in summer, and it will not become rancid.

Grandmother could not analyze the reason she preferred to make doughnuts right after butchering.

She only knew that new lard was fresh and sweet. Fundamentally her reasons were the same as those of the city consumer. It is true that lard is more attractive and easier to use from a vacuum sealed can. The vacuum seal prevents oxidation which has to do with rancidity. Some folk like the taste of lard, of sweet lard that is, and that's one point grandma probably would not like about the new package. It is tasteless. The deodorizing, bleaching, and hardening are all chemical processes.

The processor who is bringing this new lard on the market is to be commended for two reasons. First, that he recognized there might be some real reasons why consumers do not buy lard. Secondly he has done something about the criticisms and has corrected each one. This should stimulate the sale of lard for it is a well known fact that it is a most plastic fat and it has therapeutic qualities which correct certain skin ailments.

The packer in improving the quality and appearance of lard has helped the farmer as well as helping himself. Why not fry a batch of doughnuts in lard for the family?

THE FARM WOMAN

The conversation turned to agriculture. The successful business or professional man in town has decided ideas about farms and farming. And more often than not he is apt to be right.

Someone remarked that a good Class A farm needed at least six buildings. The successful broker replied that no farm needed six buildings. That is too much capital invested - no wonder they can show no returns on the investment.

Now any good farm in these parts must have at least six buildings. The house may or may not be included in the number. Certainly the dwelling should be livable and comfortable. However Dunn and Bradstreet do not consider the dwelling when rating farms, so we will omit the home.

All will agree that a good barn is needed. Any Class A farm must have livestock and livestock in this region should be well housed. In my childhood there was a separate barn for horses and cattle. Probably with the advent of the tractor the horses and milk cows on the general farm can be housed under the same roof.

Since the outlay for farm machinery is so much greater than even a generation ago every farm should have a machine shed to house adequately every piece of equipment. In connection there should be a work bench and tools for minor repairs. As one drives over the countryside this would seem a more imperative need than any other buildings on the farm. Farmsteads were improved before the era of power farming and the machine shed has not been added. One sees expensive combines, binders, and even tractors standing out in the weather the year round.

thus depreciation eats the net returns.

Building number three should be a good chicken house, weather tight with adequate light and ventilation. More than one farm woman feeds and clothes the family from the laying flock even in these times of disastrously low prices. This can only be done by good flock management including proper housing.

The next building that should be mentioned is a good granary - rodent proof. Some storage space for grain should be provided in the barn. However the fire hazard is too great to store all of the grain that should be stored, in the barn. We cannot expect a crop every season. Therefore storage space for a carry over crop should be provided.

Although the price of hogs at the present time may not warrant it, the general farm should have a hog house or houses. Hogs are something we dare not get clear out of. If we raise a few litters year in and year out the returns in a decade will likely show a net gain. Many a farmer relies on hogs to pay the taxes. If more town women requested pure, sweet lard from the corner grocer, the farmer with shoats in the feedlot would show a steadier net gain.

That is five buildings checked off the list aside from the house. No mention has been made of a silo, garage or the little square sanitary privy at the end of the clothesline. These six or eight buildings properly painted and cared for may be charged off in fifty years depreciation. Which one can be omitted on a good general farm?

THE FARM WOMAN

Almost overnight it seemed the entire valley changed from glistening green to white. Those dark green splotches in the wheat fields disappeared. The wheat is white unto the harvest, the grains are filling. Rich promise reigns in the hearts of farmers. The farm boy, who dislikes arithmetic in school, figures orally that 40 acres of 40 bushels will yield 1600 bushels; at a dollar a bushel will be 1600 dollars. His eyes sparkle, "Gee, that's a lot of money."

We go to town and find the merchants are all figuring and planning much as this small boy. Their mouths are watering over expected sales. Some of them are even coming out and pressuring farmers into a new car or a new gadget on the mere promise of harvest. But the wise farmer in this Neosho valley knows that he cannot count his chickens before they are hatched. The grain must be in the bin before we are assured of it.

These rains are not encouraging. One wonders why they cannot be boosted a hundred miles or so farther west where moisture is really needed. One may drive along and see adjoining fields of wheat after a downpour, one upstanding the other lying flat. Thus far the latter fields are as the king's wife, though put down they rise again. The question is how many times can they rise. Several factors may be contributing causes. The wheat which goes down may be on too rich soil. Or likely it may be the variety. This season gives a very good comparison of varieties. Prudent farmers will take note of this in selecting seed wheat. However as the wheat turns to golden yellow it will not absorb moisture as it does in earlier stages. It will shade the ground and prevent its drying. Too much rain may make all varieties bend.

We'll take what comes, of course. But, Oh Lord, let us reap this harvest which today bespeaks such rich rewards.

Chapter 7

'Pass the Cream'

'farm environment is the one intended for the growing child'

Certainly the most fulfilling memories were of her family. The children; James Thomas McKinney, Mary Kathleen (known to all as Kathleen) and Esther Alice were only 9, 5 and 3 respectively when their mother began writing her articles for the *Gazette*. If we were to measure their significance to her everyday life they would be everything. And so, what became everyday occurrences were fodder for her pen. In a practical sense she weathered their growing up in the most delightful way. There were many articles. The children were never named in these articles but we do have an idea who she was talking about, especially when she referred to her son, or the farm boy. Fun to read but they did grow up all too quickly.

Here are some selections from these articles, I call it 'skimming the cream' of her stories about her children:

Did you ever count the number of requests the small child can make when she doesn't want to go to sleep? Having nothing else to do, we did. Here is the list: Want a drink, twice; Have to spit, three times; Tell you a secret (having just learned what secrets are), once; toilet, twice.

And, lastly - cover me up and I'll go to sleep - which she did.

As long as we had nothing else to do this occasion did not matter. The trouble is the same thing is likely to happen when Eddie Cantor is on the air or we are lost in our favorite continued story. Then our reaction is entirely different.

1933

****

Will wonders never cease? Is this my own child who volunteers the information in the middle of the week that he wants to take a bath? Is this the child who has always grumbled about the Saturday night dip? Baths are no problem in summer with an improvised swimming pool in connection with the windmill. But we thought boys and baths were always adversaries. Is this what health habits are doing? Or the program sponsored by the teacher and the county health office? More power to you. Well, I know the novelty may wear off but for this one ablution I am thankful.

Most country children have been run down and shod for the winter. When ones feet are unencumbered for six months of the year, it is real punishment to succumb to shoes. Especially when mothers bring out last year's shoes and try to wedge dogs, that have spread at least two sizes, into them. If competition in races at school becomes too keen, boys will slip off their shoes to run in their sock feet. Country kids seldom wear tennis shoes around the dining room stove after supper.

****

Just how does one proceed to instill manners in 10-year-old boys? Or, are they immune? Three small boys volunteered to serve on the hospitality committee at a party recently. They were so hospitable they felt they must eat ice cream and cake with each group of guests. All went well enough until one boy came grumbling. "Them boys had five dishes of ice cream and I have had only four." 1935

****

The difficulty with a family budget is that there are so many unlooked for things bobbing up that never have occurred before and almost upset the budget's equilibrium. Take shoes for example. Johnny has always been able to get along on two pairs per year with three or four months allowance for barefoot time. Then the road was graveled. We all wanted gravel. But Johnny is on his third pair of shoes now and his mother wonders if they will last until school is out. This family budget is apt to be hurled out the back window.

****

Speaking of boys, do you ever fret because Junior's hands are always grimy? Let us expel that worry. Some day when you least expect it, Junior will become so conscious of his hands that he will protest some task you wish performed. We speak from experience. In this case it was getting bed springs down from the attic. Only a few minutes work but the springs were dusty. It wasn't the valuable time the scion minded so much as getting his hands so blooming dirty. And all these years we have yearned for this boy to have clean hands!

****

Do you ever become discouraged as a mother and think nothing constructive, which you try to put across is sinking in? We must confess we do. But today we are pleased. Didn't we hear the 4-year-old warn the neighbor boy who had come over to play in the playhouse. "Now you mustn't put so much cocoa in that cake. You're wasting it." The cocoa was dirt, of course.

She may use too much sugar on her cereal tomorrow or pump out precious cistern water that is not needed. Right now we have a thrill of satisfaction that seeds of thrift may not have fallen on stony ground. 1934

****

Is possession nine points of the law? "Ole," the black bantam, a gift for all the family, arrived while the older children were at school. The youngest maintains he is more hers because she got him when he came. Arguments are heated. We wonder if "Ole" enjoys such popularity or if he is a bit bored. "Ole" has the run of the yard which the other chickens are not supposed to have. He proudly struts about the barnyard. When he becomes too boisterous in his braggadocio one of the young cockerels takes after him. "Ole" bobs through the fence into the yard for safety.

3-8-35

****

Easter chicks have arrived. Fluffy little yellow balls similar to the chick of a scouring powder fame. The latter is renowned because it hasn't scratched yet but these farm chicks begin to pick and scratch as soon as they leave the shell. A few bolder ones peep out from under the brooder and make for the water fountain. Soon the fountain is surrounded. Four other drinking cups in the pen are unused. Are chickens that much like people, in that they like to gather where the crowd is? They crowd and walk on each other in order to get the very same thing that is offered a few feet away. The other fountains have no advertisers around them.

One industrious 3-year-old was very busy and quiet. She came in the house and said, "I put the chicky to sleep mother." Soon she was gone out again and came in with the same announcement. Something warned her mother she had best investigate. She had just put six chickens to sleep - their last sleep. Six prospects for early fries gone a glimmering. And the poor child thought she was helping the mother hen!

Fifteen or 20 white faced calves are kept in the lot near the barn. Frequently late calves need a little extra care and attention. On Sunday afternoons these calves often get some extra curricular attention. Young buckaroos assemble and take turns riding them.

The calves are herded into the chute in the corner of the lot while the rider mounts. The gate is opened and the show is on. If one can last across the lot he is doing well. As the rancher watches the performance he commented that such antics were not especially good for the calves but they were fine for the boys. It gives a sense of equilibrium, poise and maybe a little common sense.

When chore time comes Sunday evening bewildered calves do not want to go into the shed for their evening feed. The shed is adjacent to the chute and how are the poor calves to know that the afternoon circus is over. Yes, such sport is hard on calves, but it is good for boys.

****

After a recent renovating campaign the old timer had his first introduction to a shower-bath. He says he has busted broncos, roped steers, ridden night herd when some slight noise startled a stampede. He has performed his ablutions in the creek and in the family wash tub and in a town bath tub. But in all his 80 years he has met nothing as unmanageable as the built-in shower. The mixer is either too hot or too cold. The spray gets in his eyes and his ears. And what is more, he isn't right sure that he is clean when he emerges.

Can it be there are some advantages to the family wash tub which is brought into the kitchen each Saturday night?

****

The first real round of colds is going through the country school. Youngsters are hollow-eyed, with cheeks too rosy as they come in from games at recess or flushed with temperature as they sit through the long afternoon. Someone is coughing all the time. And, though childish hands attempt it, hankies do not stifle the coughs and senses. The virus is broadcast over the school room. Consequently about two days later more youngsters in school have acquired the infection and joined the chorus. The teacher says she always knows some one will come back from Christmas vacation with a severe cold. It never fails. And, from then on until the close of school her attendance record has one absence after another.

****

One young lady asked Santa Claus for a bicycle. She promised if she could have a bicycle and an orange she would wish for nothing else. All the relatives concentrated on a bicycle. Through some misunderstanding, the wheel was delivered two weeks early. The lass had a great time those balmy days riding around telling the neighbors she doesn't know where her bike came from. She had asked Santa for it but evidently he was bringing something else. Poor Santa, the problems he has.

12-22-34

Two children went to sleep happy tonight. One, because she has a brand new pair of shoes and overshoes. The other because she is the proud possessor of her sister's old shoes and overshoes. It is a real sign of growth when you grow into big sister's clothes. 2-21-35

****

City boys are drawn to the farm as steel to a magnet. The hoe handle is not as attractive as the pony but each is included in the day's program. They have five different kinds of birds' nests to watch, excluding sparrows. One was fortunate enough to find a plover's nest, a rare treat even to farm folk. The eggs are as freckled as a turkey egg and about one-thirds as large.

These boys are going to miss out on the wild west serial at the neighborhood theater. No matter, they are enacting their own wild west out here. The small change their indulgent fathers gave them is about to burn a hole in their pants pockets, but if it will just molder till Saturday night a conflagration can be prevented. 6-1-34

****

Trapping season is here again. Last week the young trapper wondered where his Christmas money was coming from. Today $1.75 is burning his pocket. He can get that best girl something nifty now. We might add that the $1.75 are the proceeds from possums and skunks neighbors caught in cane shocks. All the old traps have been hunted up and oiled and set by holes along the creek. Every morning at break of day the *trapper is up and out. He has caught nothing yet but hopes are high.* 12-12-34

****

These are days when the kitchen and back porch are strewn with shavings and homemade flour paste. Kite flying time is here. One would think from the amount of paste used that the kites would not need any tail. But tail they must have and the rag bag is ransacked. Country children are saving their money to buy string. Raveling from flour sacks are not strong enough and binding twine is too heavy. Two balls of string put the kite pretty high and we think four balls might put it up out of sight. 1935

****

The stairs are little used of late. How the family can hurdle all the things on the steps when they want a necktie or a clean dress is more than we can see. It never dawns on them to carry part of the collection up with them thereby making a small path. Instead they hurdle up and leap down. Mother eventually clears the steps. Immediately another collection begins to form. For one thing we can be thankful. It is not an open stairway leading up from the front door. 8-14-34

****

"We haven't any 4-buckle over shoes," said the clerk, "but here's a dandy rubber." Can you imagine a country boy doing chores in rubbers? Feedlots knee deep in mud. The cows pull one foot after another slowly as they go from bunk to hay

rack. Father carried a new born calf to the box stall for the night. Just a few steps from the door a boot came off. It was a case of falling or stepping in the mud a la sock. And no time to meditate on a decision. Father stepped in the mud.

****

What does a boy do when coming down with the measles? He wants to skate on his roller skates but his mother insists that he stay in bed. He wants to read but mother says he should not use his eyes. He can't read, he can't get up. What is there to do. All the bubbling energy that boys possess becomes pent up and bursts out. The loose tooth is worked with until it comes out. Once upon a time the lad heard if a tooth is placed under your pillow a dime will mysteriously appear in the night. Sure enough it did. He grabs everyone that comes within reach, unties said mother's apron strings and fumes and frets because there is nothing to do.

****

Big sister would not think of starting off to high school without her lipstick and make up, and her hair just so. Little sister slipped off to the country school the other morning with a discarded compact of big sister's. On the way she stepped beneath the wayside bridge and tried to get the makeup on as big sister does. When she arrived at school the teacher made her wash it off immediately. Her mother and the teacher both want her to brush her hair carefully and keep her fingernails clean and neat. The child cannot understand why she should be punished for doing something that big sister does every day.

Can you explain this satisfactorily to a 6-year-od child? Or is it one of the ambiguities of the world which children must learn but which has no reason or logic.

****

Country school soon will be out. Mothers are sitting up nights to make their daughter's dresses for the occasion. With baby chicks, garden, et. cetera, there isn't much time in daylight hours. Midnight oil must be burned. These girls have been poring over catalogs for weeks trying to decide how the dresses should be made. Last day of school would lose much of its glamour if country girls could not have a new dress. Eighth grade girls will have two new dresses this spring. Their mothers will have to commence graduation frocks as soon as last day of school dresses are out of the way.

****

The school children have been earning money. Purely local specie with no exchange value outside the school ground. No depression was felt nor was inflation resorted to. But it was fun. Some thrifty children earned a good deal and a margin of safety and rewarded all who saved that amount. Probably the child who enjoyed the contest most worked hard and earned all she could. She saved enough for a reward and spent the remainder freely - She enjoyed earning and spending. 3-8-35

****

Every once in a while some one gets "het up" about American diction. In general it is bad. This is the time of year when we say no one should be graduated (from 8th grade, high school or college) unless he can write legibly and speak correctly. It seems to us there is considerable buck passing between the home and school. Parents are prone to say that teachers should make their children read and write correctly. Teachers may say they have our children only six hours out of 24. Lastly some one may say it is the other boys they play with who contaminate their speech.

Evidently correlation is needed here. If parents set a good example at home and teachers strive for pure speech they may fail unless they have the co-operation of the child and the boy on the street. Many a lad of eight or ten will ape the language of the gang and scorn all efforts to correct his speech. Yet lifetime habits are formed at this age.

****

Did you see your baby off to school with an ache in your heart and a tear in your eye? Or did you share with her the thrill of that first day in another world? Seriously now, would you have kept her at home if you could? Weren't those sparkling eyes upon her homecoming compensation for the loneliness you may have felt? And when she tells you that the first graders all learned how to spell home - h-o-m-e. because home was the place they wanted to come when school was out.

****

Little sister is five and distinctly feminine. She brushes her teeth as regularly as the older school children do. And often several times in addition each day. Being feminine she squeezes the toothpaste from the top of the tube. If she would only listen to her 7-year-old brother, who is very masculine, future family differences might be spared. Patiently brother tried to show her that you mustn't press from the top of the tube. You must squeeze from the bottom and roll it up this way. The next time brother was less patient and wanted to know why she didn't use the toothpaste the way he told her to. Miss Five-Year-Old swished her skirt and replied, "Oh heck I guess I don't have to if I don't want to."

Some day when she is a bride a young groom will patiently give her a demonstration in squeezing out toothpaste. Later when she does not learn, he may swear. Then he will buy his own tube and announce to the world that this is his paste and woe unto the first one that uses it.

Les femmes will not learn the scientific way to squeeze a tube of toothpaste.

****

On a rainy day a farm boy invariably thinks of fudge or butterscotch or divinity. The boy and the kitchen become stuck up in the process. No connoisseur ever looked with more delight upon a rare find than did the boy upon his slightly "runny" and sticky plate of candy. What matter if the family enjoyed it. Though he knows nothing of the effect of humidity the lad has decided it is harder to make fudge on a rainy day.

****

What has become of the girls who could play church hymns after one or two summer terms of music lessons? One high school girl plays for Sunday school now. If per-chance she is not there, nor her assistant, the superintendent must call on a gray-haired mother. Don't girls learn to play hymns of the church as they study piano? Do we emphasize orchestra too much in schools today? It seems a shame that more high school girls cannot play the familiar hymns. 5-15-35

****

June is associated with roses and brides and commencements. Seniors who complete their work in the summer term sweat through examinations and have not the admiring throng to cheer them in the processional. When a Lyon county girl receives all honors offered in her division it is incumbent that at least one carload from the old home town be there to cheer her on.

Our admiration for the deans and faculty increased as they sat through the ceremony calm and serene in their caps and gowns, with hoods and stoles signifying the rank of the scholar. Not a fan did we notice in all the group. They may have used their programs to promote a gentle breeze. Our eyes were on the speaker. A Kansan speaking the Kansas language to Kansans.

The clock struck 12 as we entered the kitchen door. Only a few hours until the alarm would sound. In this year of depression, in harvest time we had stolen away 100 miles to midsummer commencement exercises. Miracles do happen.

Do you recall when 12 o'clock was deadline? You were expected to be in at that time and you were home when the clock struck. Those days are no more. Instead of father laying down the law, today's children volunteer to come home at 1 a. m. Old cars may have something to do with getting in late. A strange thing about these old cars is that so many times they will get you to your destination and flare up on the way home.

One country girl was forced to remain away from home over night. She slept little the few hours she was in bed. The first question when she reached home was, "Mother, were you worried? Did you wait up all night for me?" "No," replied her mother, "I went to bed and slept. I decided something had happened and I knew I could trust you." This girl told me that one remark of her mother's did more for her in her adolescence than any other one thing.

The thrill of knowing that her mother trusted her.

****

The dearest places in our childhood hearts are of course reserved for father and mother. But close by is the love for our first teacher. The other day a young miss said to me.

"Mother if you died do you know who I would live with? My teacher, of course," Primary teachers share all the joys and sorrows of their beginners. Occasionally we meet someone who doesn't like school. Often this child disliked his first teacher. At a reunion last week gray haired men all toasted their first teachers. There may be others we liked almost as well but no one can replace that first teacher.

We still feel much as our daughter towards our first

teacher. Didn't we take the babies for her to admire? And, if we had any troubles we would go straight to her with them.

Children are the most important crop out here on the farm.

****

Vacation is over for country kids. Homes have been turned over to children for the past week. Toys and candy and nuts and Christmas decorations have adorned the dining room. It was a relief to take down the cord and tinsel and really clean this morning. Children are glad to be going back to school. Mothers are glad, too. One mother says she almost wishes we had school 360 days in the year. Vacations are joyous affairs. but, its' good to swing back into a regular routine again. 1-36

****

Why is it that children, when wading, must wade within 1-32 or 1-64th of an inch of the top of their overshoes? Although the shoes may be waterproof rubber, four buckles high, bucolic explorers must wade in water or snow to the very tops of them. Invariably somewhere along the ditch, the depth is miscalculated and water seeps in and down to the toes.

****

A town family is enjoying a rabbit for dinner tonight; the result of the boys' hunting expedition in the country. Pork chops or T-bone from prime beef would not taste as good as this rabbit. Three boys went out across the pasture and came back carrying a rabbit. When interrogated they admitted they did not know who killed bunny as they all took aim.

She summed it up when she wrote the following:

A nation that would be really civilized would surround its children with a natural, simple environment. Its youngsters would not be over stimulated on the one hand and over-suppressed on the other. Boys need to dig in the earth. Girls do too. They need to yell and shout. They need to know where baby pigs and pups and chickens come from. They need above all some chores and responsibilities. If they must have bicycles, and what boy does not long for one, let them have a bicycle on a country lane. We are old-fashioned enough to think the farm environment is the one intended for the growing child.

THE FARM WOMAN

Christmas! Bright eyes of children! Always shall the two be associated. The faith of children that Santa will leave all the things asked for. The quick adjustments to whatever they receive even though it may not be what they wanted. Candlelight reflected in shining eyes as the little procession marches from the kitchen to the Christmas tree, singing carols. The joyous confusion as gifts are sorted and distributed. What simple things will please a child! There in the heart of a child is to be found the spirit of Christmas.

We saw the spirit of Christmas in the eyes of a maiden, too. She sat and gazed at her most prized Christmas gift - a solitaire. Lights from the Christmas tree were caught and reflected in myriad colors. What dreams filled her thoughts as she sat by the fire? The same dreams and air castles her mother and grandmother before her dreamed when Prince Charming came riding.

Christmas, for most of us is a day of merriment. Overeating and hilarious confusion are the order of the day. Fathers throw off the burden of years and show young sons how to wind the streamlined trains and how to aim the popgun.

As we see the white billows roll out from the engines of trains, we know that the train crew will have a belated Christmas. Central answers our call whenever we ring. Although the postman does not come, someone must go to the office and sort the mail. The doctor must be ready to answer a call at any moment. We can get the daily paper if we go to town after it. The radio may be tuned in at any station all through the day. Cattle and horses and pigs must be fed. Chickens must be tended. All the folks have their Christmas no doubt. But the wheels of our so-called civilization must be kept running even on Christmas day. The celebration of the workers must be attuned to their work. We selfishly celebrate all the day long with little thought for the folks who must work on Christmas day.

We sometimes think that radio advertising is overdone. Often it is. Today we are profoundly grateful to the company which dramatized Dickens' "Christmas Carol." From the quiet of a farm home no dramatization on the air has ever equaled that of Lionel Barrymore and his supporting cast.

And, to think we can sit by our fireside and hear 'round the world greetings. From the hills of Judea the Christmas story is read to us in our kitchen in Kansas. The miracles that are wrought in this generation!

Dec 1935

THE FARM WOMAN

Rural school children sweated over mid-term examinations the past week. The child who makes anywhere near a perfect score is trained for a world citizen. He is familiar with the Russian droshky, the French travois, Japanese rickshaws and Eskimo kayaks. He can trace a package of tea from the tree in Ceylon to his table. He is familiar with the industrialization of Latin America. He knows the cause of the trouble between Italy and Ethiopia. He knows the name, author, publisher and copyright date of each of his textbooks. He reads understandingly such terms as interdependence, chronologically, evaluate, bibliography, etc.

The above conclusions are based on a perfect paper. We wonder how many perfect papers there are. Can the country child assimilate all this information? One boy defined public domain as a hit-and-run driver.

Technically we should say the child was correct, who marked the following sentence as false: "Patent medicines should be avoided." Her teacher explained that by "patent" medicines we mean those blatantly advertised products which people take without the advice of their physician. The child explained she thought we could not know medicines were pure unless they were patented. Won't some of you druggists come to the defense of this country girl?

How many drugs do you use in prescriptions which are not patented? Do we not use the term "patent" medicine loosely?

Social studies certainly will broaden and enrich the child's store of knowledge. Many college professors would be pleased if underclassmen made an A on such a quiz. A generation ago school children took arithmetic problems home for help from mother and dad.

Chronicles of
The Farm Woman

Today parents are learning from the child.

Some time ago an achievement test was given in rural schools. The following paragraph was included in the silent reading test: "Reduced to simplest terms, crime is an act in violation of a law. A man who drives his car at 30-miles in a 20-mile zone is criminal. Arrest, trial, conviction taken separately or together are not necessary to change lawbreaking into a criminal act. More technically, a crime may be defined as follows: a crime is an act believed to be of such serious consequence to the well being of society and to affect so adversely the interest of the life of the state, that it has been brought within the cognizance of the law and there specifically prohibited - generally with a penalty prescribed for its commission. Likewise, the omission of an act expressly enjoyed by the law constitutes."

We had to give the paragraph a second careful reading to get much out of it. Material for the upper grades in the country schools today is couched in language beyond the ken of country children. If anything is to be expressed in simplest terms let it be told in words that these youngsters use everyday and under-stand. Seventh graders stumbling along over the prelude to "The Vision of Sir Launfal," see no beauty whatever in the poetry there. Poetry to be enjoyed must be read with a swing and its meaning understood.

We opened a second reader the other day to see this sentence, "Miriam went and got her mother." Now when we used "went and got" in high school themes our English teacher tore her hair. Times do change.

It's a liberal education in itself to send one's offspring through school these days - M.F.M.

THE FARM WOMAN

It's a strange fact that admiring friends or relatives will drive to Coffey County to see and hear a student band from one of the state's leading schools. And, be there by 10 o'clock on Monday morning, too. That meant hustling with the chores both outside and in. It meant driving 30 miles to hear a concert when most every week a musical treat is offered in Emporia. When a college freshman 200 miles from home wrote, "We will be in Burlington Monday. Wish you could meet me there," we knew there was a wistful longing between the lines to see some familiar faces on the landscape. Of course, we met him.

The concert had begun when we arrived. We sneaked to the balcony and found ourselves its sole occupants. The janitor came over to inform us we were not supposed to sit in the gallery but since the program was on we might stay. The superintendent frowned slightly when he saw us. How many blunders are committed when one does not know his way 'round. Strange folks in unfamiliar surroundings are apt to commit many faux pas.

Weren't those lads handsome? We may be a little bit prejudiced but those brilliant blue uniforms with crimson and gold trim and plumed helmets were a thrilling sight. They played beautifully. It was worth hurrying around. Where was the boy we wanted to see? During the second number we spied him. He sat straight. His posture was much improved. The bandmaster requires military bearing. Compulsory military training may be objectionable. For two decades we have watched insignificant college freshmen learn to carry there shoulders straight, chest out and chin in. They are handsomer lads. We can't observe that they are any more warlike than their round shouldered fraternity brothers.

Some years ago we despaired of this boy ever learning to play "America." We thought one doting mother might as well spend the money she was squeezing out for music lessons for movies or chocolate sodas.

Neighbors be patient. Mothers, keep on insisting that those boys and girls practice. They may make the college band or orchestra some day.
3-22-35

Chronicles of
The Farm Woman

THE FARM WOMAN

Coon season is on in the country. Farm boys take to the timber with their dogs. Dogs of all descriptions. Some with long flapping ears that may be sure enough coon dogs, some fox terriers, but mostly just dogs join in the chase. Dogs bark, boys halloo, lanterns bob up and down through the dark. They hunt all night, come in at 3 or 4 o'clock in the morning with one measly skunk! And the next night they are ready to go again. Perhaps the hunting chromosomes are lacking in our makeup. We couldn't go hunting night after night for a striped kitty. Expectancy runs high with the boys here. They may tree a coon yet. Anyhow they like to run with their dogs.

Country kids are glad indeed that examinations were held last week. It was evident that spelling, reading and arithmetic were incidental this week. The school program was Friday night. Dialogs, recitations and songs occupied the attention, to say nothing of Christmas gifts. There is no prouder child in the county than the boy who happened to draw his best girl's name in the Christmas exchange. The 10 cent limit cramps his style. He would like to spend a quarter for her gift and economize somewhere else.

All spools and tin cans and the small paint brush have been taken to school. The tin snips were borrowed from the tool chest. The air is full of secrets.

What a simple time children had a generation

ago in comparison with the child of today. Then, we wrote a letter to Santa Claus and told him all our wants. Perhaps a few country children saw Santa Claus in town. A very few talked to him over the phone. Today's youngsters hear a different Santa over each radio station. They see some skinny Santa's, some jolly fat ones. The Santa at the church sounds exactly like our mail carrier. Four-year-olds puzzle these observations in their minds. They are more worldly wise than the 4-year-olds of yesteryear. Too many Santa's are confusing. Somehow it brings a tinge of sadness to us.

Chronicles of
The Farm Woman

THE FARM WOMAN

The last day of school in the country is eagerly looked forward to in most cases. There are exceptions. For instance when it is the day before quarantine is to be lifted. The boy feels perfectly well but he must sit in his yard across the road and watch all the neighborhood gather for the last day dinner and ball games. The urchin usually chases fly balls. How his feet itch to run after those balls that go sailing into the pasture. He gazes at the baskets as they are carried in the schoolhouse. His mouth waters because he knows full well that chicken and noodles and at least four kinds of pie and three kinds of cake will adorn the tables.

Then it is the lad wishes he lived in town where all you have to do the last day is go after your report card. He wouldn't mind missing that. Or if he lived far enough away so that he might not see what he is missing. Why couldn't those measles have come a few days earlier? The misery was lessened somewhat when school girls who had had the measles brought a plate piled high with what looked to be a sample of every dish at the dinner.

The hired man took a half day off to do his Easter shopping. He returned with a complete new outfit from the top of his striped denim cap to the tips of his horsehide shoes. Easter is late this year but we do wish the weather would warm up so that a cold chill would not envelop us every time we meet a pair of white shoes.

Our heart is heavy tonight. We have just discovered that the last freeze nipped the peaches. They withstood the warm and chill winds and brightened the countryside for days. Hopes were high. Today as we pinched a blossom a black heart greets us. Another and still another.

Chronicles of The Farm Woman

This Easter season is too cool for peaches and white footwear.

Country children all over Kansas are taking seventh and eighth grade examinations today. That is, if they attend an 8 month rural school. Some of the tests will be given today, the remainder a week later. Green country kids, who have only seen inside the high school to see the senior play, must go there to take these exams. The finals are hard to pass, they know. For six years they have been underclassmen in the country school, they have watched the seventh and eighth graders review and sweat with apprehension. The environment is totally foreign. And to top it all off they wore their Sunday clothes. No farm boy can do his best in arithmetic with a Sunday shoe pinching his toe. If his own teacher was only there to smile and reassure him. He is scared to ask any questions of these strange assistants.

All these obstacles the country child must overcome if he would graduate. We signed a petition to have these examinations abolished by act of the state legislature. Evidently mothers in Lyon county were the only ones interested and the bill failed to pass.

Taking examinations the day after school closes and one week later. We wonder why this must be. And, we wonder how Teachers College seniors would fare if President Butcher gave them final exams one week after commencement. We have a sneaking feeling that con-siderable acquired information is lost or misplaced during commencement week and the week following. Much of it will return when and as needed but a good stiff final one week after commence-ments would be something, would it not?

THE FARM WOMAN

School children have longed for the first snow. They came home from school the other evening shouting because occasional flakes were falling. It was as if a kind snow man had waited for these country kids to get home before he began to send the snow down in earnest. At the first peep of a gray dawn, heads peered out windows to see if the ground was really white. With a whoop and a bounce the household was awake and dressed and outdoors. The whole landscape was white. Every weed, every branch, unsightly tin cans - all were blanketed in beauty and silence. It seemed a shame to mar that beauty and destroy that silence. But that was why the children were up and out. They rolled in the snow, they tossed snowballs and they commenced a snow man. All this was done before breakfast was ready.

The cat whined and picked her way through the snow, carefully. The ducks took a turn through the air. One would think they might not come back but they always have. The hired man says it is a sign one is getting old, if he does not enjoy the first snow.

Teachers and parents of rural school children may be relieved that there was no parade in town Saturday. But every rural school child shares the disappointment of the Editor of The Gazette, that the parade was not to be. "Mother, will you read that!" exclaimed a grade school miss in high disgust as she handed a note from the teacher. The note stated the postponement of the parade.

Now if there is anything more enjoyable than seeing a parade, it is being a part of one. We do have a fine group of children in rural Lyon county. It is too bad that the kids could not have the parade. Yet children out 15 or 20 miles are dependent on their parents for transportation. And if floats are to be in the parade, the ingenuity of teacher and parents and older brothers and sisters must be called on. Every child is willing and ready for a parade today or any time. Their time budget is crowded. Praise be for that. Oldsters are enmeshed in activities that almost bog them down.

It is hoped that a rural school parade can be arranged before long.

1936

Chronicles of The Farm Woman

THE FARM WOMAN

Every one on the farm is gathered around the cook stove today. Ambitious house cleaners have taken down the heating stove for the summer. The kitchen is the only comfortable room. Prairie grass and potatoes like this cool damp weather. But chicks and kittens and babies thrive on sunshine. Barefoot boys, with their shaved heads, shiver and make us cold. The clipped ewes seem to ask if we took off their fur coats too soon. And every one digs out a winter comforter at night - the bedding we had stored away for the summer.

The mallard drake has only one companion now. The rest of his harem are setting - on beautiful blue green eggs. The turkey eggs are pipped and we're pretty sure the guineas have a nest in the hedgerow.

The lad was tempted to take one of the killdeer eggs to add to his collection. Four good sized eggs with brown splotches which looked as if they had been carelessly painted on. Someone told him if he touched a killdeer nest the mother would never return. He merely gazed at the eggs and counted himself lucky that he had even found the nest. Last week he saw a pair of killdeer run along the ground and act as if they were badly hurt. As he neared the nest a baby, just hatched, ran up the slope as fast as the boy could go. A tiny creature - all legs. It seemed an imposition to chase it so hard but he did want a good look at it. Suddenly the tiny bird crouched down in a small hole. Not an eyelash did it move for more than half an hour. But that time the uncles and aunts and grandparents were circling and crying and feigning injuries. The child looked for the nest. He could not find it nor any other small birds. No doubt they were hiding behind a rock or under a weed. There are no clumps of grass in the pasture this spring.

The send-a-dime craze has penetrated to the country. The children came in eagerly with a whole bunch of letters. We recognized the handwriting of a dear friend. Hopefully we tore open the envelope to hear all about her exciting experiences. Our face fell when we found a typewritten prosperity letter. Send 10 cents, six letters or 18 cents postage, 1 cent each for five copies of the form. Total 33 cents per letter. Six letters are in the mail today. How shall we know which chain would be the most profitable? Six times 33 is $1.98. Instead of a dime investment it looks like two dollars. Eggs are 20 cents a dozen - 10 dozen eggs. Six letters in the kitchen stove and two dollars in our pockets.

5-9-35

TOWN DOGS & LIVESTOCK

If you have children visiting on the farm and they have taken their dog, here is what happens to them, according to the Farm Woman down on the Neosho: WAW

When girls from town come out they like to ride the pony. He is as gentle as a purring kitten. They climb on and hold tight rein in each hand and the poor horse doesn't know what to do. Neither do they. He prances a few steps. We tell them to loosen the rein. They look at us askance but by that time are desperate enough to try most anything. The moment the rein is slacked the horse knows what to do and starts down the road.

The town dog has a hard life in the country. He thinks the fat heifers are interesting and yip-yaps at them whereupon the heifers lower their heads, raise the tails and take after the hound. The boys tire of his interference in their play and they chuck him in the house. The homemaker on the farm is too busy to have a dog underfoot and she leads him to the granary.

Poor pup, surrounded by tanks, screenings, salt and likely a few mice. He whimpers, he barks frantically, he demands to be let out of that dark interior. All sounds fall on deaf ears.

The dog, center of attraction at home, is relegated to the granary on the farm.

THE FARM WOMAN

When or where have we seen such a snow? Sledding has not been as keen within the memory of eighth grade boys. Every father in the neighborhood has had an order for a sled. All orders have been filled. Two 2 x 4's cut at an angle and bridged together with a few crosspieces. And a home-made sled is evolved. A sled to haul the wood and kindling as well as a sled for joyriding.

Neighborhood visiting is done via children's home made sleds. Mothers and grandmothers have all had rides and the teacher at school must go coasting every noon. If you get up enough speed going down one bank of the creek you can coast up the other side.

The oldsters seem to be holding their own remarkably well. A high school miss dropped her comb while getting her waves just so. It was too far to the floor, for she had been coasting the day before. Mother picked up the comb for her. Mother had been coasting too.

As we watch these country kids in the back pasture it seems they are having fully as much fun as any one behind a car. They do not think so. But danger ever lurks when a sled is hitched to a car. Something tightens within us every time we see youngsters clipping along thus.

Father has had his fill of snow and ice. He would vote for a thaw to get this ice off the wheat. But the weatherman casts his vote with the younger generation. We will have coasting a while longer.

Chronicles of
The Farm Woman

THE FARM WOMAN

An undergraduate home for the holidays is at a low ebb. Try as she will she cannot glimpse the vision some of her professors desire her to receive. She is champing at the bit thinking said prof is hard-boiled, unreasonable, no pleasing him and no making grades. Many of his demands for lengthy detailed reports are the bunk. In order to make an "A" she would have to devote all her time to his course. She was sure last year what her major should be. Now in that chosen department she is not getting on so well. She is wondering if she made the wrong choice.

In the next breath she tells of the most interesting professor she has yet had. She expects to make an "A" under her. Her course is hard but she makes it clear and one can really understand what she wants you to do. We feel as if we might be this youngster's grandmother. She is treading the same halls, sitting under some of the instructors we had a few years back. And having some of the same difficulties! Only the instructor she likes so well, we found impossible.

The decision of alumni gathered around the supper table was that the student is fortunate to find two of three professors who stand out in after years. The coed is passing through a slough of despond common to many undergraduates.

THE FARM WOMAN

The football season is here and the band instructor has been smoothing out the numbers the band will play. He tears his hair as he tries to teach members of the high school band to march. Why can't they throw out their chests, hold up their heads and lift those feet gracefully? One is prompted to interrupt the practice and whisper to the young bandmaster that part of his difficulty is heredity.

The pep girls are planning their sweaters and skirts and caps. It is an important event in any high school girl's life when she is chosen a member of the pep squad.

The football squad is given stiff assignments by the coach. Farm boys who drove a team or a tractor in the summer come home weary and meek after evening practice. They are as quiet and subdued as the young mule after a full day in the furrow. Little sisters enjoy cessation from torment and teasing. A strange quiet settles over the household as the football sub retires immediately after supper.

Coaches will tell you that football develops teamwork. Fathers say that it brings out good sportsmanship. But mothers know that it calms the over exuberance of adolescents.

Likely, over every mother whose son goes out for football there sometimes or other flashes the fear of accident. The day's mail brings the account of a high school freshman, fresh out of football, breaking his collar bone. It must remain in a stiff cast for three weeks. The collar bone was not fractured in scrimmage but in a game of tag after supper with the smaller youngsters in the neighborhood. To this high school freshman it would seem much more glorious to be wounded in practice on the gridiron than in wood tag at home. 1939

THE FARM WOMAN

What about needs and desires of children? Or of adults for that matter? One child gets away with an all day sucker in 10 minutes. His sister enjoys her sucker awhile today and puts it away until tomorrow. On the morrow the first child cries because his sister has a sucker and he hasn't one. What to do? What to do?

Again two children get brand new shoes. Each child gazes at his own reflection in the toes of his shoes as they go down the street. The first child needs half soles in no time. The uppers and half soles are gone before the second child needs half soles. Child number one gets new shoes - he needs them. Then sister rebels. Brother gets two pairs of shoes to her one. What to do? What to do?

Of course the child who wears out his shoes is the one whose sucker never lasts. In the balance sheet of needs and desires the lad receives much more than his sister. But his sister usually has shoes and suckers What is just? Should we give both children the same number of shoes, and of suckers? Is little sister entitled to a surplus because she can make them last longer? Or do shoes and suckers come in altogether different categories? Shall we give a child all the shoes he needs and apportion suckers equally? But it's easier to buy suckers than shoes.

What to do?

THE FARM WOMAN

Is there a country child in Lyon county who hasn't enrolled in the chicken contest? Well, yes, there is one down this way. She hopes that it doesn't close down on Saturday before she gets to town. The waiting line extended halfway to the alley last Saturday and we haven't seen a committee as busy since the day of the school parade at the time of the 4-H fair.

Every country kid, 10 years old and over, is going to raise a brood of White Rocks this summer. There will be tall tales to tell as well as chickens to exhibit at the poultry show next fall.

Hens do not seem to want to set this spring. They have joined the modernists and refuse to sit on the nest for three long weeks. They prefer to be classed as layers, and turn the setting and chick raising business over to the mass production industries. They welcome this contest.

Speaking of contests, this chick contest seems to be about the best one we have ever heard. We are so fed up with soap contests that we've a notion to join the army of small boys and go with our neck dirty. Every time we buy a bar of soap or a package of soap chips we are contributing toward a shiny new car for some one and a new kitchen for some one else. This chick contest is different. Every child who enters this receives 25 fluffy baby chicks and has a chance of winning prizes next fall.

Every child should have the responsibility and care of some little animal or fowl. It is part of the training of the universe. The pride of possession, the observation of growth from day to day and the knowledge that a helpless creature depends upon him for protection and food; this is a heritage intended by the creator.

This contest will be followed with interest.

THE FARM WOMAN

Sunday was Mother's Day. A national institution in these United States. Sermons were delivered on the theme of motherhood. Radio programs were dedicated to the mothers of the land. Sons and daughters traveled long distances, as is possible in this day of speed, to spend a few hours with mother. Showers of gifts were bestowed. Flowers, candy, negligee or household gadgets, things which mother would not buy for herself.

All the gifts are lovely. They illustrate thoughtfulness and devotion. But no material gift, however costly, can rival in a mother's heart the sparkling eyes and the sweet childish voice which says, "I think you're the bestest mother in the whole world." Households may have their ups and downs. Storm clouds may gather and economic troubles beset them. It is such expressions as this that give mother strength and courage to carry on.

What day be dull when the song in a mother's heart echoes over and over again - "You're the bestest mother in the whole world?"

THE FARM WOMAN

Farm families can get up and hustle around in wartime when the occasion demands. Mostly they go by old time because farm routine year in and year out is geared to daylight and not daylight savings. Eighth grade commencement is one of the exceptions, and the graduates and their parents were in town in their best bib and tucker Thursday morning at 9 o'clock. Many folk had done a half day's work before they came. Water had to be left for the chickens all day and also for the young calves. They simply turned their backs on weeds and alfalfa mowing and cultivating. The dog was left in charge for the day and the whole family was off for the county seat at 8 o'clock.

The exercises didn't begin at 9 o'clock, but the graduates had to be there to get in line alphabetically for the processional and to receive last-minute instructions.

Every girl had on a brand new dress and most of them had a brand new permanent also. Twenty-five years from now likely not one girl will be able to recall who the speakers were, who presented the diplomas, yet each one will be able to tell you what kind of a dress she had for the occasion. Nature seems to have a far greater variety in sizes of 14-year-old boys than in girls of the same age. Big or little they all had their hair slicked down. Forward looking mothers had seen to it that new suits were plenty big to allow room for growth.

Everyone will have to put in good hard licks to make up for the day in town, but it was worth it. Eight grade graduation is one of the high spots in the life of a country child. 6-3-44

THE FARM WOMAN

Two hundred and forty-nine boys and girls received diplomas at the eight grade commencement Saturday morning. A group of quiet, alert youngsters, every one well dressed. Girls all had their hair curled. The boys wore white shoes.

It was "ad astra per aspera"[1] *for many of the children and parents in that audience. In order to be in our seats at 9:15 as the directions stated it meant those in the far corners of the county must leave home at 8 o'clock. Farmers must allow time for a flat tire or adjustment of the distributor.*

Eighth graders like to plan, and they should probably be given more voice in household management. One young graduate proposed that a good many things could be done on Friday. Saturday's baking was combined with Friday cleaning. Small brothers and sisters were scrubbed and shampooed. She worked hard and faithfully. Friday night it seemed that everything was working smoothly. The first thing Saturday morning a younger brother came down stairs in his best bib and tucker, expecting to slop the pigs and feed the calves in that garb. He was quickly dispatched back upstairs, mumbling. The little kids who had no definite outdoor chores sallied forth in the dewy morn. All that bathing to do over. It was too much for the sweet girl graduate. She wept.

Experience, that wonderful teacher, has taught her that farmers had best get

[1] Kansas motto (Latin) means 'to the stars through difficulties.'

right out of the wash tub into their best duds.

We overheard a youngster in the audience remark, "Mother, there are lots of babies here." There were lots of babies there. The next crop of rural school children - the hope of America. It is to rural America that cities must look for leadership.

The speaker of the morning echoed our philosophy when he said that every one hundredth anniversary of the founding of the common school by Horace Mann - the man who dreamed of a literate America. A wave of humility and gratitude comes when one thinks of the vision and courage of the founder of our common schools.

One of these graduates may not one day be president but it is to be hoped that each will cling to the heritage of freedom of speech and worship, to the right to trial by jury and to the right to private property. This the birth-right of every American child. 6-1-37

Chronicles of
The Farm Woman

THE FARM WOMAN

A country girl has recently proven to be a social genius. She went to the city for a week's visit with an aunt. The aunt lives in the suburbs. This girl who knows all the neighbors at home for miles around set out to get acquainted with the suburbanites. Because she likes people they reciprocated. She found them all interesting.

At the end of five days she decided to have a party. All the neighbors for three blocks up and down the street were invited and they came. Introductions had to be made. Some of these people had lived on the street three years and were not acquainted. Each one had some contribution to make to the afternoon's entertainment. Youngster girls were taking dancing lessons. Others sang. A young mother who played the violin had not been asked to play for months. A gray-haired grandmother sang old songs. It was a gay afternoon thoroughly enjoyed by everyone present.

The girl has returned to the country. Little did she realize that her party was an achievement in the neighborhood. All the folks up and down the street miss her. They wonder when she will return. Is there sufficient initiative and leadership to stage another successful party? Or did the guiding genius of this youngster account for its success?

Daughter is studying on the accordion this summer. Not that she is especially interested in it. But it pleases father mightily. One of fathers dreams was of being a master on the accordion. That which he did not attain he desires his offspring to grasp.

How true this of all parents. Those youthful dreams and ambitions which we were unable to fulfill, we desire to pass on to our children. For this reason many youngsters are sent to college. It also causes some adolescent flares and clashes.

Instead of permitting youth to fulfill its own dreams and ambitions we want them to bring ours to fruition. 6-27-37

THE FARM WOMAN

A local news item states that neighboring farm girl, Henrietta Becker, called her parents from New York City on New Year's eve and that her voice came in clear on the party line.

Long distance tele-phone calls are common place today. Every day con-nections are made from the east coast to the west coast, to the north and south. In the course of minutes one may be connected with London or Helsinki. But it is still rare enough to be news when a call comes through from Manhattan Island on the party line.

The story behind this telephone call may well be observed and read by all who say there is no oppor-tunity for youth today.

This neighbor girl is an intern in dietetics in Presbyterian Hospital and Medical Center and she got there entirely by her own efforts in the depression thirties. The way has not been easy but the point is she is there and will complete her training in a few months.

This girl taught in country schools for eight years. She hesitated to go to the university because she thought she didn't have money enough. She decided to try. She found employ-ment, did without many things but earned her bachelor's degree. With even less money she set out for Iowa State to work toward a master's degree. While there the dormitory in which she lived, burned. It burned on a rainy Saturday night and the only things she saved were an old dress and shoes and a raincoat. From this experience she learned that it takes grace to receive as well as to give. No one had ever given her anything before, or rather she had never before been placed in a position of needing to depend on someone else for a dry pair of hose and a toothbrush. It was a struggle, she was tempted to come home. It would have been so much easier. Instead she acquired this added grace and finished the term.

The offer of internship in Presbyterian came. She had little money and few clothes, but she accepted the offer. After she had been there a few months a vacancy occurred on the staff and she was asked to supply. For five months she was on the payroll and that was a godsend. She is on the last lap now.

The experiences along the way have been as valuable to this country girl as her academic training. She has pioneered as did her ancestors when they came to this new land from the old country. She has worked hard and has learned to trust in the morrow.

Of course we are proud of Henrietta. She is our neighbor. But what she has done, others with health and determination and a vast capacity for work, can do. Don't tell us there is no opportunity for youth today.

1-8-40

THE FARM WOMAN

The high school lad came to school decked out in his Sunday best. In a town high school this would be no uncommon sight. But in a small rural high school where clean overalls and print dresses are accepted wear. It was unusual to see a boy all dressed up. Upon seeing him someone recalled that this was the day the itinerant photographer was expected. Johnny was dressed up to have his picture taken. It was an event in his young life. He was going to send the picture to his big brother in the far Pacific, that big brother who had teased and tormented him but who had always been his pattern.

Few of the students had remembered the day. Immediately the girls began to primp and add more lipstick and the boys to comb their hair.

The picture man did not come on the appointed day or the next. He did call and say he would be there late in the week. The lad continued to wear his white shirt and tie and suit. He wanted to be ready when the man came. Then came the great day. The photographer arrived with all his paraphernalia and his line of chatter. Was there ever an itinerant photographer who did not have an incessant flow of patter? It is part of the stock in trade no doubt. He lined up all the eager customers along the schoolhouse wall and snapped them in quick succession. Girls did not have nearly enough time to primp.

Soon the man was on his

way again with the promise that the pictures would be delivered in a few days. When the pictures came Johnny's was the best of the lot. Today that picture is winging its way via air mail to an outpost somewhere in the Pacific. Big brother will be amazed o see how the stripling has grown and changed in the two years since he last saw him. This picture that little brother waited so many days to have taken probably will go up alongside the favorite pinup girl or in his billfold with pictures of his best girl and his mother.

Now little brother is wondering how long it will take to get an answer, that the picture really arrived.

5-16-44

THE FARM WOMAN

The hum of tractors accompanies the evening symphony of the cicadas, crickets and the late bird call. Farmers are impatient to get the plowing done. On moonlight nights, many worked the night through. Now, unless they have lights, they must stop soon after dark. Do you see no beauty in a freshly plowed field? Oh, but beauty abounds! This mellow black dirt is the background of the farmer's dream. His hopes are always high at plowing time.

There is no need to worry about America going Fascist or Communist as long as the younger generation craves freedom as they do. They want the privilege to say what they please, to call what belongs to them their own and they bring many problems for mother to solve. Farm kids have been earning money through harvest. It is spent over and over mentally. Watches, bicycles or bicycle repairs, new suits and new hats can be seen on parade. Farm lads have not yet joined the college boys' hatless promenade. A neighbor girl had every intention of buying silk hose, but the cosmetic counter held alluring attractions. She decided she could do without hose in this hot weather anyway.

The farm boy is growing up. His voice has changed, a slight fuzz has appeared on his chin. For years he has taken out his dad's safety razor and gazed at it longingly. Now he has need for it occasionally. He is permitted to take a team and rack in the trashing crew this summer. Another goal of every farm boy. His folks are proud of him, of course, but they somehow cannot sever that knot on the apron strings. When the heavy black cloud appeared at the end of the day and lightening flashed, the family felt compelled to start out and find the lad. They met him on the way home whistling and enjoying the thundering clouds.

As he related this incident he commented he didn't see why the folks could not have done his milking for him instead of coming out long the road to find him.

THE FARM WOMAN

Farmers did not have a holiday last Saturday. The day was perfect and too few perfect days have come along this spring. Teams and tractors could be seen in every field all day long. Some member of the family did take time to go to the cemetery. While there, one felt that the old timers who have passed on to their reward looked down in understanding. They had experienced the rush of farm work in their day.

Although Monday was equally as fine a day as Saturday it was a holiday to many farm families. You may not have realized it but Monday was the annual rural eighth grade commencement. Whether it was making hay, cultivating corn, planting soybeans or canning peas, everything was laid aside for the exercises. A casual onlooker may go to a college or high school commencement but no one goes to the eighth grade exercises unless he is especially interested in one of the graduates. The audience is composed always of beaming parents, school teachers, grandparents and neighbors. It is always a receptive audience for the speaker.

Eighth grade boys who unleashed would probably make a stampede for their reserved seats, marched in as dignified as did the K. U. seniors and faculty in the procession in the stadium the night before. It was a big moment in the lives of each boy and girl when he or she marched across the platform and received that purple diploma from the hands of Gary Wilson.

The eighth grade graduate is not handicapped as is the high school or college grad. The former feels that the world is good and there is an eagerness to find out more about it. Somewhere in the next four years he will suddenly come to believe there is little in this world he doesn't know. And if he chances to go on to college he will become self assured that he knows it all, even more than some of his professors. The world is his rare and especial oyster. Fortunately the world is waiting for one such as this. Disillusionment is swift and certain.

The eighth grade boy rides the tractor down the corn rows today. He is confident and pleased with his first educational triumph, but not overconfident. 6-5-42

THE FARM WOMAN

Summertime always brings a procession of small boys to the farm. Here often in two or three weeks they must try to make up for a lifetime of denial of the natural pursuits of childhood.

The combination slippery slide, trapeze and ladder gleaming in its coat of red and silver in a town back yard may be the envy of country cousins. But where is the ten-year-old in town who would not eagerly exchange it for a haymow, a windmill and a pony?

The boy who may be a sleepy-head at home rises at six o'clock on the farm without being called and accompanies the hired man to the milking. The information he has gleaned at the end of the third day is astounding even to himself. "I never did know I could learn so much in three days," he comments. And then he reviews his new found knowledge. A voluntary review is the key to retention of learning as any school ma'am will tell you.

This lad can tell you how many pigeons are setting in the barn, how many eggs the barn swallow has in her nest and where the turtle dove is nesting. He knows the milk cows and the horses by name and what their daily diet is. He has made a friend of the saddle horse and scarcely bounces any more as he rides. The saddle horse always seems to welcome visiting admirers. A boy and a dog and a horse are a natural combination.

The only thing about the farm routine that bothers at

all is that one cannot go to sleep at night. The tree frogs get tuned up about the time the lights go out and they make so much noise it disturbs this child accustomed to the noises of the city. Not a word is said but probably this bedtime hour may also bring thoughts of mother and father and the familiar things at home. However with the call of the mocking bird and the meadow lark he is up to find what the new day has in store.

Always boys come for four or five summers. Then the time comes when the farm no longer has the same allure. The pigeons and the tree house suddenly belong to an age of the past. More likely there is the urge to get a job and the job at the soda fountain or the grocery store keeps him in town. Or it may be that some sweet young thing has entered the picture. The sixteen year olds seldom come to the farm.

However there is a procession of small boys who come and keep us entertained with their discoveries and observations.

6-29-42

THE FARM WOMAN

As these lines are written the first round of the snowball battle at the country school is drawing to a close. The 5-minute bell has rung, which calls for cessation of activities.

Preparations for the battle have been going on for two days. The four big girls in school are lined up against all the younger ones. Each side constructed a fortification of defense. This required all the recesses and noon intermissions for two days. The big girls made a high fort, not very long. Some 20 feet away the small children constructed a longer defense and lower. Each child worked hard and eagerly to make ready for the fray. Little fingers flew as they made a large pile of snowballs for ammunition. The big girls made a small reserve, not many.

One doesn't know exactly how or when the barrage commenced. Suddenly snowballs were flying thick and fast through the air. The little ones, having numbers on their side, sent more invectives. Their fort is longer, they can stand at the ends and strike those larger girls crouched behind their tall fort. The boy who is having the most fun is little brother who ventures right out into no-man's land with a mammoth snowball and plumps his big sister right on the head. It is sweet revenge for all the edicts this older sister has enforced by might through the years. It is no matter that the big girls all pounce on him and wash his face. He got his good lick in first. When the big girls come into view such a heavy barrage greets them that they are forced to cover. Sideline referees would say that the little tikes have the edge as the bell rings. The big girls feel this way too because they dash toward the schoolhouse shouting, "It's not fair!"

If the snow holds another day there will no doubt be a change in legislation. The battle of the snows is on. 1940

THE FARM WOMAN

Americans are prone to worship big things. We boast of our tallest building, largest mansion, victorious football team, et cetera. It may be that we are getting away from this to some extent. Man is a pretty small creature in the universe after all. Time was when the family which had the largest Thanksgiving turkey was the envy of the neighborhood. Nowadays the biggest turkey will not even go in the oven of the new stove. And the Department of Agriculture is conducting intensive experiments to reduce the size of the strutting gobbler.

The young husband brought home the largest bird from the market. The wife scurried all over the neighborhood for a roaster large enough to accommodate the bird. When none could be found, she had to amputate the running gear and the wings. As the once proud turk graced the festive board it appeared that his race had lived too long upon this earth. When there are no drumsticks for the children the race is indeed falling into decay.

At this Thanksgiving season rural school children are grateful to the local theater manager for scheduling "Heidi" at this time. Shirley Temple is the idol of all country kids. "Heidi" is a favorite story. In addition the fourth grade social studies unit is about Switzerland. The dishes were washed in no time. The living room is spick and span. Everything is co-ordinated, correlated and consummated. 12-9-37

THE FARM WOMAN

All the children in the country school agree they enjoyed the Christmas program in the auditorium even more than the parades of the last few years. For grown-ups that goes double.

It was a full day. Each child came to school at the usual time with a sack lunch in his hand. Nearly everyone had on something new. A new dress or jacket or shirt or scarf, gifts that had likely been laid away for Christmas and brought out early for this special occasion. The teacher had planned a full day. Each child had a partner and designated position in the line of march. They marched to the flag stop on the M.K.&T., and rode the train to Emporia. For the younger ones it was the first train ride. A sophisticated fifth grader announced this was her third trip. The remainder of the morning was spent visiting business houses and industries in the county seat. Lunch in the park. In line for the first matinee and home after a full day.

Back seat conversation on the way home after major events is always illuminating to front seat listeners. The monkeys and the acrobats were plenty good but the outstanding feature was the pony on the stage. First of all there was amazement that the stage was large enough for a real, live pony. When one's stage experience is limited to the eight by twenty-eight foot platform at school, it is a bit difficult to imagine a stage where horses can prance and not be crowded at all. Was there ever a child, rural or urban, who did not long for a pony? You may have the dancers and the other acts if you will just give us the pony.
12-19-40

THE FARM WOMAN

Now and again one reads directions for keeping the cookie jar filled. None ever worked at this house.

It may be highly complimentary to the cook, after she has combined the ingredients that go to make good cookies to have four or five pairs of hands reach out to sample each panful as it comes from the oven. She hovers over the last pan and guards it as closely as the White Rock hen does her one chick.

A survey of kitchen, after two hours of labor, reveals soiled mixing bowls, cups, spoons, rolling pin and bread board and one cookie sheet half filled with cookies - barely enough for supper. And still there are folk who would tell us how to fill the cookie jar.

However a recipe in the current farm Bureau News has caught our eye. Castor oil cookies. Two cookies are said to be equal to a dose of caster oil. Can't you think of several people you would like to feed such dainties? At the mere mention of the new recipe the hired man shies off and says he will almost be afraid to taste cookies any more. Perhaps here at last is the answer as to how to keep the cookie jar filled. 6-24-39

THE FARM WOMAN

Did you ever sit in plain sight of the telephone and less than 15 feet away when it was repeatedly ringing your ring on the party line, when you were perfectly able-bodied and still unable to walk that distance to answer it? Well I have.

Such are the experiences in a house divided due to scarlet fever. Mother and the girls are confined to the kitchen and the stairs while the masculine members take over the living and dining rooms and the spare bedroom. The school teacher and the high school lad are scuttled to the neighbors. The hired man sleeps on the cot and dreams of his soft bed above stairs. He is also troubled for fear some other swain will try to show his best girl a good time.

Father must be housekeeper, errand boy, telephone girl, secretary and general handy man.

Children weigh requests carefully, "Bring "Tailspin Tommy" but not "Pinocchio," because I don't want to have to burn up "Pinocchio." Paper dolls are gazed upon fondly today for tomorrow with all their fine wardrobes they must enter the kitchen stove.

Never have hands been scrubbed so often with soap and water. Never have dishes had such intense scalding. The family doctor recommended it. Germs, germs are lurking everywhere, unseen. Now if they would only come out in the open in plain sight one would not feel so helpless.

Monotonous days are filled with meal preparation and dishwashing, with baths and bed making, with cleaning and sweeping, with reading and listening to the radio turned up loud, somehow they pass in quick succession, one week, then two and three are gone before everyone realizes it.

The bold red card on the front of the house tells the world that this family must be isolated. Neighbors generally give such a card a wide berth. They send in dainties with the hired man or set them carefully on the back step. But political seekers are a braver lot. They march right up to the front door adjacent to the warning placard and boldly knock. One loudly calls, "Go to the back door." Then through the back screen one explains that during scarlet fever isolation, it is more blessed to receive than to give. In fact the health officer ordered not even a scrap of paper or a signature sent out of quarantine.

There is one difference between quarantine and a grand jury. One doesn't tell the quarantine officer that he has a vacation trip planned or that there is an important executive meeting. One just stays in. And sometimes those things which seemed necessary and all important go right along without you. 1-28-39

THE FARM WOMAN

One custom country children do not enjoy is that of hanging May baskets. There is no reason why they shouldn't. They could walk a quarter or a half mile to the near neighbors. Perhaps it is because we have no doorbells in the country. Ringing the doorbell as you hang the basket is half the fun.

May, in the country, means the time when children go barefoot. They step gingerly the first few days until the feet become hardened. It is the month in which country boys have their heads shaved. All the bumps of knowledge or skill, which we used to study in high school psychology, are plainly visible. Sheep are sheared in late April or May. They appear nude and retiring. However, they are comfortable and they do not pant on warm days.

Eighth graders are breathing easier this week. Examinations are over. They know that no grades will be mailed until the last of May, yet they watch for the mail carrier half-expectantly. We know only second hand what the examination questions were. The children were not allowed to bring a copy home. As they explained it, it seemed rather a trick question to ask what sections of land were originally laid aside for school purposes. We did not know, hence we thought it catchy. How many of you know the section, township, range in which you live? Any test or examination is easy when one knows the answer.

Chronicles of
The Farm Woman

A friend from town always comes to the farm in spring. Especially does she come to watch the little red pigs as they roam around. She says the expression on the face of each little porker reminds her of some acquaintance.

Old cars are a necessary nuisance. We must have transportation. Where is the country boy who can rate a steady girl unless he has a car or a friend who has one? But old cars are a source of worry to more than one farm mother. Youth dares to venture farther from home than its elders. Mothers wonder when daughters set out if they will return safely. Blowouts can often be fixed or one can return home on the rim. When the lights blow out or an axle breaks what is there to do? Daughter knows her mother will not sleep a wink until she gets home.

Has some demon given us a glimpse of improved streamline transportation only to deny us the privilege of obtaining it? Will our economic world eventually catch up with that of industry and invention?

Many old cars on the highways today should be taken to the city dump.

5-6-35

Chapter 8

"Bread cast upon the water"

Mary worked for Community Mental Health. She helped with legislation, on the state level, to get local centers organized and established. She was the first president of the Mental Health Association of Lyon County, an agency organized in 1958. Two years later, the Mental Health Center of East Central Kansas opened in Emporia.

Mary had become interested in serving on the board of directors of the Mental Health Association. "I was always screaming about how everything was Emporia," she remembers saying, "let's make it Lyon County." Somebody looked at her and said, "Mary, we'll just make it Lyon County if you'll be president."

She was the type of person with leadership qualities, needed at the time to get everything going. One of her main objectives and goals was to really see that the organization had something to contribute to the community. She was able to give it a base from which to go forward. She served on the Board of Directors of the Center until 1979.

Back in 1941 she was on the committee to set up the state United Services Organization. And, from 1944 to 1948 she was regional director of the American Cancer Society. One of her duties was to attend the National convention of the American Cancer Society in Biloxi, MS in 1946. Mac and Esther went with her to this meeting. Kathleen and Jim were in Lawrence attending KU.

They always said helping others was like, "bread cast upon the water, it comes back to you." [1] The more they did, the more it grew and the better it got, for everyone.

Mary was comfortable with notoriety and was everyone's equal in any situation or with a group of any age.

The John Redman Reservoir inundated the most fertile land along the Neosho river. The dam was finally built in 1963, but she fought it for nearly 20 years.

Mac was on the Lyon County School board that reorganized grade school districts after WWII. Many

---

[1] The good deed you do today may benefit you or someone you love at the least expected time. If you never see the deed again at least you will have made the world a better place - And, after all, isn't that what life is all about?

small districts closed and there was much hostility. One room schoolhouses were closing and farm families were adjusting. Mary served on Neosho Rapids School Board beginning in 1942 for a period of 4 years.

In 1954 Mac was appointed to the Newman Hospital Board. He served for 30 years.

Mary also helped organize Blue Cross and Blue Shield in the late 30's and early 40's. She was the first non-medical doctor to serve on the state Blue Shield Board and possibly the first female to be on the board. She said, "the hardest to convince were the doctors."

In 1963 John Anderson, governor and friend of Mac and Mary, appointed Mary Frances to the State Library Advisory Commission. Governor Avery re-appointed her and she served on the commission for 8 years. She worked to organize and establish the state system of regional libraries and get it funded. She was instrumental in setting up the library system for the State of Kansas.

They entertained many people in their home for meals; neighbors, friends, governors, State Representatives & Senators. Mary could lift the phone and call the Republican governors, Senators & Representatives. Names like Dole, Reese, Kassebaum, Schoeppel, and Milton Eisenhower were familiar names around the house. These people were friends, not just acquaintances.

In the 40's, twice a year a group of "thinkers & doers" got together for picnics, called Basket Dinners, to brainstorm ideas. All discussed current affairs and how to improve the community and Kansas. They came from Topeka, Manhattan, Strong City, Hartford. They took turns hosting. In the group were: a lawyer, a Kansas Supreme Court Justice, homemakers, Extension specialists, K-State professors, Kansas Power & Light representatives. Families were always included. While the kids played, the adults visited and made plans. Many programs for the betterment of Kansas came from these get togethers. One of the boys called this the "Broadus Group" because all the moms were on the plump side.

They always felt that good common people make the world a better place.

Education was always foremost in their home. Mary served on the state book selection committee for elementary and secondary schools. As a result their home had a roomful of sample books on all sorts of material.

They made sure there were lots of people around during meals - neighbors, governors, State Representatives & Senators. Their children were certainly blessed to be around so many movers and shakers at the dinner table. Their son and daughters learned from and certainly appreciated the people they were exposed to, maybe not so much when they were younger but a keen awareness developed early on in their adult life.

Mary made many friends, most became lifelong friends. The following is a letter from Eloise Hamman, who is 95 years old, at this writing. She wrote:

My Friend Mary McKinney

Mary was a busy person who loved her home community of Hartford and all the common rural folks that lived there. To help them was her goal. She was educated and hoped to extend learning to all. In 1957 she helped compile Hartford's history of 100 years.

She was a great promoter of government programs. She helped educate people through Extension, 4-H, & Farm Management, naming a few.

It was through Extension I first met Mary. It was around 1940, she went to Extension and organized a program, held in the Hartford Methodist Church basement to teach the women of the community how to pressure food, using a pressure cooker, safely. Many women were afraid of the cooker and other methods of preservation weren't satisfactory. This was a valuable lesson, as preserving food extended the income & provided a veritable variety of garden produce, out of season, when there was little refrigeration and electricity available.

She encouraged the youth to join 4-H and learn to do better.

The men weren't neglected. She introduced them

My family was recipient of her suggestions & help.
to KSU's expertise thru Farm Management. Many young

farmers joined at her suggestion and many of retirement age are still members.

One daughter was accepted at 4-H Smurthwaite Sorority at KSU. Another did social work at Osawatomie State Hospital at Mary's suggestion. Mary introduced her to Cap Edwards in Topeka, an important dignitary, who accepted her application. My son was introduced to Farm Management by Mary. But that wasn't the end of it, when I became handicapped and lost my limb to cancer, Mary was there to encourage me. She came to my rescue supplying supplies given freely to cancer patients, checked my insurance and found they had overcharged me, notified rehab of my needs. Later when I became discouraged and depressed she encouraged me to get a degree at Emporia State. She went with me to enroll and kept tabs on my progress, often making suggestions to help me achieve, although I was 56 years old. I graduated in 4 years and, at 60 years, made both the President & Dean's Honor Roll, and was hired to teach Special Education at my first interview. Her job didn't end with my graduation. She accompanied me to Wellington and helped me find an apartment available near the school to accommodate my handicap.

My family wasn't the only one to enjoy and gain by Mary's expertise. A number of youth of the area were fortunate, with her help, to attend college with a grant from the Jones Foundation. Another facet of Mary's endeavors was the Mental Health Organization and, of course, her political contacts were valuable to the community.

She remained a good friend and became very dear to us.

One day she remarked, "I get the most satisfaction out of the things I do and accomplish, that no one knows about!"

She also had another great trait. In helping you it may have started with a suggestion, but she assisted you until the mission was accomplished with satisfactory results.

(Thank you Mary for your help!)

I think of her often and know that there are many others in the community who gained from her generosity, and knowledge, maybe not money wise, but her expertise & knowledge of what would help us, instructing us and educating us, because education started with a capital "E" where Mary was concerned.

Eloise Hamman
February 1, 2007

Ever the educator, Mary wanted her readers to grasp the savvy knowledge that was her political nature, and understand and enjoy becoming active in the affairs of the community. It was easy to see she relished a thirst for knowledge and diversity, so much so that she would entertain the notion that everyone should learn new and better ways of doing, and proceeded to teach them. She never stopped learning and her readers learned right along with her. She relished her pen and could make her readers appreciate her point of view with candor and assurance. Her contacts with special people in special places was her handy tool. Never afraid of calling a Senator, or a Governor on the phone.

Here follows some of her delightful suggestions, all clipped from various articles she wrote:

"I wonder how many of our readers long to attend lecture courses at some of the country's leading universities delivered by visiting notables. I wonder if those same people tune the dials of their radios to CBX every Tuesday at 2:30 o'clock. In the solitude of the radio you are carried across the seas to listen to some of the most brilliant minds in the British Empire. The series is "Wither Britain" H. G. Wells, Winston Churchill, the Bishop of Exeter and George Bernard Shaw are some of the voices lecturing to us.

"If you desire an intellectual treat tune in next Tuesday." 2-9-34

The title of this article was *Farm Woman Falls for Alf.*

"Landon and prohibition swing into the lead as out state votes begin to come in." With that announcement we decided it was safe to go to bed. Our votes did count after all. Kansas has upheld the heritage that is hers.

Last week our governor talked to the Farm Bureau in Manhattan. For one half hour politics was laid aside and we had a frank discussion of the problems of the Kansas farmer. "We cannot look for a panacea for our ills," he told us. "In the final analysis it will be a long time educational program." Critics were in the audience that day in case he injected any politics into his speech. We sat down front praying fervently that he would pass out no meat for the wolves. He didn't

Our governor may not be a Kuppenheimer model, his double-breasted coat has a few too many wrinkles but he speaks the language of the Kansas farmer.

On School Textbooks

What criteria should guide a county committee in the selection of textbooks? Shall children be asked to procure bright new books every few years? Or are books now in use plenty good enough?

Textbooks are tools in the hands of students who would increase their knowledge. A good tool is essential to good work. A good tool is not necessarily the latest model. Materials, craftsmanship, and the character and abilities of writer and publisher, as well as suitability for the task at hand, are some of the things to look for in considering a textbook.

Children are the most important crop in the nation. We expect them to become good citizens. Schools and books are provided to assist in the development of good citizenship. Textbooks are important.

Housewife Mrs. J. McKinney of Hartford is State Republican Vice Chairman, writes for the *Emporia Gazette.* This picture appeared in Life Magazine during WWII

Chronicles of
The Farm Woman

THE FARM WOMAN

Clarence Malone, Kansas representative of the USO, has mailed a comprehensive report of USO activities to all members of the organization.

Lyon county is one of the 37 counties which launched its drive and went over the top early. Some of the counties are getting their drives under way now. Each county which has made a concerted effort has reached their quota. For everyone wants the men in the armed forces to have a good time when on leave. USO stands ready to furnish clean entertainment and recreation.

More than 500 elevators cooperated with the state committee in accepting donations of wheat - "a bushel or so for the USO." Reports from these elevators are now beginning to come in. In some counties where elevators could not furnish storage facilities and wheat was stored on farms or in unused buildings, the county USO committee sent out trucks. Each truck came in loaded with wheat for the USO. Again and again one hears the comment, "this is the least we can do."

Do the boys like USO? Ask any neighbor boy home on leave or a khaki clad stranger whom you meet. If he has been around the country at all he will tell you about the USO club in Louisville, in New Orleans or Long Beach. Men can go to these clubs for a quiet time of reading and writing letters or for a gala evening of dancing and games. It is the place to go if you want to meet good looking girls. Each USO club has a hospitality committee which sees that men in service are invited out to dinner. In short the USO endeavors to provide a home-away-from-home for men on leave.

USO started from scratch a little more than a year ago. Now there is a county organization in one hundred of the counties in Kansas. There are 842 operations in the United States, and forty-one operations overseas. Each week new operations are being set up. Already clubs are functioning in Junction City, Manhattan and Leavenworth. Approvals have been granted by the National committee for Topeka, Salina, Gardner and Coffeyville. As other camps are made ready USO operations may be expected.

Boys from all corners of the United States and from the United Nations will be sent to various camps in Kansas for air training. Kansas is an agricultural state and farm families can make a definite and unique contribution to the USO effort, if they cooperate by inviting trainees into their homes for week-end leaves.

Some day the peace will come - the peace for which we are now striving. It will be more likely to be a just and durable peace if the people from the corners of the earth know one another. It is only a little thing to entertain a stranger in khaki for Sunday dinner. Yet one bit of hospitality multiplied many times could mean the friendship or hostility of nations. The stories that come back to us of the warm hospitality our boys are receiving in Australia should be an example to us.

Let us show the stranger within our borders what farm hospitality means. If and when we get an air base at Emporia this will be one contribution you and I can make.

9-1-42

THE FARM WOMAN

A feature story by Peggy of the Flint Hills[1] *in the Topeka Capital is about the 15th birthday of the USO. In the picture along with the story is Connie Smith, A Hartford girl who now works at the statehouse in Topeka.*

Fifteen years ago Governor Ratner called Ray Pierson, Clarence Malone and the writer to meet in his office. Mrs. Daisy Johntz could not be present at that first meeting. We met to talk about United Service Organizations. This was back in those days when we were talking about defense. Our boys were being assembled for defense. Mothers were concerned about the temptations their sons might face away from home. USO came into being to meet that need and forestall that worry. It was to be a home away from home, a wholesome place where lads could go when not on duty and where they could find someone interested in them.

At the national level someone had assembled representatives of the YMCA, YWCA, National Catholic Community Service, the Salvation Army, the Jewish Welfare Board and The Travelers Aid Association. These six organizations banded together to form the United Service Organizations. Governor Ratner gave us the information he had received and told us there was a job to be done, to perfect a statewide organ-

[1] Zula Bennington Greene who wrote an editorial, six days a week for 50 years, for the Topeka Capital as *Peggy of The Flint Hills.* Mary and Zula were very good friends.

ization and solicit funds to support it.

Everyone over the state knew Red Pierson, the only one of that committee who has gone to the great beyond. Clarence Malone had headed the Knights of Columbus and had a wide acquaintance. Mrs. Johntz had been president of the Federated clubs, president of the Woman's Kansas Day club, president of the Council of Woman. The writer was there to represent rural Kansas. At this time Kansas was beginning to emerge from those long, lean years of the depression and money was not as plentiful as it is today. We coined the phrase "a bushel or so for the USO" and asked people to share a bushel of wheat for this cause. They did.

The welfare of their boys was close to the hearts of every family.

At that time the committee was thinking of the immediate task at hand. Certainly no one voiced a long look into the future and pictured the USO as it is today.

The USO is still that home away from home. As Peggy says: "Boy likes to meet Girl and Girl likes to meet Boy." That is true in peace time as it is in war. Country girls who go to Topeka to work, get into the USO and there they meet boys. Thus the USO has come to be as important for girls as it is for boys.

How many married couples do you know who met at the USO? Many happy returns of this birthday. 2-23-56

THE FARM WOMAN

What a day! What a day!

Can you imagine 500,000 people lining the streets of Indianapolis to see our Kansas governor? Eight and 10 deep on either side of the street for blocks they stood to watch the Republican standard bearer and the parade. Every window was filled with faces. Business had a 2-hour breathing spell on Saturday afternoon.

It took the parade exactly two hours to pass our vantage point. Two lines of cars and floats two hours long. Bands and drum corps too numerous to count interspersed the parade. Legion bands, auxiliary bands and drum corps, kid bands, school bands, town bands and the spirit of 76 was there. Delegates from practically every county in the state. Voters enough in the parade it seemed to carry the state for Landon. We thought as we crossed Indiana last Sunday that the situation did not look so good. So few sunflowers were in evidence. But sunflowers lined the streets today as thick as they grow along fence rows and township roads in Lyon County. Indiana may have looked like a doubtful state yesterday or last week. Tonight it is in the bag.

And one thing about Republican parades in this campaign of 1936. They are purely voluntary demonstrations. There are no orders or threats of fine.

It is remarkable how much satisfaction and confidence people gain by even a glimpse of Landon. The farm folks were gath-

ered in assembly hall. The candidate was ushered in for a brief moment. A wave of inspiration and enthusiasm settled upon the audience.

The Coliseum was so packed that the doors were closed at 7 o'clock, one hour before the speaking. Thousands listened from outdoor speakers on the fair grounds. An eager attentive audience. One wonders at the boldly placarded Roosevelt marchers that are in the crowds. They apparently are not listening to the radio address. Do they adore crowds? With stolid mien they march along, not slow, not fast, a measured trudge.

We turn out the light tonight, weary but thrilled to the toes. This day is something to tuck in our memory book.

1936

THE FARM WOMAN

The legal notice in fine type has been published in many of the Kansas papers recently. It is a notice published by the Secretary of State regarding the civil service amendment to the constitution. Little if any discussion of this proposal is seen in the press or heard in conversation on the street. Yet, it is of importance to every citizen of the state.

As each voter enters the polls in November he or she will be handed a constitutional amendment ballot which will contain the phrase "The Civil Service Amendment to the Constitution." It is no political party football. Each party at various times has endorsed civil service. Governor Ratner came out for the merit system two years ago and urged the legislators to submit this constitutional amendment to the voters.

The merit system will provide careers for statecraft rather than patronage plums as now exist. Young men and women will be encouraged to enter govern-ment service as well as the professions. They will prepare for and take examinations in various branches of state government. They will do this with the assurance that there will be some permanence to their positions as long as each one does his work well. This should result in better governmental administration.

Women should be especially interested in this constitutional amendment. They want sound economy in government. And good government is similar to good housekeeping. The cook who knows how to bake good biscuits does not waste the flour as does a raw inexperienced girl. The trained homemaker practices real economy. The adoption of the civil service amendment will result in more thrift in government.

Statesmanship as a career will elevate the plane of government and give us greater returns for our tax dollar. Find out more about this amendment and vote yes in November.

8-22-40

THE FARM WOMAN

Friday in Topeka Governor Ratner signed the Oberg-Platt bill providing for the construction of a dormitory or student union building at state schools.

Under the provisions of this act a dormitory or student union may be erected without one cent of cost to the taxpayer. Such buildings will be erected by the sale of revenue bonds. A dormitory will be paid for out of income over a period of years; a student union by special assessments.

The passage of this bill climaxes the desires and efforts of a group of women of the state, the Kansas Council of Women, The American Association of University Women, the Home Demonstration council, all have labored in its behalf. In 1933 or 1934 when Alf Landon was governor and John Stutz directed the KERC, a group of women called on these two men to see if there were not some way to get a dormitory through an alphabetical agency. Both men were willing but at that time there seemed no way it could be done except by direct appro-priations of the entire amount. Through the years news has trickled in that dormitories were being erected in other states by means of revenue bonds, in Indiana, Idaho, South Dakota, Wisconsin, etc. Iowa State now houses all of its women in halls. Letters have been written, small group meetings held, always seeking a way to improve student housing.

For years students at Kansas State college have craved a recreational center. An election was held to test student sentiment and it carried overwhelmingly. The State Board of Regents decided in favor of a dormitory and student union at Kansas State

Chronicles of
The Farm Woman
Continued p. 2

college. The bill was introduced by two able men in the House and Senate. The governor placed his support behind it and now the 1941 legislature has passed the enabling act. It is a case of many forces pulling together finally achieving success.

The need for housing and recreation at Kansas State college is more acute at this time because of its proximity to expanding Camp Funston. The student population has doubled in the last few years while that of the town of Manhattan has increased little, if any. Now workmen, officers and their families, mothers and wives of soldiers and those charm sisters who follow any mass group, all have descended on the town. Hence the housing shortage. The inescapable operation of the law of supply and demand must increase rentals.

The story of women's halls at our state schools is a tale that might well be told. Years ago a small group of university alumni under the leadership of Alberta Corbin, whose death occurred last week in Lawrence, decided to do something about housing. For one thing they placed a mug on the clock shelf for any stray change. Small donations were received and hoarded toward erection of a women's dormitory. They were joined by alumni from other state schools and in the early 20's the legislature made appropriations for women's dormitories. Van Zile Hall at Manhattan, Corbin Hall at Lawrence, both named for deans of women who had labored long for better housing. Morse Hall at Emporia State and dormitories at Pittsburg and Hays were erected.

If memory serves correctly the net income or profit from these halls was to form a nest egg for the erection of a second

Chronicles of The Farm Woman Continued p. 3

dormitory on each campus. In the first days of the depression when everyone was looking around for surpluses or cached treasures some members of the legislature spied the reserve of board and room money at Van Zile Hall and suggested its appropriation for paving the campus roads. The roads did need paving.

Now through these 10 depression years another nest egg of $26,000 has accumulated. This surplus is really an achievement also. For the past 10 years Van Zile has been managed on a co-operative basis. A total of 130 women live in the hall throughout the school year and 115 of these live co-operatively for $20 per month. Living cooperatively means that the women do most of the work, averaging about one hour daily. This living and working together is an experience, as any woman will tell you. One woman who had come of college age without ever assuming many kitchen responsibilities was sure she could not make a cake for 130 people. She had never baked a cake of any kind in her life. However, she was admonished by Miss Wood, the director, to follow directions closely and the result would be satisfactory. It was. Today that woman and many others declare the training at Van Zile is as valuable as any they received on the campus.

Now another story is to be added to the story of housing. It is hoped that another dormitory may be ready for occupancy at Kansas State college next year.

3-29-41

THE FARM WOMAN

Farmers in ever increasing numbers are haunting the relief office. Much independence is sacrificed as they mount those steep stairs. When a farmer has a little money in the bank, a crib of corn and a mow of alfalfa, five or six milk cows in the back pasture, a couple of litters of pigs, 200 pullets and a cave full of fruits and vegetables, when he has all these he is as independent as nobody's business.

Debt, first of all, shears us of much of our independence. Especially debts that cannot be met when due. Three years without a crop pushes us toward despair. No grain means no chicken feed. And this year no garden has driven us to ascend the stairs to the relief office to ask for aid.

Farmers want work. As they apply they are referred to the WPA in Topeka. In one specific instance the case worker made an investigation one month ago and recommended that the farmer be given work. She supposed her recommendation had been carried out. A near-neighbor discovered quite by accident that the last chicken had been exchanged for flour and the flour almost gone. Somewhere in the mill this man's name reposes - his credit gone. Work relief, his very last hope, does not come because he has not yet been certified.

This man is a neighbor.

If I were not a Republican already this one instance would convert me.

Chronicles of
The Farm Woman

THE FARM WOMAN

A year ago many women of the county were doing Red Cross sewing or knitting. Red sweaters of all sizes and blue ones and green were being knitted for needy folks in devastated countries. Layettes, toddlers packs, children's and women's dresses were cut at the sewing room, checked out to be sewed and returned ready to be marked, packed and shipped to a central depot. All this was done by a corps of volunteer workers.

Today the shelves are not filled with row upon row of cutout or finished garments. The knitting division has packed and shipped more than 100 turtle neck sweaters size 36, and 200 helmets - beautifully made garments all. At some point of embarkation those sweaters and helmets will be issued to men who need them. It is altogether possible that some boy in the armed forces may be issued a sweater that his wife or mother or sweetheart has knitted.

Although there is not the sewing or knitting to be done at the moment the demands for volun-teer services is greater than ever in the history of the Red Cross. The demand now is for volunteers who will fold surgical dressings, hun-dreds and thousands of them under careful supervision. Exactness and accuracy along with clean hands (without nail polish) and a clean frock constitute the only equipment needed to do this work. Doctors and nurses in the armed forces must have dressings for their patients. They will have them if we, the volunteers, find time to fold them.

Other volunteers will serve as nurses' aides in hospitals, without pay. They must first study for eighty hours and then give at least 15 hours of bedside service each year. Still others will study canteen work and be prepared to do mass feeding in an emergency.

Less spectacular per-haps but fully as important are the classes in basic subjects which the Red Cross offers to any group which desires it. Before one can become a nurses' aide she must first have had the first course in home nursing and nutrition. Before one can serve in a canteen she must have finished the nutrition and canteen course. Before one can serve in a motor corps, she must have had first aid and motor mechanics. Through years of experience the Red Cross has found that the way to meet an emergency, to cope with disaster, is to have a band of trained workers ready to serve. Is it too much to ask that you give 2 hours of your time in a primary Red Cross course this autumn? Gather ten or 12 of your neighbors together and ask for a Red Cross class. Every effort will be made to furnish a volunteer teacher.

8-24-42

THE FARM WOMAN

A call has been issued for the organization of the Lyon County chapter of the Kansas division of the American Cancer society. The public is invited to the meeting. All persons who contributed one dollar or more to the cancer drive last spring are eligible to vote.

Cancer is the giant killer that stalks the earth today. He may meet his match in the surgeon's knife, x-ray or radium therapy, if these treatments are used in time.

Eleven or 12 years ago, doctors who had been working in the American Cancer society asked the General Federation of Women's clubs to organize a field army to disseminate existing knowledge about treatment of cancer. These doctors knew that if they could see the patients in time, many lives could be saved. The women accepted the challenge. The watchword of the field army became "Saving Lives." The theme of the army is "Fight Cancer with Knowledge."

Progress has been made in these 11 years. Many years ago cancer was a muted word, as consumption or tuberculosis had been a generation earlier. The field army has seen to it that a piece of literature about cancer has been placed in nearly every home. Cancer is no longer whispered as if in disgrace. Doctors report that more patients are presenting themselves for early diagnosis.

In the past two years a quarter million dollars has been raised by the field army in Kansas. That much money called for incorporation. The Kansas division of the American Cancer Society, Inc., was formed. Now the Lyon County chapter of that society is to be duly formed. Delegates will be elected to a district meeting where a district director will be elected. The district directors in turn select additional directors at large. All these folk with certain designated persons, the president of the Kansas Medical society, the state commander of the field army, the chairman of the State Board of Social Welfare, the superintendent of public instruction, the Secretary of the State Board of Health, the chairman of the cancer committee of the state medical society, compose the Board of Directors of the Kansas division.

Although the name and details of organization may be changed, the purposes of the group will not be altered. The aim is still to fight cancer with knowledge; to provide funds for research and to urge frequent physical examinations. Until cancer is conquered, this fight must go on. More power to Mrs. Lucille Davis and Claudia Williams who, with their corps of helpers, are directing this work in Lyon County.

10-6-47

Chronicles of
The Farm Woman

THE FARM WOMAN

Most of the readers of this column are probably aware that the writer recently made a brief sashay in politics. As this is written ballots over the state are being counted and in a few hours the suspense will be over, the victor will be applauded.

It was a varied and interesting experience to sit in the state headquarters and assist in a statewide campaign. To sleep until 7 or 7:30 o'clock in the morning. To eat three meals each day without having one thing to do with their preparation, never have to wash a dish, although every day the help wanted columns in the daily papers advertised for dishwashers and waitresses. To have a hot bath every day. Never once did I make my bed.

For the first time in my life I had a secretary and dictated letters. She was a kindly, patient person and usually put in commas and periods where they were needed. She kept a dictionary at her elbow and we both used it frequently.

On the other hand I saw the sun rise only once while I was away. That was one morning when it was necessary to catch an early morning train. One could tell that the sun was shining by the reflection on the buildings across the street. Not until midday could it be seen in the little slice of sky visible from Kansas Avenue. Only once were my feet set upon the ground. That was when friends took me to the country for dinner.

I was never more chilled than when the first cold spell of the season come along and the hotel furnace was not in working order. Repairs had been ordered for weeks. When they came there was no plumber to put them in place. Everyone shivered and went to bed to keep warm. The first cold snap may arrive before the farm heating stove is set up and the stove pipe in place Yet one can always send the children to gather a few chips from the wood yard or a basket of cobs from the pigpen and start the kitchen range. If the oven door is opened all the family can gather round and get warm. One doesn't do that in a steam heated hotel room.

Every eating place which we patronized has curtailed its services in the past six weeks. This was due to the inability to get help. Food prices are higher than in small towns and of only mediocre quality. On one day not a needle could be purchased in Topeka. All stores have green and hence inefficient help. Customers are learning to buy what is on hand even though it may not be exactly what they want. Everyone seemed to have money in his or her pockets. However, one could observe the strained look on the face of more than one mother when the first of the month came and she was trying to stretch a pre-war salary check over bills incurred at War-time prices.

If any of you on the farm feel that town folk get all the breaks, I beg you to thank the kind Providence that you can see the sun rise and set, pictures every day that no artist can reproduce. You can tread the good earth and gather fresh warm eggs from the nests in the chicken house. You can bake nut-like home made bread which has a certain something no bakers' products possess. By your own labors you can produce at least half of the family living. And above all you can breathe the fresh pure air that blows over these Kansas prairies.

11-11-42

THE FARM WOMAN

The five people from Hartford who attended hearings before the public works committee in Washington last week, did not see anything on the entire trip more pleasing or promising than this Grand Neosho Valley.

The route led through the Seventh Street traffic way in Kansas City, Kansas, and across the Fairfax bridge into Missouri. Scattering herds of cattle were seen on feed in Missouri and Illinois. In Illinois great corn cribs were seen and about half of them filled - wise insurance on the 1949 crop. Filling station attendants told us it was so dry farmers were delaying planting corn and soybeans. The seed bed was carefully worked - as thoroughly as ground is prepared for alfalfa in these parts.

The first night was spent in Jacksonville, Ill., where the writer's maternal grandmother attended a female seminary in 1855.

The second day we passed three state capitols, Springfield, Ill., Indianapolis, Indiana, and Columbus Ohio, and holed in for the night in tourist cabins in Cambridge, Ohio. Highways and railroads tend to parallel each other across the continent so in the night one usually could hear the through rail traffic roaring by. The route from Indianapolis to Columbus crossed two of the flood control dams on the Miami River. A series of five dams were built by the Miami Conservancy district. The legend says they were completed in 1922.

In eastern Ohio we left

the farming country as we think of it. From there on in it was mountains and industry and farming in small patches. We rode 85 miles on the Pennsylvania Turnpike for 85 cents. This is the 4-lane road that FDR built through mountains, over streams. Every crossroad and railroad crossing is an overpass or an underpass. Nothing crosses the turnpike. One can enter only at certain points. We passed through two tunnels and under any number of crossroads. One man has the gas, oil and lunch concessions the entire length of the toll road. There are no speed limits posted. Only one's conscience at the throttle, touching the floor board is the determiner.

Hotel reservations were at the Hotel Washington, Washington D. C. It is on Pennsylvania Avenue, one block from the White House. The capitol is at the end of the street 15 blocks up. The parade for President Dutra[1] came past the hotel. From the dining room on the roof one can see all the familiar landmarks of the city, the Capitol, Washington monu-ment, Lincoln and Jefferson memorials, the famous cherry trees, the Potomac River, Arlington and the spire at Alexandria in the distance.

It was almost like old home week in Washington - one saw many folk from Kansas. The day before the hearing was scheduled

[1] President Eurico Dutra of Brazil visited Washington D. C. May 18, 1949.

Congressman Rees entertained the Kansas delegation and all of the people who had gone for the hearing, in the House restaurant - about 40 people attended. The pros sat across the table from the cons. But no glares were detected over the good food. The House restaurant is not a public eating place. Only members of Congress and their guests may be served. It is in the basement of the Capitol and is for convenience. Members leave the floor long enough to eat. If a roll call buzzer sounds they leave their soup and coffee and dash for the elevator. A round table is reserved for Republicans. The day we were there Joe Martin, McGregor of Ohio, Vursell of Illinois, Ford of Michigan, the latter three members of the public works committee, Anderson of Minnesota and others sat at this table.

Washington is on daylight savings time and likes it. It seems people never go to bed yet the offices are astir shortly after eight in the morning.

Most of the work in Congress is done in committee. Committees meet at 9:30 or 10. The House and Senate usually meet at noon, although the sessions are sometimes called earlier. When the bell rings throughout the Capitol and Senate and House office buildings, members know a vote is to be taken and they scramble to answer roll call. The hearing on the Grand Neosho was interrupted for the Dutra speech before the joint session and for three roll calls in the afternoon.

Each time the committee took a brief recess - not all

the committee members were ever present at one time - the chairman, Congressman Will M. Whittington of Mississippi was there all day and the clerk of the committee sat steno typing statements made at the hearing.

Hearings on three projects were scheduled the same day. First was a project in the vicinity of the Elephant Butte dam in New Mexico. The siltation in the reservoir has created problems in the local drainage area. Furthermore, New Mexico is in arrears in delivery of water to Texas. Thus we learned that the construction of dams creates problems.

When it came time for hearings on House Document 442 - the preliminary plans for Grand Neosho River, Colonel Gee of the staff of the Chief of Engineers explained the project and answered questions asked by members of the committee. So many letters of protest from Hartford had been written to the committee that they were conscious of the town of Hartford.

After the engineers had made the explanation, the proponents were called. John Redmond led the group, followed by witnesses from Marion, Council Grove, Chanute and Chetopa. Chetopa and the river near the Oklahoma line are really suffering from the Pensacola reservoir in Oklahoma. Where floods from the upper reaches descend they stay and stay because the Pensacola dam retards the fall.

Along late in the afternoon the opponents of the project had the chance to *state their case. The delegation was led by Frank Cosgrove who grew up on the river at Hartford and now owns land above Council Grove. We had prepared a brief to show that the benefit cost ratio as shown in the report is not economically sound. The engineers estimate that the average annual benefits will be $34,400. Yet not considered in costs of damages is an annual recurring loss of more than 2 ½ million dollars. These losses were computed from questionnaires circulated in the four areas. They are not guesswork, but actual losses that would occur annually should the reservoirs be constructed.*

Smaller reservoirs, which the people in this area desire, can be constructed at less cost per acre foot than the large ones proposed by the Army engineers. Tied in with smaller reservoirs must be a plan for soil conservation. Surely anyone who has seen the recent rises in the creeks and rivers here realizes the need to hold the silt out of the streams. We need clear running creeks.

The opponents stated their case. The decision of the committee on public works is awaited.

Saturday morning we left Washington at 6:15, before anyone was awake. All day we drove through the famed Blue Ridge mountains of Virginia and into West Virginia. We spent the night in Charleston. The next morning we ate breakfast in Ashland, Ky., on the Ohio river, four miles from Ironton where my father was born in 1855. A short stop was made at Calumet Farms. The pedigree of each mare and colt was posted on the stall door. We saw the famous Kentucky bluegrass. From there we crossed the Ohio into Illinois and in less than a mile crossed the Mississippi into Missouri. It was around the junction of these two rivers that my father's family floated in 1865. They left Ironton, went down the Ohio to the Mississippi, up the Mississippi to the Missouri and up the Missouri to Hannibal. In 1868 they came by train as far as Lawrence and on to Emporia.

In Springfield, Mo., we left Highway 60 and headed for Pittsburg, Kansas, and on home - 2,773 miles. Good weather the entire trip.

Project Document 442 became public law 81-516A May 17, 1950, then 85-327 on February 15, 1958. Construction began on the John Redmond Reservoir June of 1959 and was completed December of 1965.

Chronicles of The Farm Woman

THE FARM WOMAN

Informal meetings concerning mental health have been held in the county in the past year. Plans are now being made to form a Mental Health Association.

Recently a Mental Health Workshop was held in Topeka under the auspices of the Mental Hygiene division of the State Board of Health. Since Lyon County is in the process of organizing a Mental Health Association, it was a privilege for this writer to sit in on the workshop. Some observations may be of interest.

A sprinkling of laymen were in attendance along with psychiatrists, psychologists, social workers, judges, case workers, health officers and other professional people. For three days experiences were exchanged in prepared talks and in conversations.

What is a local Mental Health Association? What is the difference between a Mental Health Association and a Mental Health Center? A Mental Health Association is a group of citizens, interested in mental health, banded together to improve existing conditions. Anyone who has heard Judge Myers report on conditions that exist in this county will surely agree that something needs to be done.

A Mental Health Center is a legally constituted body with a staff consisting of a psychiatrist, a psychologist, a social worker, and a secretary. Often one or more professional persons may serve the Center on a part-time basis. No elaborate building or fixtures are needed.

Eight or ten counties in Kansas now have these Centers. Atchison County has had a Center for 20 years. In each case county commissioners appropriate funds and appoint a board to administer the Center.

The goals of a successful Center must be clearly defined and must lie within financial means available. It is remarkable what some counties are doing on a modest budget. Shall funds be used for individuals or for large community needs? Shall funds be used for preventive counseling with a long look ahead? Shall funds be used for research? Shall funds be used to acquaint the community with information about mental health.

Individuals may be chary about advocating research if it will require tax money. Yet research holds the key to the solution of many problems in the field of health and abundant living.

In Wellesley Hills, Mass., with a population the size of Lyon County, they have found that a Mental Health Clinic as part of the pre-school check-up, may reveal a problem child at a time when simple treatment and precaution may save more serious problems later on.

A County Mental Health Association should first of all, find out how well adjusted the citizens of this county are. It is important to learn what can and should be done by concerted community effort.

Treatment is long and drawn out and expensive. Prevention may also be expensive. However, the end results of a preventive program carry rays of hope. The home, the church, the school, and all agencies of government are vitally concerned in the work of keeping well people from becoming sick. Mental health is everybody's business.

2-23-59

Chronicles of
The Farm Woman

FREEDOM FOR WOMEN

In commemoration of Women's day in Emporia's Rededication week activities, the Anthony Morse chapter, Daughters of Colonists has submitted the following article for publication. It was written by Mary Francis McKinney, The Gazette's Farm Woman:

The Freedom Train is "a moverin'" across the Kansas prairies today. Coming out of the Rocky mountains it is coasting eastward with stops at Hutchinson and Wichita.

The exhibits which the Freedom Train bears are as sacred in the traditions of the United States as was the Ark which the Israelites toted across the desert, centuries before Christ. Only the high priest could view the inside of the Ark.

As many as can crowd in the train can gaze upon our sacred documents. The Declaration of Independence in the fine handwriting of Thomas Jefferson with the signatures of men who were bold enough to assert their independence and form a new nation. The Constitution and the Bill of Rights and later amendments is the framework within which free men have carved their destiny these last 16 or 17 decades.

These documents would be mere scraps of paper if the ideas and ideals embodied in them did not continue to live in the hearts of men, women and children. We are apt to take these privileges for granted and forget that responsibilities go with freedom. "Eternal vigi-lance," said one of the founding fathers, "is the price of liberty.

It is a wonderful thing that a group of people over the nation conceived the idea of the Freedom Train and that civic-minded folk at every stop have made all local arrange-

ments, including finances.

In the week of dedication in Lyon county we are reminded of the place that women have taken in the civic life of the nation. Martha Washington, Dolly Madison, Betsy Ross are familiar figures in the pages of history. Then as now it was the spectacular, the unusual that made news. What of the great mass of women of that era and of each succeeding generation? Woman was right there alongside her mate, helping him to carve a home and civilization out of the wilderness. In the century before the Declaration of Independence men and women had evolved a comfortable, cultured mode of country living which is still a dream of luxury and ease.

Each plantation was a community within itself and vast store houses of food and staples that were secured in the markets at infrequent intervals. The plantation mistress was teacher, household manager, nurse, community arbiter, and gracious hostess. Hers was a responsible position. As civilization pushed west-ward woman trudged along with man. Cabins supplanted plantation mansions but dreams of a better day sustained the pioneer woman.

Trades and industry came in along with westward migration and the walls of the home were extended to the community or village. Instead of each mother teaching her children, schools were established. The village store replaced the plantation storehouse and today's delicatessen may substitute for the kitchen range. As all these activities have branched out and supplanted the plantation community. It is the natural thing that woman has gone out of the home into teaching, clerking, into industry and the professions. In the late war there was no discrimina-

tion against sex in industry. It was equal pay for equal work. One day that will be the rule in peace as in war.

One hundred years ago a suffrage convention was held and articles drawn up demanding equal suffrage. In 1920 this became an amendment to the constitution. That victory was not won without a struggle but the objective was worth the persistent efforts expended. Indeed each phase in the evolution of woman's place in society has been met by resistance of the opposite sex. Yet eventually man has given in and accepted woman in a new sphere. No doubt much of the objection has been due to the fact that man resists change, he objects to the things he does not know or understand.

Betty Co-ed strides across the college campus today in the new skirt length and soiled saddle oxfords, little realizing that it was the persistence of her great grandmother in pursuing a college education that broke down the barricades and made the pathway easy for her. This Betty is carrying on the spirit of the pioneer woman who helped make America the nation that it is.
5-1948

Chapter 9

I Pledge…….

My Head to clearer thinking,
My Heart to greater loyalty,
My Hands to larger service, and,
My Health for better living,
for My Club, my Community, my Country, and my World.

Rural life and 4-H go hand-in-hand. 4-H is a nationwide program led by state land-grant universities in cooperation with local county district extension councils. In Kansas, 4-H is the largest youth educational program, aside from public schools. 4-H is a community of young people across America who are learning leadership, citizenship, and life skills.

The four H's represent:

Head-critical thinking, problem solving.
Heart-self-discipline, integrity, communication.
Hands-serving others.
Health-choosing healthy lifestyles.

To not include a chapter on 4-H would be tantamount to not including the family. Mac and Mary did what was right with their children and most rural families owe a great deal of debt to the organization that fosters their young.

Most individuals will agree that skills learned in 4-H last a lifetime. Each child is taught to achieve a positive self-concept, to have an inquiring mind, exercise a concern for the community, foster healthy interpersonal relationships, and attain sound decision making skills.

Mary included many articles about 4H activities in her household. The following are excerpts:

It was no problem to get country kids to take a midweek bath if they were going to the 4-H achievement dinner. Younger members who had never been to a dinner before hung around the edge of the crowd until they spied some of the other members of their club. These older boys and girls crossed the lobby with confidence. They had attended such dinners before. How much poise experience gives us.

These future framers may not even remember to thank the Chamber of Commerce for the hospitality. The sparkle of their eyes must, in a sense, have repaid Emporia businessmen. Friendliness promotes understanding, always. Mutual understanding surely will bring a better day for town and farm.

Every day something is called to our attention which strengthens our faith in the youth of today. A group of 4-H youngsters down this way went camping over the weekend. It was a splendid opportunity to skip Sunday school. Instead they invited the pastor and congregation to worship with them. An outdoor service on the creek bank turns one's mind to the psalmist of old testament times. My faith in tomorrow is strengthened. The coming generation will find the way.

****

The 4-H fair last week was an achievement for every exhibitor. It was the summation of the year's projects. By comparison farm youngsters are learning better quality and improved standards of agricultural and homemaking activities. Some boy or girl who may not have received any prizes this year will return next August and carry off the ribbon. Such is the inspiration received at the fair.

Girls on the judging team in baking are now unconsciously judging every baked product they see and comparing it with the score card for quality products. Likewise the clothing girls are securitizing hems and seams and the becomingness of color and design. They should be better buyers of clothing than those of us who have not had such training.

All parents and friends of 4-H boys and girls are grateful to the Chamber of Commerce for their magnificent co-operation with the county agent for the fair's success. Not only the monetary contribution which was given so freely. More valuable than that was the interested visitors who came and looked and admired.

****

Perhaps you are aware that a District 4-H model meeting contest was held in the high school auditorium last Saturday. Five counties competed. The audience was small. Mostly it was composed of contestants and proud parents. The chests of the latter swelled a bit as the curtains parted showing their particular group. They frowned or bowed their heads if a slight mistake was made. However there were few mistakes. In 30 minutes each club conducted a business meeting which would put any group of elders to shame. Tabled motions were brought out. An amendment to an amendment of the original motion was dealt with. In addition to the business meeting an initiation or installation, music appreciation and group singing, a demonstration and recreation was worked into the 30 minute period.

Perhaps the demonstration which interested us most was that on correct table manners. If there is one way of distinguishing a farmer aside from his shoes, it is his discomfit at trying to eat in style. To see that farm boy seat his girl companion, unfold his napkin and know which was the soup spoon was indeed a joy. That boy will not have to be worked over by older fraternity brothers in regard to table etiquette when he gets to college.

THE FARM WOMAN

The 4-H club members down this way joined in a club tour last Monday. Why do so many things happen on Monday? We used to think it was wash day exclusively. Now we must hurry around and get the wash on the line early in order to do something else. Boys were half afraid to ask dad to go on the tour in such a busy week. Fathers really have a soft heart even though the exterior may sometimes appear gruff. Of course, they arranged for the boys to go.

Garden projects, which were promising early, look sick this week. Especially at 3 o'clock in the afternoon. Zinnias and petunias extend a friendly greeting at the garden gate. Children fortunate enough to have the garden below the pump have installed a system of ditches. It takes a heap of hand pumping to water cucumbers 25 feet from the well. The boy who disliked to exhibit his corn because he had not finished hoeing weeds felt better when he saw that other boys had weeds in the row too. Girls in baking and clothing projects brought samples of their handiwork and formed a display at the picnic grounds.

The picnic supper and playtime were the climax of the tour. As we observed these boys and girls playing together, comparing notes on projects we wondered if agriculture tomorrow might be in better hands than it is today.

Dolls lie neglected much of the time this summer.

Who wants to play with dolls when they can walk to the neighbors and watch the new baby? It seems to childish minds that the baby sleeps most of the time. They have learned the baby's waking hours and visits are timed accordingly. Now that the baby has a new swing the daily visit is imperative.

A grandmother remarks that these schedule babies may be all right but she is thankful her babies were raised before schedules became the thing. When a young mother can cook for thrashers four days and baby not cry, some credit must go to the baby's routine and the mother's good sense in establishing and adhering to the schedule.

Pity the child who cannot watch babies, pups, calves, pigs, chicks and colts grow.

THE FARM WOMAN

April 1 finds all 4-H club members lined up for the year's projects. Gardens, livestock, crops, home-making, every phase of the farm is represented in these laboratory experiments which our children are carrying on. These children are learning to work together in a community way, something difficult for us to learn. If we can hold the ship of agriculture together until these children take the reins, farm life will surely be richer and fuller. 4-H boys and girls learn parliamentary procedure at 10 years. They learn how to prepare and give a talk.

One 4-H boy is introducing sheep on a Lyon county cattle farm. The horses and the herd bulls snorted and pawed the ground at the very scent of them. The old collie who guards the place diligently was for annihilating such strange creatures. The old cow puncher probably felt the same way but he said nothing. All are reconciled now.

Thirty years ago one would have declared he would be as apt to find sheep on a cattle ranch as comics in the Emporia Gazette. Times do change.

THE FARM WOMAN

The 4-H girls are working on their clothing projects these hot July afternoons. Each year the resolution is made to get clothing finished before the weather gets hot. Always hot weather finds smudgy, perspiring hands basting, overcasting, and slip-stitching. No matter how often hands are washed, white nainsook gowns and slips become soiled and grimy in the construction processes. Long hours are spent on the first garment. Fingers are awkward. Not only must beginners sew. They must also rip. It seems as if ripping takes more time than actual sewing. The new slip stitch, which has a cross on the wrong side and a tiny, well-nigh invisible stitch on the right, brings tears in more than one household.

After the first garment is finished a dress is made. It goes much faster. For one thing the girls have learned much in their first lessons. Also gay print is much more interesting than white muslin. And dresses are worn on the outside where all the world may see. Feminine vanity comes to the fore and girls work harder. Mothers must have patience and encouragement. The struggle is hard for a few summers. When we see 16-year-olds making all their own clothes and garments for mother, all the clothing work seems terribly worthwhile. Often a certain amount of individuality and chic is developed. More than one mother of an adolescent daughter tells me she has given up sewing because there is no pleasing daughter. The latter will wear a ready-made garment e'en though it does not fit perfectly. Not so, something mother makes. Mother cannot get the vision of chic which daughter desires. Hence the adolescent flare.

It seems much saner for the 16-year-old to make her own clothes.

THE FARM WOMAN

The 4-H youngsters are off to camp this week. For days they have been stepping livelier and bounding out of bed on the first call. Girls must have their hair set and they want to take all the dresses in their wardrobe for fear they might need them. They wear slacks to camp and wear them most of the time they are there. Of course the bathing suit is another important item. Lipstick and compact are not forgotten. With boys the problem is much simpler. They check over the suggested list. The bathing suit goes in the bag first. Upon mothers' insistence they take along an extra shirt but doubt if they will need it. Hair oil was not on the list, but is it included nevertheless.

It is up to mothers to get the children to camp in this busy week. Cars are filled with children and four sacks of straw adorn the fenders and bumper. Upon arriving at camp it is interesting to watch the members. Older ones who have been to camp before know their way about. Younger ones stand back and know not exactly what to do. Little green country kids who have never been away from home overnight before. Mothers linger and hesitate to leave them. But youth ever eager for adventure stays. We wonder if a few homesick tears may not be shed in the pillow after lights are out tonight. Quiet tears that even one's bedfellow cannot hear.

We glanced at the camp

schedule. A full, well planned day; work, studies, recreation, all of it fun. What an opportunity for farm boys and girls. They will get to know the Lyon County boy who attended the national 4-H roundup in Washington, D.C. How proud we all are of him.

Mothers will be on time Friday afternoon to bring the campers home.

Thrashing is in full swing this week. Farmers come home at night tired and dirty and are glad to stand under the home-made shower which they once kidded us about. Showers aid dispositions and make the laundering easier.

Bright yellow straw stacks dot the fields and each night at least one burning stack looms on the horizon. Why farmers burn straw stacks is more than we can tell. When baled straw sold as it did last winter one would think not a straw would be wasted. As we see the flames leap we wonder if that farmer's wife will have her garden mulched next year.

7-20-35

Chronicles of
The Farm Woman

THE FARM WOMAN

August brings the windup of 4-H project work in the county. If the clothing girls have followed the advice of their leaders they are putting the finishing touches on the last garments. If they have been "put-it-offers" they are working feverishly and suddenly it seems that 4-H clothing is a burden and too much is expected of the girls. Isn't that always the wail of procrastinators?

Despite the downs of discouragement the information gained in 4-H project work is remarkable. A visitor from the city notes this especially in the ease and grace with which farm girls do so many things. They make their own clothes, get a meal without a question or direction, and stock the cellar shelves with good things for the winter's food supply. The daughter of a neighboring household excels her mother in baking muffins, cookies, biscuits and gingerbread. This 12-year-old says she prefers to bake when she can have the kitchen all to herself, when her mother is out of doors. That suit's the mother also.

Garden projects were disheartening when the hot winds came. However, carefully kept, records show a nice profit from early vegetables.

Some boys may be natural showmen. However it seems the average adolescent on the farm must be goaded into slicking up his calf for the fair. Boys do not mind feeding and watering their calves and taking every day care of them. But when it comes to manicuring their toes, sandpapering their horns and marcelling the midrib, father or mother must be there to insist that the fitting be done. The state leader says that occasionally the boy with an ill fitted calf at the fair catches a spark of enthusiasm and returns the following year to get the blue ribbon. Slicked up or no we should have more calf projects in the clubs in this county.

Boys like crops projects. Dad probably lets them use the tractor to till the crop and that just suits them. In every neighborhood one will find that there is general improvement in seeds for planting when the boys are enrolled in crops projects. Herein lies one of the great values of 4-H work. Children learn the results of research, they adopt these findings and gradually we all come to use them.

Here is a toast to the leaders of these boys and girls. They give generously of their time to what sometimes appears a thankless task. However, one local leader in the county feels well repaid for all her time and effort. The other day she received a letter from one of her girls. This farm girl is working now and she took time to write her 4-H leader and thank her for all the things she had learned under her tutelage. Her present employer complimented her upon her ability to bake bread, to use the pressure cooker and she was amazed when this girl refashioned a dress out of two old ones. There are many former 4-H members that are giving satisfactory service to their employers. They often think of their leaders and good times. The interesting thing about this girl is that she sat down and wrote a letter expressing her gratitude. No wonder my neighbor's heart is singing.

8-16-39

THE FARM WOMAN

The 4-H demonstration scheduled was on the construction and erection of birdhouses. The demonstration team did not get to 4-H that night. Instead our county agent put on a demonstration which no one present will ever forget. The hired man brought in a little newborn calf which had been dropped in the mud. Icicles clung to the tips of wet hairs. It was chilled but not frozen. The agent asked for a tub two-thirds full of tepid water. The family bath tub was brought in from the nail on the back porch. The calf was immersed in the warm water and massaged gently to stimulate circulation. The head needs be held up, out of the water. Soon the head began to move and eyes to roll. "Baaa" "Baaa" echoed through the house. More water was added from the teakettle, from time to time, to keep the temperature constant. After 20 to 30 minutes that calf was lifted out of the bath and rubbed briskly with burlap sacks. The patient was wrapped in a blanket and placed by the fire, warm and relaxed. Next morning early the calf was up and calling for breakfast.

Farmers who have been raising calves for 30 years looked on at the demonstration. Parents and children alike learned something about chilled calves or lambs or chickens which they had never known before.

For demonstrations such as this we are grateful for a Farm Bureau and a trained county agent. Some farmers still scoff at these young whippersnappers from an agricultural college who come out and endeavor to teach us something. What they do not realize is that in four years of scientific training these men and women may learn more things which otherwise would require years of experience. Not that the agents do not learn from farmers. Probably almost as much as from experience as we learn from them.

Then it is, we have a well-rounded whole, the combination of scientific training with the practical. True balance is attained with the former supplementing the latter.

Chronicles of
The Farm Woman

THE FARM WOMAN

Lyon county 4-H kids are off to camp. There was no need for an alarm clock this day. Lists of suggested equipment were checked and double checked. A 10-year-old saw that a camera was on the suggested list. Immediately she told her mother she would have to have a Kodak. Younger boys wondered why a wash pan was needed when the camp was right long the river. Girls did not forget their lipstick nor older boys their hair oil.

For three days these youngsters will follow camp routine, learn something of group activity, group organization. It is a case of when learning is fun. The 4-H club is smoothing and polishing the rough edges and giving poise to country boys and girls.

The younger generation will return home Saturday. Sunday the farm home-makers are off for a 3-day vacation camp. Think of it! A farm woman up and leaving home at this time of the year for three days - well not exactly three days because most of the Sunday chores will be done before she leaves and she will return in time to catch up the loose ends on Tuesday. Is this Utopia? Or an aftermath of the deluge? Are these women endeavoring to regain a portion of their childhood that they missed? Or are they merely becoming carefree and frivolous? Pharaoh of old thought when the Hebrews petitioned him that they might go on a three day journey in the desert, that if they had time to leave their work and spend three days vacationing he was not giving them enough to do.

Let's hope the homemakers' burdens are not increased.

Older girls are impatient for mother to get off. For three days they can run the house exactly as they please. No doubt the living room furniture will be rearranged - and that monotonous daily grind that mother insists on will not be followed. The dishes may pile up on the kitchen table. The old hens may have to wait an hour or so for their daily rations. Some of the things that mother does every day may be omitted. These girls will learn considerable in three days. Likely they will be as glad to see mother return as they are to see her off.

THE FARM WOMAN

The 4-H club members are concentrating on project work - especially those enrolled in home economics. It might seem a hardship to have sisters enrolled in Baking I. Yet there are advantages. The family reports that one recipe is merely a sample. Whereas twice the amount really satisfies. Corn muffins, fruit muffins, plain cookies and gingerbread are on the summer menu. It often defers bread making another day for mother. This is one of the objectives of 4-H project work. Boys and girls take over some responsibility about the farm thus relieving another of that duty. Each batch of muffins is scrutinized, scored and recorded.

Canning girls are processing all varieties of fruits and vegetables that come their way. Mothers may pack things into jars most any way to get them sealed. Daughter looks to appearance and arrangement. She wonders where judges draw the line between fancy pack and neat arrangement. Fancy pack is ruled out in judging.

There is something about a row of canned products which bring a glow of achievement. It is something to display, it looks ahead to the winter's food supply, and its attractiveness whets the appetite. In another year or so these girls may take over the summer's canning.

Girls enrolled in clothing projects labor on through the long afternoons. As one chats with mothers of 4-H youngsters it would appear that clothing brings more grief and tears and household upsets than any other project. It may well be because beginners are required to rip and rip again. Now if a pan of muffins is too brown or unsalted the family may eat them grumblingly. There is no undoing them. But alas! The crooked seam must be taken out and done over and the cross stitch, slip stitch around the bias facing at the neck is a veritable Waterloo. If girls can persevere the first two years of 4-H clothing they come to enjoy it. They construct attractive costumes; redesign cast-off garments and consider cost, suitability, etc.

One mother has stipulated a definite goal in clothing, or no camp. That daughter is working diligently because camp is the high spot of the summer. Another child decided it was so dreadfully hot to sew in afternoons. Anxious to get the job done the mother excused this girl on wash morning. She came in from scrubbing to find daughter sleeping blissfully. There was a sudden and effectual awakening.

Every girl, as she grows into adolescence dreams of how she would like to have her room done. Room improvement projects make these dreams a reality. Curtains, rugs and bedspread are selected and constructed by the occupant. Thus 4-H club work offers to every farm girl projects in all phases of homemaking.

Sometimes in late August the annual 4-H club fair will be held. Results of the year's projects will be displayed.

7-22-37

Chronicles of
The Farm Woman

THE FARM WOMAN

This is 4-H mobilization week. All over this nation it is hoped that boys and girls along country lanes not now members of 4-H clubs, may be enrolled.

Ask any farm boy or girl why he belongs to a 4-H club and he will not doubt reply, "to have a good time". Fellowship is the underlying principle of the organization. Along with the good times, rural youths learn something of parliamentary procedure; they learn to stand on their own two feet and give a talk or a demonstration. If one can stand on his feet and express himself before his neighbors, he can likely express himself anytime, anywhere.

The 4-H club is the youths own organization. They plan the programs and carry them out. Sometimes one may think a weak struggling club is not worthwhile. However, last year's struggling group may be an outstanding club today. It is part of a great nationwide organization. Six or eight years in club work makes a better citizen of any boy or girl. In the background of any successful club is an interested community leader or leaders and interested parents. These leaders give generously of their time and talents. They attend leaders' conferences and training schools. They attend club meetings. They assist members in projects, in agriculture and homemaking. They see that the projects are completed and records handed in. Records in 4-H are the same abomination to boys and girls that farm accounts and income tax returns are to parents.

The motto of the 4-H is to make the best better. Through the years youngsters have been getting purebred dairy heifers or certified seed for the crop project thus improving the dairy strain and the seed crops. The symbol of the organization is the four leaf clover, each leaf standing for one H: head, heart, hands, health - make for a well-rounded personality, one who loves the land.

For more than a quarter of a century county agents and home demonstration agents over the nation have sponsored 4-H clubs in the counties. Here and there counties employ club agents who devote their entire time to 4-H work. The writer has been of the opinion for several years that Lyon County should have a club agent along with Butler County, Sedgwick, Shawnee and others. What better invest-ment could the county commissioners make of your tax dollar and mine than to invest about $3 per farm child in a 4-H agent? Yet there has never been sufficient concerted action on the part of parents and leaders in the county to convince the commissioners of the soundness of this investment.

There are two obstacles to 4-H mobilization. The first is the inability to find volunteer leaders. It does take time and it means some sacrifice but the rewards are rich. What more could one ask than to see the transformation from gawky green country kids of a generation ago to the friendly poised youth of today? The second deterrent to greater membership is parents. Those parents who have not caught the vision. Who cannot be bothered with taking children to meetings or encouraging them in their projects. They forget that each child grows but once and in 4-H he learns as he grows as he associates with neighbors.

3-8-44

THE FARM WOMAN

Every girl in the eighth grade procession the other day had on a new dress. Only a few dresses really stand out in a woman's life and the eighth grade graduating dress is one of them. The confirmation dress, the wedding dress, perhaps the first formal complete the list of the readily remembered dresses. Boys were not to be left out of the clothes parade either. One boy informed his mother he wanted a two-tone suit for the occasion.

Some of the girls were thrilled that their dresses were ready made. At least three girls in the procession selected the material at Emporia stores and made their dresses. The three were 4-H girls from over the county. Dorothy Roberts selected a blue printed rayon and made it as one of her 4-H dresses for this season. Dorothy has been doing 4-H sewing for five years and she has now graduated in that line to the point where she does all of her sewing. Her trinket box is filled with 4-H ribbons many of them blue ones received in clothing.

Elsie McGrew, north of Emporia in the Dow Valley community made her dress with the help of her mother. It is not a 4-H project but Elsie is carrying clothing along with swine and others probably. Her problem at 4-H fair in recent years has been to exhibit her Hampshire pigs where the showing counts 50 per cent toward the award and then skin out of those duds and into the style review. Such training as this makes for versatility.

The third dress that we know about was made by Kathleen McKinney. Kathleen is taking third year clothing. Her intentions were all right, but about the time she was ready to put in the hem she was needed in the hayfield so her mother whipped in the hem. And, confidentially the hem isn't done as well as the rest of the garment.

Much of the credit should go to the 4-H leaders who take time from their workaday routine to teach these girls the rudiments of the needle and thread. It is pretty tedious those first years. And yet the first thing anyone knows these girls are doing all their own sewing. Here is a hand to our 4-H leaders.

How many other girls in the class of '42 made their eight grade graduating dresses?

6-4-42

Chapter 10

Winds of Change

Good common people make the world a better place.

During her lifetime Mary had witnessed great changes to life on the farm. We are also witness to it, by her articles, but what was really happening in her world was far more understandable if we look back 100 years, at the turn of the century, when there was no Mother's Day or Father's Day to celebrate. Only one in ten adults could read and write. We also know that more than 97 percent of all births took place in the home and the average life expectancy was forty-seven.

Only 14 percent of the homes had a bathtub and

most women only washed their hair once a month. The average wage was twenty-two cents an hour. The average worker made $400 per year. Only 8 percent of the homes had a telephone.

There were only 144 miles of paved roads in the entire country and most of the roads in the county were made of dirt or gravel. The maximum speed limit in most towns was ten miles per hour.

In 1927 the cost of a Model T was $475. If you had a fender bender, you could replace the rear fender for $1.75.

The estimated annual income per capita in the country by 1928 was $538.

The economy was bad and every one did there best to cope. But a family who didn't manage the few dollars they had would not fare well. When the stock market crashed in October of 1929, no mention of it was made in the local papers. In 1930, more than 2,352 banks would close and not reopen. In 1931, the number was over two thousand more. Newspapers reported suicides of farmers who could no longer face their debts, but they usually left a wife and children behind to face them.

Generations are shaped by the significant emotional events that occur during their lifetimes. Living thru the Great Depression they were indelibly stamped with a fear of going into debt or living above their means because of the scars left by their common experience with economic disaster. It is easier when we understand where their values lie and how those values changed their generation. Once we are imprinted with a set of values, that is pretty much it for the rest of our lives. Ask anyone who experienced the Depression about the stock market, and they will tell you that it can crash and you'd better have some savings tucked away.

Mac made a decision to move his family to the farm, so that they could be more self sufficient when money values were hit by the sinking economy. He made the perfect move. They would have milk, eggs, butter, vegetables, fruits, and meats; chicken, pork, and beef. They had little else to buy. It was never easy but life became better on the farm.

The Dust Bowl years left only faint scars. Experiencing a dust storm was awesome with foreboding black clouds towering from the West, blowing in quickly. They were fortunate the epicenter was more than 150 miles away from Hartford. During the long years of the drought, soils in the dust bowl states of Nebraska, the western parts of Kansas, Oklahoma, Eastern Colorado and the Texas Panhandle became so powdery that almost any wind sent them swirling in the sky. In 1934, dust storms covered buildings in New York City and ships at sea with an ashy film. A severe windstorm would strip an unprotected field down to plow depth - robbing the fertile topsoil.

To a farmer the welcome sight of rain or tiny sprouts and the music of the wind rustling the grains are simple gifts. Hail could destroy an entire crop in less than an hour.

Values, customs and a way of life have taken on a remarkable transformation. The contrast between old and new is startling. There have been radical improvements; in transportation, telephone, television and other marvels. Little refrigeration was available; iceboxes were a luxury for years, before electricity. Farmers have the Rural Electrification Administration to thank for making electricity available to rural America.

One can now drive through the country and seldom see a chicken in a farmyard, and almost no farmer keeps a cow to produce milk for the family. The old days are gone, mourned by some who look back fondly upon that era.

In the years 1934 and 1935 there were 3,115 rural schools in the state of Kansas with 10 or less students, and 145 of these had 1 or 2 children in each school. The teachers that taught in the one room, rural schools were very special people. During the winter months they would get to the school early to get a fire started in the potbelly stove, so the building would be warm for the students. On many occasions they would prepare a hot, noon meal on top of the stove, usually consisting of soup or stew of some kind. They took care of their students like a new mother hen would care for her newly hatched chicks; always looking out for their health and welfare. Since Fairview country school was across the road from their farm, the school teacher roomed with the McKinney family. Mary always fixed a hot lunch, which her children took to the teacher on a tray then they carried their own lunch back to school to eat with the teacher.

The vast majority of one-room schools in the United States closed their doors in the late 1940's or early 1950's and are no longer used as schools and have either been torn down or converted to other purposes.

World War II changed the entire countries commitment to work and country. Another "significant emotional event" that would change an entire generations values. Those who lived through it's torment would remain patriotic for their lifetimes because of the profound patriotic fervor generated during the war. FDR's infectious confidence taught an entire country how to believe again, to endure, and to triumph. Hard work and values built something else. They lived their values everyday. They honored family, faith and hard work. Work was valued. Farmers and Americans, in general, worked hard to improve life in our country. Good common people make the world a better place.

Life is fragile and families struck a bond when they made stockings for the G. I.'s so far away from home, or knit caps for them. Simple efforts to link their lives with those who were giving of theirs.

Our very existence is fragile and the freedom we take for granted is not, after all, a given. Mary writes:

Country people are ready to make the supreme sacrifice, they give their sons, their substance and their patriotic devotion to the end that America shall be free. 9-22-42

****

Wherever groups of women gather these days, whether it is a church function, a Red Cross meeting or a political gathering, one soon learns that the woman on her left has a boy in Ireland and the one on her right a son who was at Bataan. Sons in service are the thing nearest and dearest a mother's heart in these trying hours.

She keeps up her usual routine of homework and outside activities and avidly does Red Cross or USO work, always with a prayer for the welfare of her boy and his comrades in service. She reads not only the headlines but every word of the day's war news.

"Today is my boy's twenty-second birthday," one mother writes, "How well I remember that day twenty-two years ago and how his father nearly burst all the buttons off his vest. Little did we think then that we wouldn't even know where he was when he was twenty-two."

"The last we heard John was in Hawaii but that was weeks ago," another writes. "You cannot know how hard it is to write every other day but I do it faithfully trying to tell the details we think he would be interested in."

Or, have you seen a mother's face light up as she tells you she has had a letter from her son in Australia? It wasn't much of a letter, just one page saying he was well and for her not to worry. It had not been cut by the censor at all. That island in the Pacific and all the tiny dots of islands between here and there suddenly loom large in our consciousness. Boys from our neighborhoods are stationed there and everything that affects those boys, affects us.

Women are carrying on in this war as they have in every great emergency. They perform the routine tasks, the extra duties they are called upon to do with indomitable courage. But their hearts are with loved one in service.

7-2-42

****

The sun shines brightly today, the smell of spring is in the air and garden fever is running high. This year every garden is to be a Victory Garden[1]*. Each seed and sprouts, each weed that is uprooted will be a direct aid in the war effort.*

School children have asked that each family who intends to raise a garden paste a placard in the front window. It may be that if you have always raised a garden the placard may be brushed aside as nonsense. The main point, of course, is to plant and tend a garden. The placard is merely a symbol of

---

[1] Canned foods were rationed regularly during the War, by planting Victory Gardens, for family consumption, larger supplies of canned goods were able to feed the troops oversees. Posters read "our food is fighting!"

one's intentions. If you display the symbol in your window and your neighbors display it in theirs, a bond is thereby created. All are working together for food for freedom.

We are all children of the soil and what a joy, what a privilege it is to be able to have a victory garden. Food will win the war. It's all out for victory gardens here in Lyon county now. 3-7-42

****

This week some five hundred farm women are coming down to earth again. There is the separator to wash, the bread to be mixed and all the regular chores. Each one is planning a victory garden and if father doesn't eat all the vegetables mother thinks he should, it will be well of him to watch out. He may have a few vitamin pills slipped in his coffee or his custard pie. Mama has entered heart and soul in the victory garden drive and the family will have to follow suit.

****

In case you may not have realized it, the woodpile on the farm has all but disappeared. In its stead has come a bright and shining tank of bottled gas. The wood box and the Round Oak stove have been supplanted by a circulating gas heater with a fan attached. No more does Johnny trudge home from school to fill the wood box and the cob basket. Today Johnny merely turns the thermostat up or down to suit his fancy.

When the mercury plummeted to 22 degrees below zero

each member of the family grinned as the thermostat was turned up higher. The warm air currents zoomed out to combat the cold air that penetrated floors and walls and window casings. The family was snug and warm and after three days the cold wind passed on. One of these days some of these old houses in the country will be insulated to save fuel and give greater comfort to the occupants.

Nothing dramatizes the change that is taking place on the farm as the gleaming gas tank that sits in the yard, unless it is the yard light that blinks out at night as if to complement the stars. Every few days one hears that the poles have been set and the transformer hung and the meter installed for another neighbor. Aladdin had nothing on the local electrician. A few days of litter and bustle and the magic is produced. Only those folks who have experienced the transition from kerosene lamps to electricity can know the thrill it brings.

These are great days on the farm. 1-1947

****

In the days of my childhood farmers probably lived as well as we do today but we did not live as city folk and that was the thing above all else that we longed to do. Today's generation is wiser in that they do not have that foolish hankering as the guiding star in their lives. In one short generation the daily paper, good roads, the radio and electricity and now freezer lockers have brought city living right to the farmer's doorstep and into the kitchen.

Twenty-five or thirty years ago all hands laid off everything else for the butchering. Six fat hogs were slaughtered and scalded and scraped in turn and hung in the shed overnight to cool. Someone had to watch the carcasses all night to protect them from hungry neighborhood dogs. There were six hogs' heads to be worked up and six back bones and six pairs of spare ribs. In desperation most of the tenderloin was ground up into sausage. The hams and sides were cured, the sausage could be fried down but every one had to stuff in order to eat the fresh meat eaten before it spoiled. No one ever heard of canning meat in those days. The last ham was usually opened on the Fourth of July. The cured meat lasted until the fried chicken season.

****

It's a great day on the farm when we can have varieties of home grown foods the year round, thanks to freezer lockers.

12-26-40

****

The winds were changed during World War II and by far the most disturbing aspect of that war was to send your only son off to his demise. It takes a profound toll on your being to find he has been ravaged and maimed by this war. Jim received extensive wounds while with the 87th Division of the 3rd Army. The following article appeared in the Emporia Weekly Gazette, May 10, 1945, p4, c7.

JIM TOM MCKINNEY IS BACK IN U.S.

Pfc. James T. McKinney arrived at Charleston, S. C., Sunday afternoon, according to a telephone call to his parents, Mr. & Mrs. J. C. McKinney, of Hartford. He had been on the water two weeks.

Private McKinney was wounded in Belgium in January. After some weeks in an evacuation hospital behind the lines he was moved to a modern hospital in Reims, built by John D. Rockefeller after World War I. Out of his ward window could be seen the renowned cathedral. From his observation, the town has suffered only slight damage in this war. Later he was transferred to England. He hopes to be sent to a hospital nearer home.

THE FARM WOMAN

The choir recessional to the tune "God Be With You Till We Meet Again," had more significance than common last Sunday morning. The pastor had announced that orders for his chaplaincy had arrived and this would be his last worship service with his flock.

Every day in numberless ways the war is brought close to us. Our boys leave in the draft or they volunteer in the Navy, the Marines or the Air Corps. They send word that they have arrived safely in distant lands or the War Department notifies parents that a boy is missing or that his is a prisoner of war. All these things bring the war close to a rural community.

Then the doctor is taken from our midst. Cold fear clutches at the hearts of families who are thus left without a physician. A slight cold can develop into pneumonia so quickly. An infectious disease may reach epidemic proportions if unchecked. A slight scratch may be the open door to staff or streptococcus infection. And who will bring the new babies into the world safely? A large number of a country doctor's obstetrical cases are still delivered in the homes of the patients.

The doctor is gone and now the only resident pastor is called into service. There was probably not a dry eye in the sanctuary as the benediction was pronounced. Not that one of the congregation would detain the pastor if the war needs him. For country people are ready to make the supreme sacrifice, they give their sons, their substance and their patriotic devotion to the end that American shall be free.
9-22-42

THE FARM WOMAN

Christmas is here again. Likely plans for the day have been changed in every house-hold in the past three weeks, but the day is being kept.

For many families in the county this Christmas is different and the difference has nothing to do with the war. The magic of electricity has been brought to many farm homes during the past year. As one drives along graveled township roads colored lights gleam from decorated Christmas trees in the windows. Now country children can enjoy those delights which town cousins have taken for granted. And oh what joy this brings. Not only have colored lights been added to the tinsel and baubles on the cedar bough, but electric current has brought trains and toy irons and wood burning sets and maybe a huge refrigerator for the family.

Eyes of children sparkle as brightly as they ever did in peace time. If there isn't a new electric train the old one has been repaired. Father tinkers with it in keen enjoyment and forgets muddy fields and world affairs. Mother in the kitchen, bustles over roast goose and mince pie and cranberry sauce. Young children complain because big brother home from college is allowed to sleep late. An immediate resolve is made to go to college when they get big just to get even with him. Big sister insists that nut cups and other extra wrinkles be added to the table decorations. A box of goodies has been mailed to loved ones in camp with a prayer that it may reach its destination.

Packages under the tree reflect indirectly the grimness of these days. They are placed there with the same spirit of love and devotion but they are articles each one needs. Useless things are not for this season. There is not the embroidery and the handwork of former years. Mother and sister are sewing for the Red Cross.

A mist clouds the new moon and the stars tonight and it seems to portray the writer's feeling at this holiday season. War clouds may dim the brilliance of the star that the wise men saw but that star shines on nevertheless and points the way to world peace. May we have the vision and courage to follow it to a happier day. 12-25-41

THE FARM WOMAN

Teachers and children and families are swinging into school routine again. Country children do not seem to get to school as early as in former years. With big brothers and sisters and hired men off to war even first and second graders have more responsibilities at home. High school students find so many interesting things to do that it is difficult to get time for regular school subjects - English, math and history.

If children find difficulty in adjusting themselves, so do administrators. The war effort wants more rigorous physical training, yet the gas rationers want less. The war effort wants more mathematics taught, yet teachers are hard to find. There is some thought that thrills should be done away in wartime and it may seem that they should.

The other day it was our privilege to spend some time at the art exhibit at the Topeka fair. One section was devoted to soldier art. Pencil sketches of buddies and sweethearts and cartoons of army life. One boy exhibited a series of water colors sketched at Darwin, Australia. The barber under the trees, the jeep, the sentry on duty, the soldier cleaning his gun or listening to a radio program from home. Those sketches were rolled up and stuck in a section of pipe. Somehow that section of pipe landed at Winter hospital with that wounded soldier. He wants his mother in Texas to have them. Can't you imagine how proud that mother, that family will be.

The point in telling this story here is that art is one of the frills of the curriculum. So also is music and drama. Yet this boy didn't go to Darwin and sit down and sketch these watercolors. He may have been the bad boy that was forever drawing pictures in his books. Likely he had a teacher or teachers who encouraged the development of his talent. Letters from lonely outposts tell of the dread monotony of the days, especially off duty hours. Fortunate is the lad who can play a musical instrument or draw or whittle or write to pass away the hours.

After seeing this exhibit it would seem that art should not be suspended for the duration.

9-24-43

THE FARM WOMAN

Time was when folk from town came out to the farm and took to the garden as part of the general farm tour. They looked at the pigs, the chickens, the calves and the garden. Always they enjoyed eating the fruits of our labors.

This year, however, there is a new note. Visitors who come ask to see the garden. They gaze at the cabbages, the beets, the beans and the carrots and the space where the peas grew, and count off to us the number of points we have in the garden. Suddenly points have become precious and vital to the city consumer. No longer is the farm garden admired for its straight rows, its lack of weeds and its crisp fresh vegetables.

Today it is appraised in the approximate number of points it will yield. Points are a foreign language to the average farm family. A few red points may be used for a little lunch meat for the picnic and some blue points for a can of pineapple but most of the red and blue stamps become void before the farm customer looks at them.

Amateur gardeners show real interest in seeds after one explains the greater yield from adapted varieties. Invariably they report going to the seed store and buying seeds. They didn't know there was any difference in varieties of peas or beans or radishes. It is to be hoped they remember the importance of adapted varieties for Mrs. Dora Aubel, wartime home economist, says that we should plan a five year food supply now. Not that the war will last that long, we hope, but the rehabilitation of peoples in stricken areas will take years. The rest of the world looks to us for food. Also it is to be hoped that all this wartime emphasis on food will result in a healthier and better fed nation. The back-yard garden could well become a part of the family's seasonal exercises in any year.

7-16-43

Chronicles of
The Farm Woman

THE FARM WOMAN

A mother of sons was awakened by her 19-year-old on a rainy night recently. "Mom, you won't get mad will you?" he whispered. "Why, what has happened now?" she asked. When one has reared five sons one always may look for the unexpected.

Then the story came out. A summertime job requires that the lad work from six until two o'clock in the morning. As he left for home he came upon two soldier boys who had planned to sleep in the park. The rain had driven them into doorways along the street. Magnanimously the boy invited them to go home with him. They demurred. He insisted, explaining that his mother would understand. They had no funds - only half of a round trip ticket back to camp. The offer was accepted.

The lad explained to his mother that she need not get up. He would bed them down on the floor. When she arose the next morning there were three forms, each rolled in a comfort on the living room floor. It was a novel experience to have total strangers bedded down this way.

She fixed a company breakfast with all the trimmings and called the three boys. Introductions were made and experiences' exchanged there in the breakfast nook. One boy was from New York City, and the other from California. After a second cup of coffee and more visiting, the boys were taken to the bus station to go back to camp. It was another week-end and another of the experiences the boys from the east and the west are cramming into these days of preparation for combat.

There were tears in the mother's eyes as she bade them good bye. She was thinking of her two sons in the service, one in the navy and one in the marines, both of them probably on the high seas. A prayer ascended that some stranger might be able to do as much for her two lads.

8-28-42

THE FARM WOMAN

Lyon County may take another bow. Last week at the annual dinner at the Farm and Home week in Manhattan, Mrs. Ray Gardner, of Hartford, was awarded the title of Master Homemaker.

For years past the Kansas Farmer has sponsored the award of master farmer degrees and the last few years has chosen outstanding women as Master Homemakers. Candidates for the position are nominated by neighbors and friend and selected by a committee of judges.

Those who have attended parties and dinners at the Gardner home, who have observed the smooth effective manner in which her home is managed, who have seen her drive 10 miles every Sunday to teach a Sunday school class, the folk who know her - are delighted to learn of this honor which she has received.

And over the line in Chase county another homemaker was selected for this honor. It is Mrs. Curt Benninghoven, more familiarly known as the turkey woman.

Wherever groups of farm women gather in the state or in the nation, Mrs. Benninghoven is apt to be found. Moreover she quietly makes her presence felt in these gatherings. Recently she was one of 25 rural women invited to Chicago by the editor of the Farm Journal to discuss problems of the hour. She is a member of the State Planning Board as well as a leader in her community. One never knows what the size of the Benninghoven family may be. At the moment they are rearing three foster children, but nieces, nephews, cousins, and friends in need may be found there at various times. The poetry and rhythm of the Flint Hills is music to her soul. Articles from her portable typewriter appear in trade journals as well as in the Kansas Magazine.

The recognition given these two homemakers symbolizes the spirit of America which is to be found in farm homes throughout the country. This spirit is the bulwark of the nation.

2-12-42

Chronicles of
The Farm Woman

THE FARM WOMAN

Some days ago the family drove to town. Nowadays, when a trip to town is made on tires, careful thought is given to supplies needed and all errands to be done. We have suddenly become transportation conscious, even as were the first settlers on the prairies. In those days a 6-months supply of necessities were purchased when the oxen made a semi-annual trip to the nearest trading post. Did grandmother ever forget to order anything? And what happened if she did? The oxen could not be sent back to town.

The eggs, the children, the library books, music, Red Cross sewing, shoes to be repaired and two good sized boxes of waste paper all were tucked in the back seat. We felt especially proud of the bulky boxes of waste paper. They contained love stories and yesterday's comments on the war situation, all of the empty cartons with box tops included, Christmas greetings and every bit of waste paper that had come into the house in weeks. The back porch was overflowing with it and it required some force to crush and bind it in awkward packages. It was our bit for the war effort and we glowed inwardly with patriotic fervor. Eggs are higher than a year ago and this time there might be some change left over for defense stamps. Yet this anticipation did not give the thrill that saving waste paper did.

We had read in The Gazette that the Boy Scouts took waste paper to the auditorium so the first stop was made there. The city clerk knew nothing about waste paper. Neither did the custodian. His expression signified that he spent all his days getting rid of waste paper that collected in the auditorium and he did not want any more added to his burdens. The police matron suggested that there was a place out near the overpass that took waste paper. We drove slowly across the overpass reading every sign but none indicated they wanted waste paper. Upon inquiry a man was found who directed us to the back of a grocery store, east of the Katy tracks. No one was to be found. We were using precious tires and gasoline and patriotic fervor was cooling rapidly. However, it was decided to make one more inquiry. The proprietor of the grocery store knew what to do. She stepped next door and called the man who would relieve us of our bundles. He came and in a matter of fact way took our contribution to the war effort.

It was the intention to get down in this column that some publicity should be given to the depository or depositories in Emporia and each town in the country where farm families could take waste paper. However, that may not be necessary. Fulton Lewis Jr., who no doubt makes the statement upon authority of the Unites States Department of Agriculture, says that farm families should call the country agricultural agent, who will call and collect all waste paper in rural areas. Just one more little chore for the county agent. Perhaps if the task becomes Herculean the home demonstration agent will assist.

It is well to know what to do with waste paper. If any reader of this column calls the county agent be sure to tell him that it was Fulton Lewis Jr., who said to call him.

1942

THE FARM WOMAN

Last month every farm family went to town to get ration books. If one ever wondered why so many pockets were placed in men's clothing, the reason is plain now - to keep all the records and certificates the government says one must have. Mother's purse, always overflowing is crammed now.

Let's see, there is ration book I and II for each member of the family, the gas ration book, the tire inspection records, the certificate of title, the photo-static copy of the car license, the driver's license, the kerosene ration book, the ODT War Necessity certificate for a farm pickup, the certificate of title, the photo static copy of the truck license, the tractor ration book, the permit for tax exempt gasoline, the draft registration card and classification notice. These things must be carried in the pocket or purse.

It is well that the Farm Bureau lesson on keeping farm accounts gave several helpful hints on filing special papers. The top buffet drawer is filled to overflowing and the clock shelf cannot hide another thing. Extra special items are always placed on the clock shelf. Now we can take the empty un-rationed cereal boxes and make a series of file boxes; we can take a half dozen or so of the franked envelopes that come in the mail, fasten them together with a couple of chicken rings and thus we can find what we want when we want it.

Someone has remarked and justly so that farm

families have the edge when it comes to ration book II. In fact one will find most farm homemakers solicitous for the apartment dweller who has only forty-eight or ninety-six points to spend. Farm consumers are not going to rush to grocery stores and buy a lot of tin cans just because they have points. Instead they are planning larger and more complete gardens for their families. The Mason jar has always been more popular on the farm than the tin can. It will continue to be. The only thing that has contested the popularity of the fruit jar is the freezer locker.

As your attention veers longingly toward the farm and its abundant home produced food supply remember that many hours of labor go into producing and processing these items. And remember this also. If war ration book II gives us the advantage, war ration book I discriminates against us. Most apartment dwellers will admit that they have more sugar on hand than they have ever had. The reason is that they buy their bread and much of their food already processed and sweetened. Farm families do not complain but the present allotment of sugar permits little baking. Farm women do not buy cakes and pastries at the bake shop.

Now if the OPA would let us trade a slice of ham for an allotment of sugar!

3-8-43

Chronicles of
The Farm Woman

THE FARM WOMAN

Most farmers down this way are poised at the edge of their fields as a group of race horses at the starting line. One starts in before the dry signal is given and gets mired down before he goes 50 yards. He works and tugs to get back where he started and to solid ground. Another may get clear across the field on the first lap and stuck on the second round. A shower of rain calls them all back to the post. They champ at the bit and stomp in impatience to be off and down the corn rows.

Weeds thumb their noses at the farmer, which he wants, and dare him to take in after them. They wax sturdy and strong and in some fields are going to take the corn.

It's a great life on the farm these days. If it doesn't rain the wind blows a prairie gale. Farmers are not on strike and they are not idle but they are puttering around at chores they do not want to be doing now. What they want to do is to get the ground worked. The first cutting of alfalfa is in full bloom, the corn needs cultivating and much corn is yet to be planted. Ground that once was harrowed for the seeding now must be disked again to get rid of the weeds. How do the policy makers in OPA know how much gas a farmer will need to plant and harvest a crop? The farmer himself doesn't know for much depends upon the weather.

This matter of the farmer and tractor fuel rationing and all other wartime blanks and permits is a dedicated subject in these parts. When a farmer is shorter handed than he has ever been. Imagine the temperament of the farmer who had driven 15 miles to apply for his quota and arrived at the ration board at three minutes after five, war time. It is probably a good thing that last week was a rainy week.

One neighbor commented that he and his wife became so tired of looking at the weeds and at each other that they decided to take the day off and go visiting. Upon their return in the evening they felt refreshed and heartened as did all those on whom they called. It helps to exchange experiences with one's neighbors even in war time.

6-3-43

THE FARM WOMAN

If a furlough is the thing a soldier or sailor looks forward to most of all, the same is true for the folk at home. Every day happenings on the home front are likely to be dated from Johnny's last leave.

A neighbor boy has been at home on a 20-day furlough after almost two years in the Caribbean area. Two years of dull and monotonous outpost duty, so dull that the company longed to be transferred to an area of activity.

A letter to home folk one day said it was rumored they might be moved. No further word for weeks. Then one night there was a collect telephone call from Kansas City from the sergeant. Would they accept the call? They would and did. In a few hours he was home. He was a shy, slight lad when he left. The family knew that he would be changed after all the months in service. However, they were not prepared for what they saw when he arrived. How the soldier had grown, his hands, his feet, his shoulders, he was larger all over and solid flesh. He talked loud. He didn't say how glad he was to get home and see all the folks and little brother and sisters. He was glad to get away from that island outpost. He didn't seem to crave any of the goodies his mother had prepared especially for him. All he talked about was women and rum. And profanity was part of every sentence.

What trying hours those were for his mother. Tears never more than two blinks below the surface could scarce be held back. Was this the price she had to pay for war? The preacher came to call the next day and the mother uttered a quiet prayer of thanks that her soldier son was not at home.

Saturday night there was a dance at the USO. The soldier did not call anyone of a dozen girls that went to school with him and ask for a date. Instead he remained in the fringes of the crowd. Finally he did ask a near neighbor, the mother of three children and one of the hostesses of the evening, to dance with him. He was too bashful to ask any of the girls. He went to church with the family on Sunday and was attentive throughout the service.

After he had been at home a few days the soldier did not shout as loud. He confessed to his mother that he was out of the habit of raiding the ice box, and eating between meals no longer appealed to him. By the time his furlough ended he and the family found more of common ground. Mercifully they discovered that neither women nor rum nor hard liquor were of any real interest to him. Beneath that loud, brash exterior was the same fine lad they had known. He wanted to get into the thick of things and get this mess over so that he could come home and have some fun.

This lad is probably typical of boys in foreign service. Will we receive these lads with open arms in our communities? Will we look beneath the exterior or will we draw a cloak of shallow self-righteousness about our shoulders and look down in long-nosed piety? Our attitude will be one of the postwar problems. 1-26-44

Chronicles of
The Farm Woman

THE FARM WOMAN

Five sale bills were lined up along the counter of the local hardware store. A farm sale listed every day this week. Back of every farm sale there is a story.

Farmers are retiring and moving to town in greater numbers than we have seen since the first decade of this century. Forty years ago it was the dream of every landowner to retire to town and spend his last days around the pot-bellied stove in the village store. He would turn the farm over to a son and live in ease from his share of the income. Unless he got away from the farm by 1910 or 12 there hasn't been a time since that one could go until now. The over expansion of land prices, the adjustment to power machinery, low prices, drought and floods have kept the farmers chained to the land, if he could hold on at all. Now debts are liquidated, there is a demand for land and some men are seeing the dreams of a lifetime come true.

Mostly these families are buying four or five-room cottages near the edge of town. Their dreams are not of grandeur but of a little place with a garden and chicken pen and close neighbors.

Others are retiring to town because sons and hired men have been drafted and they are too old to carry on alone. Nothing to do but sell out and move to town. This number is considerable and the question in this writer's mind is how will their land fare? These men have an accumulation of knowledge gained over the past generation. Can a young farmer, however willing, do as well with their acres in wartime as they have learned to do?

Secondly, where are the young farmers coming from? A year ago there was an influx of defense workers who thought they would be safer on the land than in a lucrative defense job. One by one they have folded up. The cream and egg check could not begin to cover the things that the defense check did after all its deductions. They have gone back to war work and are again taking chances with deferments.

Some men are having a sale - and this applies particularly to specialized farming such as dairying - because they keep detailed records and find they are going into the red. Current prices of labor, ready-mixed feeds and milk prices do not leave a margin upon which to operate. No doubt if more farmers kept accurate records on dairy cows there would be less milking today. As it is the profitable projects on the farm carry the unprofitable ones along and if the farmer has enough cash to pay taxes and meet his note when it is due he does not bother to delve further into accounts.

Regardless of the reasons, farmers are selling out and moving to town. The government has requested that we increase production. Draft quotas are larger. Harvest time alone will show how the task can be accomplished.

2-26-44

THE FARM WOMAN

The following is part of an article written by M. F. McK at Thanksgiving, Nov. 22, 1945.

A few months ago we could think of nothing to be so thankful for as the end of hostilities. That end came. Our boys no longer face enemy mortar and machine guns. No longer do suicide planes from the air or submarines under the surface menace ships that sail the seas. Nor do our planes and ships and artillery rain fire and destruction upon the enemy. Each day brings news that our boys are getting home.

All America and Kansas has this at Thanksgiving. And yet we are not satisfied. Boys on distant shores who no longer charge the enemy suffer from ennui and boredom. When they do get home they can not get an apartment or a car. These things which they have dreamed about are not obtainable even when they have the money to pay for them. Jobs are not as plentiful as they thought. Re-conversion to peace does not seem to move as fast as did reconversion to war. Peace we all want. Then why can't we move forward to peace even faster than we did to war? Ah, peace we think is permanent. There is jockeying for position at the starting line. The way we get set now may set the pattern for years to come. And yet forces in the earth may change those patterns faster than anyone dreams.

No one in our country is hungry. Yet hunger we

know abounds in the world. No one in our country is cold. Yet folk will perish from cold this winter. No roofs and windows or houses are destroyed. Yet millions are homeless in other countries. Some are scantily clad but that is from choice. It is not a matter of choice in countries devastated by war. America has both privileges and responsibilities at this Thanksgiving season.

This might be a good time for a backward look at the first Thanksgiving. Those Pilgrims who celebrated the first Thanksgiving did not have electricity or running water or steam heated homes and offices. In fact there were no office jobs. They had come through a year of suffering and hardship. For that they were thankful. They had strangulated hopes and dreams. They had faith that those dreams would come true.

So on this Thanksgiving Day let us be thankful for those who have lived out the year. Let us remember those who gallantly gave their lives that free peoples might survive. Let us kindle our hopes and dreams anew. Let us resolve to do justly, love mercy and walk humbly with our God.

Everything is not well with America today. It was not on that first Thanksgiving. But with the help and interest of every American we can go forward to a greater day.

THE FARM WOMAN

Next to the return of our own kith and kin from the war, likely no one is welcomed with quite the zeal as the return of the family doctor. Especially when that doctor is a country doctor who still comes into the home at any hour of the day or night he is called. The country doctor mingles with the crowd in town on Saturday night. He sits in his pew at church on Sunday morning. His joys are in the simple happenings of the community. His sorrows and disappointments are well hidden from view.

The country doctor still has a unique place in the hearts and lives of citizens in a rural community despite the headlong drive to socialized medicine. He comes only when he is called. He still delivers babies in the homes of the community. He is the first to greet us in this world. He counsels and treats minor and major ills as they come along. He holds our wrists as the last fluttering pulse dies away and the heart is stilled forever. He knows all members of the family and the individual characteristics of each one. He practiced psycho-somatic medicine long before one read that word in the Readers Digest.

No one murmured when our young doctors joined the armed services. We wanted our boys to have the best medical attention. And the best they received. The record of the medical corps is one of the brilliant achievements of the war. The medics surmounted insurmountable difficulties.

They preserved the spirits of the wounded as well as restoring torn and shattered bodies. If no longer needed in the armed services they chafe to get home where they know they are needed.

As younger doctors begin to return to their former practice one should pass out orchids (or perhaps more appropriately carnations), to the older doctors who have held the home front. They met us at the hospital when an emergency arose. They treated long lines of patients every day. They have driven themselves to the point of exhaustion. And they have coped with the ills of the community for three long years. May they soon be able to take the vacation they have been dreaming of and enjoy it to the full. They did not fail us when we needed them.

12-22-45

Chronicles of
The Farm Woman

THE FARM WOMAN'S TRIP I

Some notes on a trip to New Orleans and the Gulf Coast:

Good roads, and new cars, as they come on the market, will open up new vistas for many an American family. Three weeks ago the family was gathered up along with Aunt Alice, and we were off to Biloxi and points South. It was the Farm Woman's first trip south and observations or conclusions are that of the novice.

Arkansas fooled us. Sawmills were everywhere. And new houses - little houses, comfortable homey-looking modern houses dot the highway throughout the state. While the rest of the country is talking about the housing shortage, Arkansas is doing something about it. At Harrison we had the best tourist cabins of the entire trip, hardwood floors, maple furnishings, radio, telephone, bath. On our return trip we stayed in Jayhawk cabins in another Arkansas town. Sure enough they were operated by former Kansans. The cabins were furnished with all the rickety, cast-off furniture that relatives and friends had discarded; partitions were paper thin, rooms were clean but weary travelers slept on Aunt Bertha's cast-off iron bed.

The second afternoon found us in Tallulah, La., and on to Vicksburg, where we crossed the river. Later we learned that the road was better and that more traffic crosses at Greenville. We returned via Greenville.

In 1968 when my branch of the family came to Kansas from Ohio, after a 3-year stay in Missouri, one brother went down the river to New Orleans. There he met and married a Canadian. It is his descendants that we visited.

We were taken to visit old homes in Natchez, mansions

that were built by wealthy plantation owners early in the 19th century. Natchez sits on the high bank of the Mississippi. The plantations lie over the river in Louisiana. Owners ferried back and forth across the river. One is impressed by the details of craftsmanship in these structures built long ago. Wide halls, ballrooms 75 feet long, spacious dining rooms where genial hospitality abounded. Cypress thresholds and windowsills show no sign of wear. Bricks were handmade on the site. Today many of the old buildings have been coated with a cement mix. We saw Rosalie House where Grant had his headquarters for two years. Grant was respected because he ordered that the town not be destroyed. China, beautiful French china, which was locked in a closet and furnishings stored in the attic were untouched and may still be seen today.

Much cotton in the delta was not picked. Not once in the ten days did we see an individual picking cotton. Help is as scarce and hard to get in the south as it is here. There has been a mass exodus of Negroes and they are not returning. The southern woman is doing her own housework and longing for the day that dishwashers, washing machines and modern kitchen fixtures will be available. A native Mississippian commented that the best thing that ever happened to the south was that the white man had to go to work.

Southern scenery is continuously enthralling to one from the prairies. Pine woods and sawmills, turpentine forests, pecan and orange orchards and tung groves. We saw eerie fairylike areas where the moss hangs from live oak trees and from stately pines. Cypress trees with lacy colorful foliage and knees projecting up from the swamp as though they were fairies sitting in convention.

We did the French quarter in New Orleans on foot in half a day. It is the kind of place where one can spend hours and days on-end absorbing history. The gardens glimpsed from the street through gates to the patios. Iron grill work, just as it is pictured, adorns the buildings. Shops abound.

A few camellias were in bloom and here and there an azalea blooming out of season. Everyone was working in their yards.

February and March is the peak of the season. It is then that the Natchez Pilgrimage is held, the New Orleans Mardi Gras and the greatest numbers of visitors at Bellingrath Gardens, a few miles out of Mobile. At the height of the season these gardens have 8,000 visitors a day. They have grown from a fishing lodge surrounded by three rivers. Mrs. Bellingrath chose to use her green thumb and plan shrubs while others fished. She sought the aid of landscape architects and laid out one of the beauty spots of the nation. A black swan glides along with its white mate. There are advantages in visiting these places out-of-season. There are not crowds and one is not hurried.

11-1946

THE FARM WOMAN

A hush settled over the grandstand at the Topeka fair the other day when the master of ceremonies stopped to announce that Mrs. Ida Eisenhower had died suddenly at her home in Abilene.

Mrs. Ida Eisenhower, mother of sons, modest, shy, industrious, devout, had slipped quietly from the scene. A jubilant fair crowd paused to pay her homage and honor. It seemed altogether fitting and proper, a beautiful thing to witness. Only a handful of that great surging crowd knew Mrs. Eisenhower personally, yet each one felt that he knew her because of the achievements of her illustrious sons. Her circle of activities was not extensive; her son's circle the globe. The name Eisenhower has a well deserved niche in American history. Herein lies the greatness that is America.

It is likely as the sons gathered at her bier the remark of Abraham Lincoln came to mind, "All that I am or hope to be I owe to my angel mother." Indeed these five sons owe much to their mother, now departed. She taught them by example and precept the simple and enduring virtues, industry, thrift, integrity, piety.

For teaching to be successful it is essential that it create a spark of response in those taught. The success of the Eisenhower brothers is that they measure up to responsibilities which came to them. What more could any mother ask?

Ida Eisenhower died as she had lived, quietly and serene and full of years.

9-1946

THE FARM WOMAN

Twenty-three years ago Watkins Hall, a woman's residence hall, was opened at the University of Kansas. The hall was a gift of Mrs. Watkins, a wealthy benefactress who lived on the rim of Mt. Oread, next to the campus.

Watkins Hall was a dream and an experiment. As Mrs. Watkins looked out from her living room each day she saw the stream of students pour in and out of Fraser Hall. As the stream grew larger she saw Spooner Library, Dyche Museum, Bailey, Blake, Green Halls spread across the campus. Now a dozen other buildings have been strung around the hill-top. Still classrooms and laboratories are jammed.

Mrs. Watkins did not get much schooling in the classroom. As she saw the student body grow she knew there were many boys and girls in Kansas and surrounding states who had keen minds, who wanted to go to college and who could do so with a little help. Thus the dream and the idea of a women's residence hall grew. It was translated into reality in her dooryard. A home to house 42 girls in pleasant and genteel surroundings, the girls to do all the work and keep the house shining. Since she believed that college should prepare one for life as well as give a taste for the classics, Mrs. Watkins planned that the girls should cook in groups of six. The small group would more nearly approximate that of the family. So seven small kitchens and dinettes were installed. Today 49 girls live in the hall. Three girls live in many of the rooms and there are seven in each kitchen.

Mrs. Watkins liked the way the first hall worked out so much that in a few years she built Miller Hall, an exact duplicate of the first and right along side it. The Battenfelds built a residence hall for men as a memorial to their son: Joliffe Hall was given, the Unitarians gave Ricker Hall and the endowment association reconditioned a number of houses for residence halls for men and women.

Details of housekeeping and management must be worked out carefully in each hall. Many hands make work light. One girl who lived at Watkins during her college days says that the training and experience of living in the hall was the equivalent of at least one year of college.

It has become a tradition at Watkins for the girls to entertain their mothers one weekend in May. The campus in gorgeous spring garb provides a beautiful setting. The lilac hedge is in full scented bloom and tulips raise their brilliant colored heads in tulip beds. The girls do the meal planning, the cooking, the entertaining. Mothers, unaccustomed to the role, try to relax and remember what the guest is supposed to do. Can her little girl do all this without any help or advice? The little girl can and does. Each mother sleeps in her daughter's bed. When it comes to clambering to the top of a double-decker mother grunts and groans but she makes it and hopes the framework holds.

On Sunday morning a group breakfast is held. All the girls and mothers sit down together. They talk of Mrs. Watkins, the hall, campus activities and things that are close to the hearts of girls and their mothers.

It was a wonderful dream that Mrs. Watkins dreamed as she watched from her home at the edge of the campus. As a result of that dream, girls from farms, towns and cities learn to live and work together while they sit at the feet of the goddess Minerva.

3-11-49

THE FARM WOMAN

How families do get around these days, especially if there is a son or loved one in camp half way across the nation.

Highways are ribbons that crisscross the nation. Almost as swift as a magic carpet, cars traverse these ribbons to get to the base before the son and heir is shipped east or west. There are no side trips en route - the whole point is to see a soldier or sailor or marine. If the lad can get a 3-day pass they take any outing he suggests.

Just one month ago a car headed east from San Francisco, skipped Reno in order to spend the night in Fallon, Nevada. There is a naval air base near Fallon and the driver's college room-mate was stationed there. The great American desert today is dotted with camps and bomb ranges and experimental areas.

They lounged in the Cannon Motel and hashed over good times of a former day, football games, and the prospects of their alma mater this season. They talked of weddings and shows and friends now widely scattered.

This sailor is a handsome lad. Many a female heart flutters as he parades down the street. In true sailor fashion he has a girl in every port. In Fallon they were getting ready for a fall festival and rodeo. Townsmen were growing beards and handlebar mustaches. Always desiring to be part of the world around him, the lieutenant was growing a beard.

He knew at the time they would be heading for Korea,

and that fighters could not cross the Yalu. He was hoping for a leave and one more look in on home folk before he was sent across.

These lads were not teenagers. Both were veterans of World War II. Neither one is sure just what we won in that struggle. "I'm glad I'm going instead of somebody else," the airman commented, "but I sometimes wonder why we are over there. We can't cross the Yalu and clean out those birds. It just makes you wonder what we can do."

A few nights ago a radio announcer reported that a Navy Lieutenant was rescued by a Navy helicopter off a sand bar near Hang Chon.

One disadvantage of a radio is that it is a one-way conversation. One cannot ask them to repeat. However, when the morning paper came the next day there was the story in black and white. The naval airman rescued in Korea was the lieutenant we had visited in Fallon. We didn't even know he had embarked and here he is rescued in daring fashion. It is sudden and shocking, yet likely not one fraction as sudden or shocking as the plight in which the flier found himself.

His eyes and his question come echoing back. Can you, gentle reader, tell the lieutenant why he is there and what good he is doing?

10-6-51

Chronicles of
The Farm Woman

THE FARM WOMAN

A big change has taken place on Kansas farms in this year of 1955. It was anticipated with fear. Now it is accepted with delight.

The egg bucket has left the back porch. Eggs on the farm are now receiving the care that fragile, perishable products should receive. An egg room with even temperature has been devised, likely in the cellar or cave. A jar of water provides humidity. An egg scale shows the weight of an egg. Eggs are gathered frequently, three or four times a day. They are placed with the small end down on open racks to cool. They are cleaned and sprayed with an invisible seal.

This change in the handling of eggs was precipitated by the Kansas egg law which was passed at the last session of the legislature. For years Kansas eggs have been at the bottom in the national egg markets. County agents and produce men staged educational meetings year after year, trying to generate enthusiasm for a voluntary change on the part of producers. It all seemed to no avail. However, enough steam was generated to get a law passed. We are prone to think we do not want so many laws and regulations. In this case it took a law to induce the farmer or the farmer's wife to change the care and handling of eggs.

There was much apprehension before the law went into effect. Some said it would be just one more thing that would make it harder for the farmer to make a living.

Chronicles of
The Farm Woman

What has happened? The price of eggs did not sink to 15 cents as it did a year ago. One neighbor says she has received 15 cents or more a dozen, more than a year ago right through the summer and fall. Her pullet eggs are bringing as much today as larger eggs did a year ago. There is little spare change in the farm wife's purse today. A little egg money is left over after paying for ready-mixed feed which induces hens to lay more eggs. That spare change in the farm wife's purse is reflected in increased retail sales.

The unfavorable reaction to this egg law is coming not from the farmers who feared it before it came into effect. The complaints are coming from consumers who are now buying eggs of known grade and quality. Many factors enter into retail price. Studies which have been made indicate that grading, cartons, etc, have added from 5 to 7 cents to the retail cost. The question for families on a salary and families of business people to ask themselves is would they prefer to go back to ungraded, unknown eggs in the market? Or can they rejoice at buying a product of known quality and value, knowing as they do so that this means the farm family has more money to spend?

11-12-55

THE FARM WOMAN

Harvest is over. And what a harvest. Old timers have never seen anything like it. Every field yielded more than the grower expected. Upland and bottom fields shelled out the grain with little difference in yield.

After five of the driest years of record, grain which sprouted unevenly, which was beset by chinch bugs and grasshoppers, came through to make record yields. This is one of those crops that will be talked about in years to come, when men gather and discuss high points in local history. This grain on allotted acres, all carefully measured and checked, all sold or stored with the accompaniment of a marketing card, must be a headache to planners. For, in many instances, the total yield on allotments of acres reduced with a slide rule, is greater than yields on free and un-allotted acres of other years.

Soon after World War II one young farmer moved to a worn out hill farm. Neighbors shook their heads and smiled knowingly. They had seen a succession of farmers go broke on that farm. The land was so poor and thin that it would raise nothing but cane and not much tonnage at that. This young man had a plan. He hauled loads and loads of manure. He seeded lespedeza and clover. He applied lime as needed. Today the entire farm is terraced. Brome grass flourishes in waterways. The wheat yield on that once worn out land was 50 bushels an acre. It is such land treatment as this that makes upland fields yield as much as bottom ground.

This year self-propelled combines made their appearance in numbers in this country. A few have been seen here and there the last few years. Today they are a common sight. The farmer sits atop this monster as it slices off a 12-foot swath and beams as the grain pours into the bin above his head. Twenty acres in an afternoon seems unbelievable. Yet that was repeated day after day.

A neighbor, watching this great hummingbird glide down the quarter-mile stretch, shook his head and remarked that it was taking better than half an acre each time it sliced off a 12-foot strip. That was mental arithmetic, something this man uses every day in his operations. No slide rule or book of tables for him. When one has stepped off the distance or followed a walking cultivator, there is time to figure out things in the head.

This man recalled the first reaper he ever saw. Cyrus McCormich's reaper appeared on the scene to supplant the cradle. Pulled by four horses, the reaper cut the grain and laid it on a platform. Two men stood on the back of the reaper, bound the grain by hand and tossed it off on the ground to be gathered up later and stacked. All grain used to be stacked. A wheat stacker was a skilled artisan. Each stack rose row upon row, symmetrical and firm. A good stack was waterproof. Grain could not be threshed before it had gone through a sweat. This took six to eight weeks. It *could be kept in the stack as long as desired. Bugs didn't bother grain in the stack. Great bins and sprays and insecticides were unnecessary. If the farmer did not need the grain for feed or flour, and didn't need the money, he kept his grain right there in the stack. It was money in the bank. It was not uncommon to see three wheat crops stacked side by side. The two-year-old stack would be black but the grain would be top quality. This was the ever-normal granary, the insurance against crop failure.*

The bigger the machine, the quicker the work is done, the larger the investment, the greater the tension on the operator and his family.

Gone is the drudgery and hard manual labor as in harvest of yore. Today the flip of a switch or the pull of a lever and the grain is not touched by hand from the field to the grain bin or terminal elevator. With the disappearance of back breaking labor comes the necessity for machinery know-how. The combine operator must be a skilled mechanic. One or two hours each morning must be spent checking, greasing, tuning up the machine. Tightening up one loose nut on a bolt may prevent a shut down for major repairs.

The payoff comes in getting the grain stored safely as soon as it is ready. Some years ago the families in the neighborhood had an ice cream social on the Fourth of July. Everyone brought freezers and mix, and froze the cream on the spot. Wheat was in the shock and threshing would begin in the morrow. As the group sat there reveling in the homemade delight, a cloud came up on the northwest, black and menacing. No rain fell here, but up on Rock Creek they had a cloudburst. The flood came and not one shock or bottom wheat was saved.

Remembering that flood and other experiences, these farmers mortgage their future for large combines. Another crop like this one and the combines may be paid for. 7-11-56

THE FARM WOMAN

The highways are dotted with cattle trucks. Loaded trucks are headed east to market. Empty trucks going west. Cowboys are out before dawn rounding up the dogies in far corners of the pastures. In the past 90 days cattle have made the maximum gain on bluestem. Now to market they go.

Occasionally these same trailer trucks haul a load of sheep or hogs or horses. The strangest load we have seen was a load of honey bees. Several weeks ago we looked out early one morning and saw a large cattle truck parked in a neighboring wheat field. It was before harvest and the wheat was green. White statues began to dot the knoll. Sixty hives of bees were unloaded and set in line. They are visible for miles around and are a neighborhood curiosity.

Adjacent to this wheat field is a large field of sweet clover. It was this maze of golden bloom that attracted the beekeeper to this area. Before the sun was high in the sky, a number of bees could be found on every clover plant. Day after day they work early and late. They fly in and out of the hives in an endless procession. And they sing while they work. One neighbor ventured too close when he went to take a look at the bees. He did not roll up the windows of his car and a busy bee darted in and stung him. It was a warning not to interfere with their operations.

Now the clover is ripe

and the seed is harvested. The yield is several times what it might have been without the bees. The bees have made nearly 6,000 pounds of honey - sweet clover honey, crystal clear. Surely it is nectar for the gods and a rare delicacy for man.

Now that the clover blossoms are faded and gone, the bees frequent the alfalfa fields. Alas, the dry years have discouraged alfalfa seeding and there are not many acres for the bees to work. Wild flowers also contain nectar and some wild flowers yield a bitter, pungent product.

How does one move a swarm of bees? That was a question which buzzed around the neighborhood. In the dark of night while the bees slumber, the openings of the hives are covered with screen wire. The hives are stapled together with special staples. They are loaded in the truck as if they were bales of hay; perhaps they are handled a bit more carefully than bales of hay. They are unloaded and placed in position. There the truck driver's part in the proceedings ends. The beekeeper removes the staples, places a rock on the top of each hive and removes the screens. The bees get to work immediately. Their queen will have it no other way.

When cattle trucks pass on the highways it is likely that they are hauling cattle. Yet they might be hauling bees. 8-7-56

THE FARM WOMAN

More and more students of land use are coming to accept the fact that ponds in the headwaters of every creek, properly terraced land, planting of trees in gullies that cannot be terraced and cleaning streams, all of these will lessen flood damage in the bottom.

Experiments have shown that terracing and strip cropping hold from 20 to 35 percent of the moisture right there in the land. A good pond properly constructed in every draw would save many a farmer from hauling water today.

What a drudge water hauling is. It is even more disheartening and endless than dishwashing. The cattle never get quite enough to completely satisfy their thirst as water is doled out from the tank wagon. There may be some water remaining in the tank when evening comes, but a cow likes to stand and drink deliberately. There is no deliberation in a pushing, crowding mass which greets the tank truck. Once crowded away many do not go back even when they can. Hogs want an excess of water to wallow in. No such excesses are allowed if one hauls every drop of water consumed on the farm.

The country has always been considered a land of doubtful rainfall. 1901, '13, '14, '34, '35, '36 and now '39 have seen water barrels headed toward the creek. It is high time we constructed adequate ponds. If a soil conservation district is obtained for this county the specifications for an adequate pond can be secured. A large pond is really an engineering problem. The engineering assistance will be available but the cost of construction must be borne by the landowner.

There is a remote possibility, but no assurance that one would be moved to Lyon county. Such camps are now established in surrounding counties. Dr. Henry Link, the consulting psychologist whose name has become a household word since the publication of his book, "Return to Religion," states that the Civilian Conservation Corps is the only New Deal alphabet that can be justified. The late Henry Hatch, who was always an inspiration and who frequently clarified my thinking, made this observation which is worth considering. A CCC camp is expensive even though it does not cost directly out of pocket. In a democracy do we dare say that any governmental expenditure does not cost us anything? He questioned such expense being placed on the land when the same work could be done by the farmer at far less cost. CCC boys carrying out these practices tend to make the farmer think such expense necessary and too expensive for him to do on his own. In the long run he thought this would make farmers spineless and dependent. Also ofttimes the absentee landowner wanted these practices followed but found it difficult to get a tenant who would follow them or vice versa. Henry Hatch was a dweller on the land. Dr. Link deals continually with products of the city.

He justifies CCC extravagance under the head of human conservation. Certainly we want to conserve the youth as well as the soil.

However one may regard the CCC, it must be conceded we need more soil conservation practices in the county. A vote "yes" in the referendum will provide a soil conservation district. No one need co-operate unless he chooses to do so. There is no connection between Soil Conservation Service and the Agricultural Adjustment Administration.

In early 1933 FDR's `New Deal' project, the CCC, brought together the unemployed young men and the land, in an effort to save both. After the Pearl Harbor attack, it came under review and was liquidated in 1942.

THE FARM WOMAN

What did that red letter day on the calendar mean to you?

That red letter day meant a holiday for workers in offices, factories and stores. It meant anticipation for homeward bound travelers. It meant statistics for safety directors. It meant headaches for highway patrolmen and traffic police. It meant picnics. It meant family reunions. Or it meant another day.

Headstones slant and lean but the cemetery is neat and tended with care. The cemetery was a boulder strewn garden on Memorial day. The holiday was conceived to honor those who gave their lives on the battlefield in order that we might enjoy the rich heritage of freedom. No matter what judgment history may finally render about the justice and righteousness of the cause, these men and women served and died for us. It is a debt that cannot be amortized. Along with the soldier dead, we have come to honor relatives and friends who have passed this way and gone. Soldiers on the battlefield, pioneer fathers and mothers, and generations who held steady in golden years and years of panic, drought, flood, depression and war.

Our destiny today was largely fashioned by those who have left this early scene. The destiny of generations to come is in our hands. How shall we alter and modify the scene before us to build for a better tomorrow? We are carving a destiny for those who come after us for which we shall be held accountable.

06-04-56

Chronicles of
The Farm Woman

FLY THE FLAG

I may not pass my neighbor's home on the Fourth of July but I know that her flag will be out and waving in the breeze. She admits that she is a flag waver. It is her way of saying that she is proud to be an American. She thinks every home should have a flag pole and fly the flag. And, why not?

This young neighbor attended a country school. It was always a privilege and an honor to be chosen by the teacher to put up the flag in the morning or lower it at the close of school. Occasionally the whole school stood outdoors and gave the flag salute as the banner rippled in a brisk wind. Do today's school children give the flag salute every day? Do they ever give it out-of-doors?

Why is this neighbor more interested in the flag than the rest of us? (Alas, on some holidays we forget to take the flag off the shelf and hang it out.) She says she doesn't know when her interest in the flag really began. She has always been interested in it. She remembers that her father was very particular about the way the flag was folded and put away. She remembers that there was a manual on how to display the flag in the country school library. Since there were not many books in the library, she read the manual from cover to cover.

She remembers that a soldier in the armed forces described Retreat, and the thrill that it gave him day after day. He saw action in the Pacific and one of the vivid memories that he liked to recall was the lowering of the colors while the bugler sounded Retreat.

This young neighbor did not know Adeline Hahn, but how proud Mrs. Hahn would have been to know her. Adeline Hahn was an adopted American and a loyal patriot. Did she ever send a letter or card or Christmas greeting without a tiny gummed American flag attached? Not to the writer's knowledge.

Many persons through-out the land have a small American flag on their desks today because Adeline Hahn gave it to them with fervent good wishes. When she handed a Governor or Senator or Congressman a flag, they caught her spirit of love and devotion to her adopted country. When a plain citizen did something she thought commendable, she presented him a flag for his desk. She was a flag waver and proud of it.

The patriotism of this young neighbor reminds me of the spirit of Adeline Hahn. Citizens should display the flag. It is a symbol of pride and faith in our country.

Let us get out the flag.

7-3-58

Chronicles of
The Farm Woman

THE FARM WOMAN

One of the main topics of conversation down this way is the reservoir which the Army engineers would install to drown out the town of Hartford and many of the bottom farms in southeast Lyon County.

The report of the Army engineers is now before Congress and hearings are due to be scheduled soon. The residents realize that it is a question of survival and they propose to do something about it. The women of the community have rolled up their sleeves, taken up their brooms and gone into action. They are going over the House document containing the report of the Army engineers, with a fine tooth comb. They are reading the Congressional Record and learning the personnel of committees in the national Congress. Incidentally they are learning more civics than they did in either grade school or high school.

The women are assisting the men in circulating petitions, answering questionnaires, writing letters and galvanizing any sleepy neighbors into action.

The Happy Housewives Club (an afternoon social club) led off with a cash donation to the cause and a pledge to do anything they could to help. Friday night when the local executive committee invited the flood control committee of the Emporia Chamber of Commerce and the County officials of Lyon and Coffey Counties, the Happy Housewives cooked up an oyster stew for the group with home-made pie on the side.

In a small town and rural community, homes and businesses are more closely integrated than in an urban area. A dam at Strawn would mean much more than the covering of 27,000 acres of real property. The term real property is a cold impersonal term. The water behind the dam would destroy homes with all that the word holds dear. It would mean the disruption of businesses and of habits and routines that have become a part of the community in these 90 years.

The people of Hartford area feel that the matter of flood control needs further study.

2-3-48

Chronicles of
The Farm Woman

Farm Women are learning to Sew the Modern Way

In the sweltering days of July and August before this welcome respite came, members of the 46 Home Demonstration units in this county met for easy-to-sew lessons. In two hot sessions the 92 leaders took 800 members into new paths with a sewing machine. Pins were used by the score but never a single basting stitch by hand.

Two young leaders who did not study sewing in high school, who are just now learning to sew, presented these lessons to one unit. First they attended the training school where the lesson was presented to them by a specialist. The specialist in this case was our home demonstration agent, Jean Carlson. After taking this lesson these young farm women practiced. They had to know how to straighten cotton material if they were going to teach us how to do it. After the corn was canned, the supper dishes done and the children in bed, they dampened and rolled and straightened material. They cut out a dress and followed each step they had been taught. It worked. Then they were ready to present the lesson.

Their presentation was well organized as an extension lesson should be. They took us through these steps in order. Unless cotton material is "sanforized" it should be shrunk before the garment is cut out. This is done by wetting the material thoroughly and rolling it in a sheet. It can be straightened in the same procedure. After the material has ripened in the sheet it is pressed straight and smooth. The pattern is laid on the material and there is an art in doing this. All markings are noted and followed. Then each piece is stay-stitched with the grain of the material. Next a slick way of easing in fullness is demonstrated. A zipper is a bugaboo for most beginners. Step by step in putting in a zipper was demonstrated. The hem was not put in by hand. It was put in by another slick trick with the machine. Then we were shown how to make a belt, cover a buckle and cover buttons. Finishing touches give a garment a professional look.

Older members were keen observers at these meetings. Gray-haired, grandmothers have much to un-learn.

We were carried back to our first extension sewing lessons with Frances L. Brown in 1912 or '13. Here the beginner had to make samples of hand stitches, even and uneven basting, side stitch or tailor's basting, running stitch and backstitch. All that is out the window now in today's easy-to-sew lesson.

The remarkable thing about today's lesson is that it produces a smarter looking garment than that of yesteryear which was carefully basted by hand and French seamed throughout.

Our hat is off to these gallant leaders who disregard temperature to show us easy and better ways of homemaking. - M.F.McK.
8-16-55

THE FARM WOMAN

Some farmers down this way have recently begun to sell Grade A milk. It is a family venture. Each one has his specific tasks that must be done on time, night and morning every day including Sunday.

The capital outlay is considerable. The barn must be up to standard, well lighted and easily cleaned. The milk room is a joy to behold. A hot water heater and large vats in which to wash utensils, a great cabinet to cool the milk, and everything bright and shining.

The 7-year-old is enlarging his vocabulary. He can tell you that the bacteria count is 3,000. Today's children no sooner learn to count than they are discussing bacteria numbers - phrases that did not come to our ears until college.

This family did not go into this venture hurriedly. They considered many angles - the outlay for equipping the barn and for more cows. They will have to milk promptly at 5:15 night and morning, every day, winter and summer. Feed for cows producing Grade A milk costs no more than if they are producing Grade C. After weighing all these things, the decision was made.

Now the entire household moves on schedule. Getting the milking done so early in the morning means that chickens are fed and watered, breakfast is over and all morning chores are finished before most folks in town are stirring.

4-30-52

THE FARM WOMAN

There is no single operation on the farm which has not been changed drastically by the impact of the machine age. In the space of one generation methods have been and still are being transformed.

The old timer was quite content and self-contained. He had a plow and a team, a cow and a sow and likely was master of all he sur-veyed. There was little market for his produce so he raised largely for his own needs. Of necessity and desire he had few wants.

He scoffed at a riding cultivator and he knew his way was best. When it came to picking corn on the frosty morn, he had his team harnessed and hitched and was in the field when the first streaks of dawn appeared. Ears hit against the bang boards as he and his team went up and down the rows. He who could husk 100 bushel in a day was looked up to by his neighbors.

Today the corn picker is going up and down the rows, gathering corn from a last straggling field. It does not glide noiselessly along. Instead there is a rhythmic groaning as it moves along over the stalks sending the golden yellow ears up the hopper and into the trailer tagging along behind. The trailer, which holds 100 bushels is filled in one or two hours. When it is filled, another tractor with an empty trailer is waiting to exchange. When it comes to the bin, a third tractor sits alongside an elevator to move the corn from the trailer to the bin.

Farming today is the life of Riley, no doubt about that. However, one must have neighbors who will come with tractors and trailers and pickers and most of all, their own time and labor. Machines do require an operator with know-how.

What a drab world this would be without neighbors - even in the machine age.

1-28-52

Chronicles of
The Farm Woman

THE FARM WOMAN

Fifty years ago today Austin S. Bernheisel published the first issue of the Neosho Valley Times at Hartford, under his masthead, as editor and publisher.

He had come a few years earlier to Neosho Rapids, a young printer fresh from Pennsylvania. By coincidence, known only to fate, he met and courted the charming daughter of one of Hartford's leading businessmen. He walked the seven miles from Neosho Rapids to Hartford to court Miss Susie Flickinger. Some years after he became established in Hartford, they were married. They set up housekeeping in the house that has been their home through the years.

The present generation thinks of the Bernheisels as publishers of the Times; somewhere along the way the name was changed to Hartford Times. They have been a congenial, hard working team. On Thursday, paper day, Mrs. Bernheisel is at the office. On the first of the month she helps with the collecting. It is suspected that some of the flowery write-ups of hometown products are from her pen. The subjects of the write-ups may blush and know it is better then they deserve, but they like it. More than one fledgling from the home community has been heartened and stayed by words of encouragement from the hometown editors.

The country editor writes the news of events after they have occurred. If he omits a name the correction is made the following week. The country weekly gives out news that most of us know already. Yet we miss it if it is not there. It keeps us straight on meetings of the Aid society, the Past Noble Grand's, the Home Demonstration unit, and other community events. Local advertisements get results. The local paper binds the community together and gives it a zest for living.

A half century ago the spirit of adventure was strong in the heart of young men in the more stale eastern seaboard states. Many of the pioneer papers in the state were changing hands. An enterprising young man and a good credit record, a flair for printers' pie, a generous supply of intestinal fortitude, some good strong adjectives and nerve, could embark on a newspaper career.

It is significant that in this period papers changed hands frequently and then came into ownership that has lasted 40 years or more. The Redmond's in Burlington, The White's in Emporia, the Roses in Lyndon, the Littles in Alma, the Satterthwaites in Douglas, the Bernheisels in Hartford and one could go on and on in the state. There is no doubt that this continued ownership has had a telling effect on the present generation of Kansans. As editors' adjectives have grown less vehement so has the younger generation. News-papers mold public opinion to a greater degree than the preacher in the pulpit or the radio orator. The editor's affirmations are down in print. We still like to see in black and white the things with which we do or do not agree.

Today we pause to hand a bouquet to the Bernheisels at the golden jubilee of the Hartford Times.

12-21-45

Chronicles of
The Farm Woman

THE FARM WOMAN

This is Home Demonstration week. It is also Family week and Well Baby week. All are closely allied.

For a quarter century home demonstration work has been gathering momentum in Kansas leaving improved rural living in its wake.

Gertrude Allen, the first home demonstration agent in this county, pioneered in promoting well-fed families. She introduced us to the pressure cooker and taught us to use it without fear. For 10 cents a day we could rent the cooker and in that one day, store a good portion of the winter's food supply on the cellar shelves. She taught us how to garden and how to plan a garden for the family's needs. She taught us to can beef and pork and chicken and to make liverwurst, summer sausage and corned beef. The locker and the home freezer have supplanted the pressure cooker in many instances.

Children, then as now, were considered the most important crop, rosy cheeks and bright eyes attested to adequate nutrition. Times were hard in those depression years but farm families were well-fed.

Miss Allen and the presidents council in those first years stressed the same basic aspects of homemaking that units study today. The construction and buying of clothing has grown until several hundred custom-tailored garments are now made each year. The woman who has tailored a suit or coat is a discriminating buyer of ready-to-wear garments. We studied labels and thread count and learned how to spend wisely.

And, how we struggled with home health and sanitation in those early years. W. Pearl Martin, the clothing specialist, created a furor when she suggested that women should milk the cows and that a clean apron should be put on each day to do the job. Miss Martin and Miss Allen would both thrill at the grade A milking barns in the county today. A shining kitchen and running water have largely replaced the pitcher pump and homemade sink of the 30's.

Interior decoration and room improvements were studied then as now. Today's members are more bold in the use of color but basic principles remain the same. Fine old walnut pieces were brought down from the haymow, refinished and given a place of honor. Last year more than 400 pieces were upholstered in Lyon County.

Charter members have reviewed phases of home-making a number of times. Always there is a new facet, and older members enjoy the lessons they have had years before as much or more than new members.

Miss Allen was followed by a succession of competent trained agents - Marie Shields, Ellen Blair Welch, Gersilda Guthrie Stapleton, Anna Grace Caughron and now our beloved Miriam Cade. Home Demonstration Agents, we salute you.

5-6-52

THE FARM WOMAN

Last week a small group of farmers who belong to a farm management association in this area, met to study and review 1957 performances and results. One hundred and fifty-two farms in 14 northeast Kansas counties were the basis of the summary.

After five years of drouth the gross income showed a sharp increase in 1957. At the same time total farm expenses have tended to level off in the last two years. No doubt any farm machinery agency could verify that fact. At a time when the manufacturing centers have wide unemployment the farm picture looks downright rosy. However, there should be no headlong rush to the farm.

Time was, when a farm family raised their children and lived on the production and income from an 80-acre farm. The country school district bounded the interests and travels of the family. Save for an occasional trip to town to exchange a load of corn for staples, the farm family felt no need of roads or machines or communications with the outside world.

Today the farm family wants the same gadgets and appurtenances of civilization as that of any town family.

Much is said about the family size farm. What is a family size farm? Let us say that it is a unit of operation which can meet current overhead and provide for taxes and family living. This calls for 300 or more crop acres (even more in certain areas). Is that a startling fact? These are the farms that showed most efficient management and best returns in 1957.

The farm units that are disappearing are the middle-sized farms, quarter and half sections. The number of small farms has declined only slightly in the last ten years. The owners of these farms have off-the-farm income which equals or exceeds that from the land.

As farms have increased in size there has been a corresponding increase in the efficiency of farm labor. The same laborer tills 50 more crop acres today than he did in 1944. Right along with the increase in labor efficiency has gone an increase in machinery and investment. The average investment per man on the farm today is $50,000. This is the reason there will be no headlong rush to the farm.

Last year was a good year for livestock men. Time was when a cattleman had grass and hay and sorghums. He did not fool with wheat or other cash crops. In 1957 the cash crop from livestock farms was almost as much as from livestock, from 30 to 50 percent of gross income.

These are great days on the farm. The old gray mare has vanished long since. Things aren't what they used to be.

4-25-58

THE FARM WOMAN

The last old-timer in this neighborhood has retired and moved to town. Hiram Wesley Zink, familiarly known as "Tobe," has laid aside his milk stool and the riding plow and has joined the bench-warmers, for Tobe has never learned to loaf.

It was no job for a large moving van when the Zink's moved to town. Instead, neighbors came with trucks and trailers and carefully loaded household furnishings for the short haul to the new home.

The chronicle of neighbors has loomed large in all events in a long life. Neighbors came in time of birth or sickness or death. They came in time of harvest or butchering. Neighbors came to welcome them into the community and to bid them farewell when they left.

In this nearly nine decades in this county, Tobe has observed farming from the time of the settlers to the larger units of today. He remembers the band of Kaw Indians who camped on Eagle Creek, near his birthplace, every winter during his childhood. The chief of that tribe was called Tobe, and Hiram Wesley was nicknamed Tobe, little Indian chief. The nickname stuck.

Tobe could always plow a straight furrow with either a walking plow or a riding plow. He converted from walking to riding horse-drawn equipment, but when tractors came in vogue, he stayed with horses. He realized that the day of the horse was doomed. However, he thought he was too old to change. In fact, he would have had to change his entire plan of operation had he converted to power farming.

His plan was that of pretty much self-contained family living. A bountiful garden along with milk and eggs and meat supplied most of the food for the table. The weekly egg and cream check more than covered necessities. Each year a few head of cattle, born and raised and fed on the farm, were marketed. It was a good life with few of today's tensions.

A rainy day was a time to check the pasture fence or hoe weeds along the turn-row. Each decade saw the pace a little slower, but as steady and consistent as the path of the sun.

Needless to say, Mrs. Zink, a native of Nebraska, has had much to do with the success of the plan of family living. Gifted with a green thumb as well as with the needle, all this in addition to being a good cook and housekeeper, she has been an energetic homemaker.

Tobe has much folklore and information gleaned from experience that cannot be acquired from books. He scans the sky and observes wild creatures to see what the weather will be. He may tune in the weatherman to see if scientific findings agree with his observa-tions. He relies on the almanac and the zodiac. He swears by many home remedies.

Tobe is not surprised or dismayed with trouble or disaster. Simply expressed, his philosophy is that "if one does not expect much, then one will not be disappointed."

As this neighbor moved to town, a chapter of farming in the era of the horse is closed. We will not see his like again.

10-1-58

THE FARM WOMAN

Surely one of the most encouraging things that has happened to this area in a long time is the decision of the Southwestern Bell Telephone Company to erect a two-million-dollar structure in Emporia.

A sketch of the building hangs in the Chamber of Commerce office. The erection of this building required no bond issue, aroused no community controversy, and yet it will be the most costly edifice in the town. We now live in the electronic age and this building will have the last word in electronics when it is completed.

Then we can sit at our telephone and dial numbers in hundreds of cities throughout the nation, just as we dial our neighbors or dial the operator in Emporia today. (Hartford has had a dial system for a number of years.)

Approximately 10,000 telephones are served by the Emporia office at the present time. Thus an expenditure of $200 per phone will bring this new marvel within our reach. There are 1,500,000 stock-holders of A. T. & T. scattered throughout the country. Slightly more than $1 per stockholder will be expended on this one new structure with its equipment and connections.

******

The first telephone in Hartford was promoted b y the banker's son soon after the turn of the century. No doubt he had seen the telephone at the World's Fair. He had seen a telephone in Emporia. He figured that what was good enough for Emporia and other cities was good enough for his home town. Three forward looking farmers on the south side of the river, agreed to put up $200 each in advance rent. For this they were promised telephones.

Some siren voice on the north side of the river prevailed upon the young man to string his wire and poles (straight round poles which were shipped in) on that side of the river instead. When the three farmers on the south side heard of this, they waited upon the young man. In forceful language they prevailed upon him to abide by his original plan and agreement. The poles and the wire were moved and the first line came down the south side of the river. Sometime later the Hartford Telephone Com-pany was formed and this marvel of communication became a convenience in many households.

******

Falling upon sad days in operation and management, the Hartford exchange was acquired by the Emporia company. Local operators continued to operate the battered and time worn switchboard.

The last operator at Hartford was Mrs. Marion Smith. When dial phones arrived, she moved on to increased pay and shorter hours. One wonders if she does not miss the intimacy and the affectionate depen-dency with which the customers regarded her. Every advance in civilization has its heartaches as well as its advantages.

******

The Neosho Rapids telephone system was locally owned and locally controlled. Each patron purchased his telephone and paid his share of the cost of wire, switchboard, etc. Patrons went to the timber and cut poles which were supposed to be at least three inches in diameter and 12 to 15 feet in length. It must have been that nothing was said about poles being straight. All manner of crooks and curves could be observed in poles along the line. Elm poles were wont to leaf out when spring came. Post holes were dug by hand and the poles set and tamped. Wire was fastened to the poles by little white knobs. Lines were extended to the central office and lo, we were in touch with the outside world.

Members paid 75 cents a month for operation. Little thought was given to maintenance, replacements or a sinking fund. Fifteen or 20 years later, members were glad to sell to the Emporia Telephone Com-pany in order to get better service. Of course, this improved service cost more but subscribers figured it was worth it.

Soon after this consolidation farmers on the south side of the river were asked to change over to the Hartford exchange. Then it was that the farmer-owned telephone came off the wall and became a plaything for farm children.

9-13-57

THE FARM WOMAN

The new telephone building is a far cry from the day when Alexander Graham Bell called the first message over the wire. It is a far cry from the day of Miss Sadie Carpenter who was the chief and only operator at Neosho Rapids for years.

The position of operator not only gave Miss Sadie a livelihood, albeit meager; it provided her with a pastime and a social outlet, as well. She ate and slept and lived within earshot of the switchboard. The hours were supposed to be from 6 a. m. until 9 p. m. for emergencies. And emergencies were always arising. Yet I'm sure that Miss Sadie liked her job. She was the hub of the community.

People called Miss Sadie to learn the time of day. They called her to locate the family doctor. They called her to learn the latest news. She gave a line call to warn residents of flood or fire. Sometimes she butted-in on conversations, which the two parties felt was none of her business. They may have told her so in no uncertain terms. Their telling her off did not faze Miss Sadie.

Listening-in was Miss Sadie's pastime. Young swains who were talking to their best girls rebuked her. No matter, Miss Sadie kept right on listening in. No doubt there may have been some secrets that she kept to herself. However, she reveled in spreading the news, always she had eager hearers.
9-13-57

THE FARM WOMAN

Among the changes in the American way of life is one that affects the activities of boys in the summer time. Mary Frances McKinney, whose delightful essays on farm topics have long been a regular feature in the Emporia Gazette, discusses the change in the career of the town boy who used to go to the country to spend the summer on the farm. She notes what the machine age has done to these boys:

For a half century and more boys have been coming to the farm. Some have come for extended visits. Others have come to work for wages. All came and stayed because they liked the farm and the hum of summer activities.

These boys hoed weeds in the corn and in the garden. They rode the horse to get the cows in the evening. In fact, the horse became a daily companion. Likely they learned to milk the cows. They fed and watered the chickens and gathered eggs. They carried skim milk to fattening pigs. Before the days of running water, they carried water in a bucket from the well, and they emptied the slop bucket.

After observing for a time, and after some practice with the farmer as tutor, a boy might be trusted with a riding cultivator or a hay rake. A boy was never allowed to run the mowing machine. It was too dangerous for the boy and for the horses. It was not uncommon to have runaways. Frightened, terrified horses would come lunging into the barnyard, dragging a single tree or part of the cultivator. Torn-up horse-drawn equipment bore testimony that boys had been on the farm.

Today all is changed. Boys still long to come to the farm. They are willing and eager to learn. But there's the catch. What must they learn?

There are no milk cows on the farm today. Milking has become a specialized business, taken over by dairymen. The old saddle horse one day lay down and died. Chickens have become the specialty of poultry men. The garden is a postage-stamp garden. Gadgets have replaced many of the routine chores a boy was expected to do.

There are still weeds to be hoed and occasionally a boy comes along who likes to hoe weeds. He is likely a lad who likes solitude, who likes to get close to Nature, or he wants to get toned up for football.

Most boys ogle the tractor with its hydraulic lift and rubber-tired attachments. They want to run the self-propelled combine. Along with their eagerness to learn is the confident daring of teenagers. However, they lack the judgment and understanding needed to operate power tools.

A farm boy tags after his father, watches him grease and adjust equipment. By the time he is 10 or 12 he can grease the combine, drill and four-row planter. He knows the hum of each piece of machinery. His sharp ears may be the first to detect the trouble when something goes wrong. Machine know-how may be a gift. Continuous association with farm equipment polishes and tunes a mechanical bent.

The farmer has thousands of dollars tied up in power machinery today. He cannot afford to let a town boy who wants to come to the farm, handle this equipment. The risk of damage is too great. Even greater is the risk of what might happen to the boy.

At this writing, in the machine age, there is not much that a town boy can do on the farm. And that is lamentable.
4-29-59

Chapter 11

Bunnies & Birds

Grandparents have a store of knowledge to cherish.

As their children were wed, they rejoiced. Esther was the first to wed on June 24, 1951, just after she and husband Walt Stockebrand were graduated from KU. They were to live in Garnett, Kansas, where Walt had a car dealership. Tom, their son, was born there.

Kathleen and Larry Whitmer were married August 3rd, 1952. Jim & Zara were married August 30th, 1952 in Tonganoxie, Kansas. Kathleen and Larry settled on their ranch, in Zenda, Kansas and Jim and Zara moved to Tulsa, Oklahoma. They were to each have three children. Scott & Monte Whitmer born to Larry & Kathleen, then Jim and Zara had Meg McKinney. Along came Esther Whitmer on Kathleen's sister Esther's birthday. Janet and Ric were born to Jim & Zara and they rounded out the seven grandchildren that were to make Mac and Mary very proud grandparents.

Mac and Mary cherished their grandchildren, it was such a joy to welcome them to the farm and spend the time to visit with them. Grandchildren are God's way of compensating us for growing old.

When she wrote to the Whitmer grandchildren she signed her name with bunnies and birds, they always knew exactly who wrote the letters.

The following articles were written as a direct result of having many grandchildren to entertain on the farm.

Chronicles of
The Farm Woman

THE FARM WOMAN

For generations it has been the prerogative and pleasure for grandma to welcome each new baby into the family. Not so many years ago one messenger went for the doctor while another went for grandma. The newcomer arrived at home in the glare of the Rayo lamp, and was promptly wrapped in a wool flannel band. A woolen undershirt and wool blankets. Grandma ran the household for the twelve or fourteen days that the new mother stayed in bed.

Today grandma is sent for when the mother and baby will arrive from the hospital. Today's grandmother is a push-button grandma. She is as busy as any of her sisters in the pre-gadget era. She does not have to carry in water and wood, nor hang clothes on the line, nor polish kerosene lamp chimneys. Yet all day long there is one button after another to flick. The wise grandma will arrive a day ahead of time in order to get her bearings among the gadgets.

First there are any number of lamps, most of them with 3-way bulbs. The TV has four channels in its range. One learns how to turn it on and off and leaves the adjusting to other members in the household. The air-conditioner hums on the hot days of Indian summer. The furnace blows on and off the next day because it is cool. The exhaust fan speeds odors and steam to the great outdoors. The food freezer and the refrigerator clicks off and on regularly.

The electric coffeemaker, the electric skillet and the electric toaster must be plugged in and set. The electric churn, the electric mixer and the refrigerator electric ice cream freezer, each made our acquaintance. The bottle sterilizer must have water and be turned on. The dishes must be rinsed before they are placed in the electric dishwasher. The dishwasher doesn't wash milk buckets or jars or churns or skillets or baby bottles.

In the broom closet are brooms and mops, the electric sweeper with attachments and the electric waxer. In the basement is found the automatic washer and dryer. The washer must be set and detergent added. When the buzzer sounds it is time to shift one load from the washer to the dryer. The sewing machine sits close by. In the bottom of the sewing cabinet are overalls and socks to be mended. Grandma would not feel right if there weren't some mending waiting for her.

Each new gadget is carefully explained and demonstrated by the head of the household. Alas for grandma if she cannot recall the adjustments after being instructed. She is then directed to the instruction book and must spend time reading directions for care and operation of each piece of equipment.

The new baby is proudly carried in, in her basket with ruffles and satin. One wonders whether she will protest the trembling anxious arms of grandma when she has had the calm expert care of the nurse aid in the hospital. She does not protest. Right away she and her grandmother become bosom friends. She calls for attention at 1:30 a.m. after sleeping nearly four hours. And she wakens promptly at 4:30 a.m. again. That is the hour that is hardest for grandmother to rouse herself. Besides, grandmother knows that in little more than an hour, older brothers and father will be waking. Grandmother learns: While that bottle is warming she sets out the coffee pot and puts the coffee in it. She sets out the skillet and lays the strips of bacon in it. She sets out the toaster with the bread and butter close by. This means a few minutes longer to snooze when the household begins to stir.

Once the household rouses there is a continuous round of activities. Breakfast, caring for the milk, dishes, bottles, start something for dinner, baby's bath, washing, drying, folding clothes, an outdoor walk with older children, naps in the afternoon. Grandma needs her nap as much as any member of the household.

Gone are the flannel bands and flannel shirts and gertrudes. Today the push-button grandmother meets new gadgets as well as a new grandchild.

11-7-55

THE FARM WOMAN

Boys come to the farm in summer as sure as the wheat stubble is turned under after harvest. Children and the land belong together.

No man-made toys are needed to entertain a child on the farm in summer. All outdoors beckons to him. The trees, birds, bugs, the water hole in the creek, the pond, and most of all, the freedom to roam at will.

Another boy cares little about machinery. A true disciple of Izaak Walton, he sets out right after breakfast with a fishing pole, a can of worms, a stringer, and a quart jar of drinking water. He sits on the bank of the pond serene and content. Solitude means much to this lad. Soon after noon he comes in, hot, thirsty, hungry, with a string of small bullheads. Nothing could be more delightful to the taste than those bullheads fresh from the skillet.

One can scarce imagine all the things this boy observed as he sat quietly in the sunshine, all by himself on a scorching summer day.

The tree house is only a few feet above ground. It is a crude platform made of a few boards nailed together. The child who climbs up there with an apple in his pocket and a book in his hand may be worlds away in space or time. No one may enter the tree house or the boy's reveries.

And these are but a few of the varied delights of boys on the farm in summer.

THE FARM WOMAN

Summertime is synonymous with young visitors on the farm. From the time a young boy and girl start to school until they are 14, the farm holds them enthralled. At 15 or 16 they begin to find jobs and have so many interests that extended visits to the farm must come to a halt.

A 10-year-old from the city has come into a strange new world. For three generations at least, none of his forbears have been farmers. He speaks English, good English we might add, but his vocabulary con-tained few pastoral terms when he arrived. If the words were used it was from a consumer's stand-point. He is an apt student and learning fast. He has milked a cow, gathered eggs, picked up potatoes. Now he knows where these foods, which his mother buys at the super-market come from. He has learned to feed the hogs and enjoys watching pork chops and bacon on the hoof. He may be here for the slaughter, as one of the spring pigs is about ready for the locker.

This lad rode in the pickup as it followed the combine in the wheat field. He knows wheat grows and ripens and is harvested and taken from the combine to the elevator. He knows that one field yielded 61 bushels and another made 40. After the harvest came cultivating and now he knows corn and soybeans and sargo when he sees them growing. Both plowing and hay were waiting. Plowing is sandwiched in, in the morning before the baler is started. He has watched each step in the meadow. First the hay is mowed, then it raked and baled. The bales are piled on a trailer as they come from the baler and are hauled to the barn and stowed away.

He has gone to the pasture and counted the cattle. He knows cattle must have salt and water and grass. When they have good grass they grow sleek and fat and make good beefsteaks, which he likes.

This lad has no fear or caution. When a fat groundhog sauntered across the road the farm boy gave chase. The groundhog darted under a board and the visitor grabbed his tail. How was he to know that a groundhog is vicious when cornered? He has found two bunny rabbits. This called for a hutch fashioned from hail screen and scrap boards. Rabbits eat alfalfa, tender soybean leaves and carrots, tops and all.

There is a sharp contrast between this boy from the city and 10-year-olds in the neighborhood. The 10-year-old boy on the farm has definite daily responsibilities. He gets the feed for the cows. He brings the cows from the pasture. He can grease the cultivator and the plow and almost remember all the places on the combine and the baler. He can drive the tractor or the pickup when his father is at his side. In fact the 10-year-old on the farm knows the steps in each activity as the season progresses. He has grown up with these things and it all comes naturally. He must often make on-the-spot decisions. He must be self-reliant.

What does the 10-year-old visitor do when he is at home in the city? He gets up early because he likes to get up. He gets his own breakfast and then rides his bicycle. He plays with the store-bought toys. He watches TV. He goes to the swimming pool when his mother or father can take him. He looks forward to a drive every evening. There is no supervised playground in his neighborhood. There is not one single daily activity that depends solely upon him. According to his account his existence is pretty tame alongside that of farm boys. There are 35 in his room at school. Only one other child in that fifth grade has ever been on a farm. This boy is not from New York city. He lives in a first-class city in Kansas little more than 100 miles from the farm. 7-22-55

Another special boy on the farm visits and wants a horse!

THE FARM WOMAN

A 4-year old grandson came to the farm with one unalterable purpose in mind. He wanted a pony. He figured that if he could just get to the farm, his grandfather would get him a horse.

When some mention of the length of his stay was made, he did not refer to days or weeks or months. He was going to stay until he got a horse.

It is a well-known fact that grandfathers are indulgent, especially when a boy comes up with a request as sensible as this. In any age or clime a boy and a horse and a dog belong together.

The boy and his grandfather looked. A good horse is hard to find. The grandfather explained that he wanted to find a gentle horse, yet one that was not old and wind-broken. Further-more, he was not going to take one third or even one-fourth of his wheat allotment to get a pony. The child nodded in agreement.

When it came time to return home, the boy was not ready to go. His mission was not accomplished. With some reluctance he gathered up his belongings. He left with the assurance that his grandfather would keep looking.

How far does one range in looking for a good horse? This child's great-grand father roved as far as Zacatecas in Old Mexico in his search for horses. The year was 1883. With seven men in their party, they loaded out of El Paso with supplies, and headed south. Through Chihuahua and into Durango they drove, finding nothing suited them.

In Durango they heard of a ranch at Paso Hondo in Zacatecas. They set out to cover the 42 leagues[1] *to the hacienda. When they arrived, they were greeted by the superintendent, a lawyer from Mexico City. The holdings comprised 99 leagues of land, 40,000 horses, many sheep and some cattle. This land had been in one family since 1751.*

The visitors were offered their pick of 2,000 four-year-old geldings for $11 a head in paper money. At that time 75 cents in U.S. silver was worth one dollar in Mexican paper money. In addition to the sale price, three tariffs were demanded - The Zacatecas war debt, a municipal tariff, and a state tariff.

The Kansans' money was deposited in a bank in Chihuahua. They drove to the town on Zacatecas to wire their bank in Chihuahua. The message had to go to Chihuahua by way of New York City. It took three days for a wire conveying the money.

Several weeks were required to round up the horses, make selections and

---

[1] a measure of distance, about 3 miles

brand them. A horse to be branded was lassoed by his forefeet, thrown to the ground and a Mexican sat on his head. The ranch brand was placed inside a circular brand, then a counter brand and a road brand. Eventually 434 horses were selected. Seven Mexican helpers were hired to accompany the herd. The first day the superintendent and some of his men went along to get them started.

The second night out a bunch of dogs stampeded the horses. The next morning 186 head were missing. They had gone straight back to the ranch. They were rounded up and three days later joined to the main heard.

When they reached the Rio Grande in eastern Chihuahua, the Mexican helpers would not cross the river. Another tariff had to be paid as they crossed the river. Thirty miles from Presidio at the Point of the Waters on Alameda Creek, they went into camp for the winter. They made camp on December 8. On March 11, 1884 they started up the trail to Dodge City. Most of the horses were sold in Dodge. Some were brought to Lyon County. In all they were 20 months on the trail.

Today's child has the same intense desire for a horse that prompted his ancestor to seek horses in far places. Frontier days or space age, the thing a small boy wants most of all is a horse.

And now word comes that this boy has his horse, a gentle mare seven years old. Joy abounds.

M.F.M. 1959

THE FARM WOMAN

Summertime on the farm means visitors and vacationers. How dreary the season would be without them.

Fond grandparents drive halfway across the continent to see the harvest and more especially to see the newest grandchild. Grandfather knows more tricks and more things to do. He can make a whistle from green willow. He can whittle a lot of things from scraps of wood. He knows how to trim the pony's feet and he can look at the sky and tell almost as much about the weather as the weather-man. He goes up and down the garden rows and insists that the boys get every tiny weed in the row. The boys grumble and complain and would like to wait on the weeds to grow.

Most of the year daddy is the pattern and the authority in the household. However, in the two weeks that grandfather is on the farm, he is followed, quoted, adored. The young father must take a back seat when grandfather is on the scene.

******

And what of grand-mother? Surely, when she comes more than a thousand miles she can cuddle the baby and spoil him a little. The wee one is wise beyond his days. When grandmother is near, he whimpers to be taken up (and is). When she is gone he lies contentedly in his bed. It is a riddle known only to babies.

Older children cannot understand why grand-mother likes to do dishes? How can anyone like to wash dishes? Grandmother lets them lick the bowl when she bakes a cake, and she bakes a sample which they can eat as soon as it comes from the oven.

She patches overalls and

mends and darns and listens to hurried practice of piano lessons. She watches the children at work and play. For grandmother, this is a favorite vacation.

******

In other families it is the grandchildren who come to the farm. They romp about the yard and garden. A dozen times a day they dart into the henhouse to look for eggs. Hens cackle and scurry for cover when eager searchers darken the door. One would think that egg production would drop off. If some hens are too flustered to lay it is no matter. Egg production is no longer one of the major projects on the farm. Bright-eyed explorers rush into the house with brand new eggs.

The seven-year-old rises early with grandmother. Vacation is no time to sleep. She eats two brand new eggs for breakfast. She climbs the trees. She finds a bird's nest with tiny live birds in it. She pulls carrots right out of the ground for dinner. She finds a few red ripe strawberries growing on the vines and gathers them to eat.

******

Life on the farm is filled with adventures, not only for grandchildren but for the young father, as well. He wants his children to see the haunts of his childhood and to discover things that he took for granted. He wants them to learn where milk come from, and how foods and crops grow. He finds that life on the farm has changed while his back was turned.

There is no longer a milk stool in the barn. It has been supplanted by a milking parlor with gleaming milker. Calves are produced by artificial insemination. Farmers fertilize crops according to the results of a soil test. The newest gadget is a hay crimper to make hay cure faster. Bales from the pick-up baler are stacked on a trailer and elevated into the hay mow. The self-propelled combine is a miracle to behold.

Rain or shine, these are great days on the farm.

7-1-58

Chronicles of
The Farm Woman

THE FARM WOMAN

A six-year-old down this way has embarked on a journey of momentous proportions. He has boarded the school bus for the journey to school - school with the unlimited possibilities that learning and knowledge may afford.

This lad is no sluggard. He is up in the morning with his father. He hurries through face-washing and tooth-brushing with the scant attention a six-year-old has for such formalities. He tells his mother that if she doesn't hurry breakfast he won't be able to eat. There is plenty of time for breakfast but mother doesn't seem to understand that he is in a hurry to go out and wait for the school bus. He may get left if he doesn't.

The boy does not have to wait alone. Four-year-old sister wakens and dresses herself so that she can go out and help big brother wait. Just as her pioneer forbears on the distaff side came to these prairies to help the men of the family, this little miss helps her brother wait for the bus that carries him to the magic world of learning.

Well, this child knows when the bus makes its return trip, they will play school and she will get a full report of the day's activities. The children in the first grade didn't learn to read words the first day or the first week but they learned to match things. Matching is important.

May we hasten to tell this first grader that, although he did not learn to read the first week of school, he will be reading many things for himself (and his sister) by the time school is out in the spring.

Three seven-year-olds visited the farm this past summer. Two of these children attend large elementary schools in sub-

urban areas in different states. The third child is a Kansas farm girl. One child read the entire front page of the newspaper to her grandmother and had to ask how to pronounce only three words. This child likes to read aloud. This grandmother likes to be read to. The child's father was reading newspapers, magazines, and professional journals to her when she was 18 months old. He contended that she enjoyed those things as much as she did Mother Goose and he enjoyed them far more. Nor was the child stinted on Mother Goose. She learned all the rhymes. Now that she is in the second grade at school, she does her own reading and has to ask only new words.

The second girl has been a library patron since she could carry a book. A bookmobile visits their shopping center every week and the entire family checks out books as regularly as they buy the week's supply of groceries. One comes as natural to this child as the other. She, too, likes to read aloud. She reads with more ease and more expression than many eighth graders of a bygone day.

The third child, the Kansas farm girl, can also read well. However, it was evident that she has not had library service or the wide selection of books that a library offers. One learns to read by reading. Her book supply was limited. We could but wish that these Kansas kids who ride the school bus, could also have the regular services of a bookmobile.

10-15-58

THE FARM WOMAN

The latest news down this way is not the lagging harvest with wheat fields still so wet in spots that the combine suddenly sinks down six inches without warning.

The red hot news is the new black and white pony in the neighborhood. No man or woman has ever been more thrilled or excited than the lad who called on the telephone to tell us the news.

"Do you know what?" he asked. "We've got a horse. Grandpa bought it and brought it out at 10 o'clock last night. It is a mare that was in the parade. She is eight or nine years old. I forget which. She's got shoes on and I don't know if she is bred or not. She is real gentle and she likes us kids. She belongs to all three of us but I can handle her the best. We've been leading her around here everywhere to get her acquainted and I've been on her some. We won't ride her down today. I'm kind of tired and I know she must be tired too. Are you going by? If you do, be sure to look in the brome pasture, because that's where she is."

All those sentences tumbled out in quick succession. That terminated the conversation.

A boy and a dog, and a horse. This is a combination that has existed since the Spaniards introduced horses to these shores. The dog has been a friend of man and boy since the dawn of recorded history.

Grandfather does not fancy boys going after cows on the tractor or on a bicycle either. The thing one needs to go after cows as afternoon shadows lengthen into evening, is a good horse.

The boy rides bareback to the far corner of the pasture, to get the cows. Cows are always as far away as they can get when evening comes. No matter to the boy who has a horse to ride.

As long as there are grandfathers who know and like good horseflesh; as long as there are boys whose pride is in a good horse; and as long as there are cows to be brought in from the pasture on the summer evening the world will not want for peace and contentment.

7-17-57

Chronicles of
The Farm Woman

THE FARM WOMAN

Grandmother's Doll

When days are dreary and cold, as day after day has been this winter, activities are apt to be changed. When country folk are shut in on account of weather, television programs come in for closer scrutiny, magazines are read from cover to cover, catalogs are studied, and books are read. Women whose hands are always busy have quilts and clothes and crocheting to show for their hours of work.

One grandmother's thoughts turned to grandchildren in faraway states. She would like to visit them, but that is impossible in winter. She would like them to come and see her but older ones are in school. She decided that she would make a large, soft, cuddly, rag doll.

Now the grandchildren have dolls galore. This doll was to be something special.

She has large brown eyes which have been embroidered carefully. She wears infant-sized clothes, including training pants and ruffly ones for Sunday. Lace-trimmed petticoats and dresses fasten with buttons and buttonholes. A gay bonnet fastens with sturdy ties.

When the doll and her wardrobe were completed, all were carefully packed for a journey. A large package was mailed to a 4-year-old grandchild. A letter accompanying the package explained that this was grandmother's doll, come to visit for a week. The child could play with her, dress and undress her, sleep with her for a week. Then the doll must return to grandmother.

Betsy Wetsy and Tiny Tears did not get much attention during the week that grandmother's doll visited. At the end of the week the doll and her clothes were packed and mailed back to grandmother.

Now the dolls clothes have

been washed and ironed and mended. Again the box was packed. This time the doll is on her way to the coast for a longer visit. Another letter accompanies the package explaining that since grandmother cannot come for a visit, she is sending her doll. Since it is so far and since there are more children to visit, the doll may stay three weeks. Then she must return. When children come to visit grandmother next summer, they can play with her doll.

From all accounts this is a joyous plan, joyous for three generations, grandmother, mothers, children.

There is the excitement of a package in the mail, the opening of the package, the fun of dressing and undressing a new doll. Then comes the excitement of wrapping a package and sending it to grandmother.

Isn't this a cheery project for dreary winter days?

2-21-59

Chronicles of
The Farm Woman

THE FARM WOMAN

If he thought the cold weather would hold, a young lad down this way would revise his Christmas list. He would like to ask Santa Claus for a pair of ice skates instead of the space ship that is now on his list.

If that request should be changed to ice skates, it is going to send Santa Claus and the local toy store into frantic gyrations to find and deliver the skates. Months ago, when Mr. and Mrs. S. Claus began planning for Christmas 1958 they were certain that missiles and rockets, helicopters and jet planes, satellites and space ships would be much in demand. They thought that dolls and sleds, books and skates, which have been standard items for more than a century, would be taking a back seat; and that all the new-fangled battery-operated gadgets would catch the fancy of the young fry. Like as not this may be true for most children.

However, this farm boy, as for at least three generations before him, is an individualist. It is for this reason that he may change his request for that most-wanted gift for Christmas.

The lad has heard his grandfather tell how they used to skate on the creek for weeks at a time. The creek ran the year around when grandfather was a boy. They might build a small fire to warm their fingers. They never thought of a wiener roast or a steak fry in connection with a skating party. The boy might put some molasses cookies or an apple in his coat pocket to nibble on. All the neighbors gathered to skate. Up and down the ice they flew. On a bright, cold, moonlit night, that was the life.

The boy isn't sure whether his grandfather knew Abraham Lincoln or Daniel Boone or George Washington. With children yesterday was grandfather, last year was Abraham Lincoln and Daniel Boone, and just before that was George Washington. He is sure that skating on ice on the creek must be one of the worlds delights. Grandfather has told him so.

The almanac says we are to have a cold winter. Grandfather swears by the almanac. If the almanac is good enough for grandfather it is good enough for the boy. Even the weatherman on TV is loathe to talk of warmer temperatures.

Santa, can you bring ice skates? The kind that will produce as much fun as grandfather tells of having in the good old days?

12-15-58

Chronicles of The Farm Woman

THE FARM WOMAN

Going to grandmother's for Christmas is a childhood delight no matter the station in life or the generation.

Grandmother used to tell of going to her grandmother's in Ohio. Pies ranked high in her reminiscences. That grandmother must have spent a week baking pies, - apple, mince, pumpkin and custard. There were hog bladder balloons, knitted wristlets, mittens and stockings for all the children. The house overflowed with uncles and aunts and cousins.

My mother in turn told of going to her grandma's in the early days in Kansas. They started out in the lumber wagons soon after daylight. Boys would get down and run alongside the wagon, but the girls were not permitted that pleasure. They wrapped up in comforts in the wagon bed and giggled and tee-heed as girls always will. The mother and father rode on the spring seat. All the aunts and uncles and cousins came and every one received a present. Simple gifts they were, but grandmother had remembered them all. No one was cautioned about overeating and stomach-aches often resulted. Thereupon the caster oil bottle was reached down from the pantry shelf and a bitter dose followed sweet overindulgence.

In my day it was fun for a country girl to go to Emporia the day before Christmas and sit in Newman's at my aunt's counter and watch the eagerness and joy with which shoppers purchased long stockings, yarn, handkerchiefs and gloves. Do you suppose any country child is permitted that indulgence today? Or to be at grandmother's on Christmas even when all the Welsh friends came to call? I remember thinking that my grandmother had more friends than any one else in the world. Christmas day my parents would drive in and it was exciting to be there to greet them.

Going to grandmother's is as thrilling for today's children. We start out soon after daylight, but now we drive half way across the state. Little wigglers sit quietly in expectation. Each 25 miles one asks, "Daddy, are we home yet?" We arrive at mid-morning to greet the aunts and cousins. Grandmother remembers the collection of each grandchild. She has the pictures from the past year's calendars for one, the year's stamps are divided between two grandsons who are philatelists. A well thumbed book for another with the explanation that it was one of his father's favorites when he was his age. A bundle of quilt pieces for the child who likes to sew. For one daughter-in-law there is a gift which that son gave to his mother when he was a lad. That gift is hallowed with the love and adoration the mother has heaped on it. One can see that all through the year grand-mother has been remembering Christmas.

As down through the generations food looms large on the horizon. Plum pudding and pie and stuffing and cranberry sauce. Today's children overeat also. They may be thankful that it is the licorice flavored cascara that is reached for instead of castor oil.

Thus it is that grandmothers play an important role in keeping the spirit of Christmas.

THE FARM WOMAN

Small boys adapt to all kinds of weather. Cold winter weather is an adventure to them, especially since older folk seem to talk more about wintertime things than summertime. It is possible that the small boy is under foot to hear winter tales, which in summer he may be off in his own pursuits.

Even a bitter cold day, one lad down this way was out to see what he could see. He was sure to keep warm. He gave a detailed recital of his preparation to meet the cold. He put on four shirts, two pairs of jeans over his underwear, three pairs of socks (not all of them mates), shoes, a great big pair of boots, coat and cap and one glove. He could find only one glove. Somebody must have done something with the other glove, because he was pretty sure he had both of them. Oh well, he would put on the one glove, and put his other hand in his pocket. Although it was below zero, he had no intention of letting the lack of one glove keep him in the house.

Unless his mother could spot the missing glove or locate another pair, she will have a few more gray hairs, come spring. Keeping gloves and socks sorted, matched and mended, is one of the trying chores of a young mother.

In one way or another the hurdle of the lost glove was surmounted. The boy and his dog set out. Wild friends seem more friendly in cold weather. Scores of meadow-larks in the feedlot, hopped here and there and did not fly when the boy and his dog passed by. Cardinals flitted about but did not disappear at his approach. Snowbirds and sparrows chirped as if they were glad to welcome an observer and friend.

Rabbits were no more content to stay snug and warm in the brush pile, than was the boy to stay indoors, and be quiet, and watch television. Rabbits' goings and comings could easily be traced in the snow. The dog, which had paid little attention to the songbirds, sniffed around the brush as if he might relish a chase and a good rabbit dinner.

High aloft, against the clear blue sky, a hawk soared quietly and effortlessly. In a graceful turn his silver feathers gleamed in the sun, as he put on a performance es-pecially for the small onlooker. The hawk does not make all the noise and hullabaloo that jets and other planes do as they cut across the heavens. All around was a stillness that this boy liked.

All at once, the blue sky turned to gray. The hawk flew away to the timber. Night came on fast. It really wasn't the night or the cold that drove the boy home. He suddenly remembered that they were having baked chicken and dressing and fresh-baked home-made rolls for supper. That thought prompted him to quicken his steps as he raced his dog to the back porch.

Now, let's see, where were those gloves put?

1959

The McKinney Family 1973
Jim, Esther, Kathleen
Mary Frances & J.C

50th Wedding Anniversary Photo
Larry & Kathleen Whitmer, Zara & Jim McKinney, Esther & Walter Stockebrand
Mary Frances & J. C.

Chapter 12

Looking Back

The Junto[1] October 18, 1983

How many of you have used a buggy for transportation?

I am a child of the horse and buggy days. Father raised registered Hackney horses. They were high steppers. Loula Long Combs drove her Hackneys in the American Royal for years. Both my mother and father liked and understood horses. I was a fraidy cat. That was one of the crosses they had to bear. Many times mother

---

[1] In 1727, Benjamin Franklin convened a group of friends who met regularly to discuss issues of science and other matters for mutual improvement. Franklin called the group the JUNTO. The Junto program committee invites paper submissions on any aspect of history and science.

would drive a team that had only been driven two or three times. Father or the hired man would hold their heads while mother settled herself and had a firm grip on the lines. I probably hid my head in the lap robe. When we arrived at our destination she would get out and tie the team to a hitch rack. When we were ready to go home she would ask some man to untie the team and hold their heads.

When automobiles appeared on the scene the Hackneys were frightened and would try to run away. Dr. Northington, here in Emporia, had one of the first cars I remember. Father and Mother were driving a prized sorrel team along the road one day when his car appeared. A large hedgerow bordered the road. Father turned the team into it and told Mother to take hold of the lines. The horses reared and snorted. I sat between them and cried.

Occasional trips were made to Emporia. It is 15 miles. My grandmother lived at 406 State Street. She had a barn where horses were put. Mother walked up town to do her shopping. Two aunts worked in Newman's Store. They walked home for lunch. Grandmother had everything ready. They ate, washed the dishes, ran a Bissell sweeper over the rug in the dining room and were back to work in an hour. We always ate with them when we were in town.

We always had a hired man. He slept in an upstairs bedroom. Mother did his laundry. He lived as one of the family. The alarm rang at five o'clock every morning. The hired man would dress and go to the barn to feed and curry the horses and harness them. Mother built a fire in the wood range and prepared breakfast. There was always warm soft water in the reservoir for washing dishes. The first thing washed each morning were lamp chimneys. Two or three chimneys had to be bright and shining every day. It was my most dreaded chore.

We had a Jersey cow called `Butsy'. Mother did the milking. She liked to milk. Besides, `Butsy' had an aversion to hired men. She demonstrated this hatred every chance she had. Mother skimmed the rich milk and churned it into butter. She made more butter than we used and sold it to friends in Hartford for twenty-five cents a pound.

Registered Clydesdale Horses were used for farm work. Loose prairie hay was stacked in the meadow where it was mowed. It was an art to stack such hay. It was slippery as could be. In winter the hired man hauled hay from the stack to bunks in the feedlots. It was still slippery and had to be loaded on the hayrack with care. Alfalfa hay was stored in barns. It was a great day when some ingenious person invented slings to spread on the hayrack for alfalfa. A track and lift had been installed in the top of the barn. The wagon was driven up to the barn door, the sleigh attached, a horse hitched to the rope pulled the load up and along the track. It was released and the hay dropped in the mow. A large load had three slings of hay. You cannot imagine the backbreaking effort that saved.

Corn fodder was cut and shocked in the field. In winter this shock corn was hauled to feedlots for the cattle. In those days cattle knew how to husk and eat kernels of corn off the cob. They also ate most of the fodder. Pigs were placed in feedlots to trail after the cattle and eat corn that was on the ground.

Many farmers had more shock corn than they needed. Father would buy it and send the hired man to haul it. Sometimes he had to go five or six miles. In winter I had a homemade sled. When snow was on the ground, I would go to meet the feed wagon, hitch on behind and ride along. It was great fun.

The pasture was three and one-half miles from home. Father was a cow man. A good cow man knows his cows and the cows know him. In winter he is with them every day. About the first of May the cows were led to the pasture. Father, on a saddle horse, led them. A lead cow usually leads the procession. Newborn calves are not able to follow that distance. They were hauled in a lumber wagon. When I was fourteen it was my job to ride in the wagon. Mr. Winans was our hired man. (Why we called him Mr., I will never know. All other hired men were called by their first names.) Mr. Winans was afraid of horses. Clydesdales are even tempered but, with all the bawling going on, they pulled on the bit. Something happened and I laughed. He said, "Now damn you, laugh."

We arrived in the pasture and should have driven to the middle of it. Most of the calves found their mothers immediately when they were let out of the wagon. One little scamp took out and ran all the way back to the feedlot. Father seemed to know we would find him there. Sure enough, when we came home the calf was in the lot. They tied him securely and took him to the pasture in the buggy.

Every Sunday afternoon we drove to the pasture to count the cattle and look them over. A lariat was in the buggy in case a cow had to be roped. Also, a hammer and staples were carried to repair the fence. A bucket of loose salt, to refill salt boxes. Somewhere father heard or read that a small amount of phenol diluted and sprinkled over loose salt would prevent Bangs disease. He sprinkled each bucket of salt that went to the pasture.

Occasionally a cow will come up with an enlarged teat soon after calving. That meant that the teat had to be milked out. Father would rope the cow and snub her to the buggy. She would pitch and rear. I was told to sit in the buggy and hold the reins. What an ordeal!

The country school was the center of culture that existed in rural areas years ago. There were 116 rural schools in Lyon County in 1910. We lived across the road from Fairview School District 29, established in 1868.

A great pot-bellied stove was in the center of the room. Two large pictures were on the walls above the blackboards. One was of George Washington, the father of our country. The other was a of Abraham Lincoln, who freed the slaves. I recall seeing copies of these prints in a number of schools. We respected these men as leaders of our country. We had to memorize Washington's "Rules of Conduct". We also had to memorize the Gettysburg Address and the familiar quotation from William Cullen Bryant's Thanatopsis, and many more.

Our next door neighbor was my first teacher. She had graduated from Hartford High School and passed examinations to teach. Some of you may have known Mrs. Vernon Milner who lived at 820 Lawrence for years. There were two boys in my class. Nearly every grade was represented.

When the bell rang we lined up outside the door and quietly filed in to our seats. Opening exercise consisted of songs, a chapter of a book the teacher was reading aloud, the Lord's Prayer and the flag salute. Each class went to the front row to recite. We stood to spell words aloud in spelling class. Often the arithmetic class was assigned to work problems on the blackboard. The one room school was actually a review process. By the time a pupil reached the sixth or seventh grade he had heard the lesson material discussed and recited by those ahead. It was not as difficult as for some students today.

Children walked to school. They carried their lunch in a syrup bucket or tobacco tin with handles. They ate a cold lunch and rushed out to play. Noon's and recesses were great fun. I lived across the road and the folks insisted I go home for lunch. I felt I was underprivileged. I cannot recall that we had much homework.

Each evening we sat around the Rayo lamp on a table in the front room and the Emporia Gazette and the Atchison Glove were read aloud. As soon as I could read, I had to take my turn in this evening ritual.

Often on Friday afternoon after the last recess we would have spelling matches. Two leaders would choose up sides, and everyone was on a team. Sometimes it was ciphering or diagramming or geography. Competition was keen and exciting. We had to know the capitol of every state.

Box suppers were an annual event. Good cooks fixed delicious treats and put them in gaily decorated shoe boxes. A swain was not supposed to know which box his best girl had brought. Boxes were auctioned off. Older men would try to make a young man pay dearly for his girls box.

When mother came to the district as a bride she was told to fix a dainty lunch and pack it in a shoe box. No mention was made of decoration. She fixed the lunch and put in a plain red shoe box tied with string. When the auctioneer came to this box he assured the crowd that this woman put in her time and effort on an extra delicious meal. No doubt father bought it after much hilarity. The proceeds of a box supper were used to buy something extra for the school such as library books or an unabridged dictionary.

The year that Oklahoma was admitted to the Union, our school had an elaborate program. An 8th grade boy played the part of Uncle Sam in striped pants and a cutaway coat and top hat. A girl in the first grade was Oklahoma, the new state. Other dignitaries were represented. The schoolhouse was filled with onlookers.

Sometimes pupils worked at noon and recess to string popcorn and cranberries for Christmas decorations. Holly and Yule trees were drawn on blackboards in colored chalk. A cedar tree was cut and brought in to be decorated. Each child had a part in the program. Proud parents were on hand. At the close of the program the teacher had treats for each pupil.

The last day of school was quite an occasion. Some of the men played andy-over with the pupils or other games. Planks were set on top of some desks for the good dinner the women of the district brought. After dinner and a short program, report cards were handed out.

I had four teachers in the country school. Each one was a graduate of Hartford schools who had passed examinations to qualify them to teach. Eunice Hunt walked out on the MK&T railroad track. I cannot recall that she ever missed a day of school. They kept the railroad tracks clear. In the coldest months she gave me fifty cents a month to start the fire in the mornings. I once asked her if she ever felt sorry for herself, having to walk so far each day. She replied, "that thought never occurred" to her.

In order to graduate from the 8th grade, a pupil had to pass county examinations. Graduation exercises were in Emporia. I remember that I wore an embroidered voile dress and a straw hat with lotus blossoms around the crown. Only a handful of rural 8th grade graduates attended high school before World War I. Country boys and girls who went to Hartford had light housekeeping rooms with kitchen privileges. Many girls who did attend dropped out of school to get married.

Not long ago I was asked if 1983 isn't the worst year the country has ever had. This is a sad year for farmers, especially those who are deep in debt for land and machinery.

My mother was six years old at the time of the grasshopper invasion in 1874. Not a leaf or blade of grass was left. The hoppers got into houses and ate curtains and bedding. Somehow they survived.

I vividly remember the year 1907. The recession of that year was called a money panic. In April of that year my three-year-old brother who had always been robust and happy became ill with pneumonia and died. Mother was a graduate of Kansas University. One of my father's sisters said the reason little John died was that no one with an education knew how to raise children. (Little cabbages have big ears. I shall never forget that remark.)

Father frequently had a note at the Citizens Bank. A note was due. Tax paying time loomed in the near future. He and mother decided to pick out a carload of cattle and ship them to Kansas City. Neosho Rapids is four miles from the farm. The cattle were driven to the stock pens there along the Santa Fe. A cattle car was set out on the siding and the cattle loaded. The train was due to leave in early evening. Father came home after the cattle were loaded to change clothes to accompany the cattle. Mother and I took him over in the buggy.

Soon a headlight appeared up the track, although it was not yet dark. The conductor and the engineer were mad that they had to stop the train to pick up one measly car. The brakeman detached the engine from the rest of the train and opened the switch to get the car of cattle. The fireman opened the door to the fire box. Great flames billowed out as he scooped in more coal. The steam whistle blared.

Father could shout and be heard nearly a mile. He shouted to the conductor to break that train in the middle and not put frightened cattle right next to the engine. His shouts were ignored. The train was coupled and the whistle roared "A' aboard". The train was beginning to gain speed as it reached the station platform. Father swung on board.

It was a troubled homecoming for mother and me. She unhitched the horse and put it in the barn.

Some of the cattle were dead on arrival. Some were maimed. I know that father put in a claim. What he received, how they paid the taxes and interest I do not know. Somehow we survived.

That is my feeling for troubled farm families today. Somehow they will survive.

One of the most touching stories she wrote in her last articles dealt with visiting the cemetery on Memorial Day and this excerpt about a little old woman:

For years a little old woman visited Maplewood Cemetery every Memorial Day. She carried a basket of short-stemmed red roses on her arm. Slowly she walked about the older section, pausing to read the name and inscription on one stone after another. Gently she tossed a red rose on the grave of a departed friend, a red rose for memories of associations and good times, perhaps of suffering or kindness and forbearance. She was in no hurry She walked until her last red rose was gone.

This woman had been brought to Kansas as a young girl. She had seen the survivors of the Civil War return to Emporia. She had watched Decoration Day parades as one of the impressive highlights of the year. She saw the cemetery grow in size as she outlived her generation.

Today this little old woman sleeps with her contemporaries. The memory of her annual pilgrimage with a basket of red roses on her arm, lives on. 5-31-60

Christmas Remembered

Second Prize Winner

Christmas 1907

By Mary Frances McKinney, Hartford Kansas

Christmas of 1907 came during my first year in school. A native cedar tree decorated with strings of popcorn, cranberries and colored paper chains, stood in the corner. We all thought it was elegant. As part of the program, shepherds and wise men came to the manger to pay homage to Mary and Joseph and the infant Jesus (a fine doll belonging to one of the girls).

Sleigh bells were heard, and in popped Santa Claus with a pack upon his back. He had a gift for each pupil and a sack of candy and an orange.

We did not have a Christmas tree in our home. Father said it was nonsense. He enjoyed trees where they grew.

As Christmas approached, Mother explained to me it had been a hard year. My little brother had died. The country was in the midst of a money panic. There was no money to buy presents. However, Mrs. Santa Claus had taken the doll which Frances L. Garside (mothers friend for whom I was named) had sent last Christmas and was making new clothes for her.

I did not want to go upstairs alone to sleep on Christmas eve. I promised Mother that if she would let me stay up, I would close my eyes and would not peek when Santa came. Sure enough, I heard him slip in. In a few minutes Mother said, "All right, Mary, you can open your eyes." There was my beautiful Katherine Cole (named for Aunt Fanny's real niece). There were dresses and petticoats, panties and a nightgown and cap. No doll ever had a sweeter wardrobe.

Years later I realized that K. Cole's wardrobe had been made from scraps of my dresses and those of Mother's.

Chronicles of
The Farm Woman

THE FARM WOMAN

Is it only natural for mothers to be concerned about daughters, especially daughters who are far away?

One hundred years ago a mother in Illinois grieved for her daughter who had come out to the Kansas Territory the year before. Letters did not satisfy her. Early in 1859 she insisted that her husband make the trip to Kansas to see how things were.

When the father arrived, he liked what he saw. In fact, he liked it so well that he returned to Illinois to bring his wife and five children to Kansas to stay. Thus were one pioneer mother's anxieties about her daughter, relieved.

Today a Kansas mother is concerned about her far-away daughter who is pre-occupied with child care and tending. When grand-mother remarked that the young mother has to work too hard, the young woman spoke up sharply, "Who are you to say that I have to work too hard? You had to carry all of the water that we used. You not only had to carry it in, you had to carry it out. I turn the faucet.

You had to wash on the board. You had to dip the white clothes in and out of the boiler. After rinsing them and running them through the hand wringer, you had to hang them on the line, and take them down again. I lift the clothes in and out of the automatic washer and dryer. You had to heat your sadirons on the cook stove. And they were sad! I set the thermostat on the electric iron. I can sit to iron.

You had to fill the kerosene lamps every day or so, and polish the lamp chimneys every morning. I flip a switch.

You had to carry in all the wood and cobs you burned, and carry out the ashes. I push a button or adjust a thermostat.

You had to help with the butchering every winter and help take care of all that meat and lard. We pick up a side of beef or pork and have it processed and frozen at the locker plant.

You had to spend a lot of time in the garden. You canned and brined and dried most of the fruits and vegetables we ate in the winter. We have a small garden that looks like a postage stamp in comparison. It could be that we have more bugs to fight.

You used to help with the milking every night and morning. You had the hand separator to wash and sun and put together again. I buy milk in a paper carton. You had to keep cream in the well to keep it sweet. You churned butter with a dasher in a churn. You made cottage cheese on the kitchen range. I get these things in the dairy case.

You had to gather eggs in the hayloft or under the mangers or wherever the hens laid them. You had to set hens and take care of them and little chickens. I buy eggs and chickens.

You went to Chautauqua[1] one week out

---

[1] **Chautauqua** (pronounced *shə-tô'kwə*) was a popular educational movement of the late 19th and early 20th centuries in the United States. Chautauqua assemblies expanded and spread throughout rural America until the mid 1920s. When the Chautauqua came to town, it brought entertainment and culture for the whole community, with speakers, teachers, musicians, entertainers and specialists of the day. Kansas Humanities Council

of the year. That is about all you had for entertainment besides church and school programs.

You did all of these things before we were old enough to help you. Yet I never heard you complain. Every single one of those things was harder than any task I have to do. I may get flustered pushing all these buttons and wiping runny noses or changing wet pants. But I don't feel sorry for myself. Please mother, don't feel sorry for me."

Will this young woman's plea relieve her mother's concerns? 1-14-59

---

hosts Chautauqua events today. Former U.S. President Theodore Roosevelt is quoted as saying that Chautauqua is "the most American thing in America."

Chronicles of
The Farm Woman

MARY BUTCHER

Mrs. Thomas W. Butcher passed quietly from the scene some days ago. For more than eight decades she observed the unfolding of the machine age, and the changes these developments brought about in our day-to-day living.

As a young girl in Sumner County, she herded cattle on the open plains. With her horse, she had to be continually on the lookout for rattlesnakes and predators. She had to see that the cattle did not stray. This called for resourcefulness and self-reliance.

Always a keen student of world affairs, Mrs. Butcher stood for culture and the good life. She was firm in her convictions. Yet she respected the opinions of those who might not always agree with her. She retained an interest in the land, in crops and cattle, and those who lived on the farms.

During the years that Dr. Thomas W. Butcher was president of the State Normal and the Teachers College, she was his companion, and gracious hostess to all the great and near-great who visited the campus. In recent years, as a memorial to Dr. Butcher, she and her family have brought illustrious and renowned speakers to the Teachers College.

The Butchers reared three children during their tenure at the State School. Today those children follow their various pursuits in Emporia. Thus Mrs. Butcher could gather her children and grandchildren about her frequently. To them and to the community she has left a legacy of appreciation for the good things in life, and the certain knowledge that one must struggle to attain.

10-3-60

Chronicles of
The Farm Woman

THE FARM WOMAN

The open house which Mr. & Mrs. Kenneth Staley held a week or so ago was perhaps the crowning achievement in a long list of attainments for Mrs. Staley. For the party was, in part, the celebration of her retirement after carrying mail on the rural route out of Neosho Rapids for 34 years.

Kenneth Staley carries on his work and his hobby, much the same as he did before they moved from the farm at Neosho Rapids. His hobby is evident to any passerby who takes a second look. For a yard and flowers, such as can be seen, reveal that a gardener extraordinary lives there. His hobby is a green thumb, nursed by hours-on-end of tender loving care.

Adeline Birdsall was teaching school when her father died in the mid-twenties. Walter Birdsall had begun carrying mail soon after the Act providing for rural free delivery had passed. He literally had to sell farmers up and down the river bottom, on the value of receiving mail every day. All that the farmer was asked to do was put up a box for the mail. Many of them were accustomed to picking up the mail on infrequent trips to town. They saw no reason to put up a box just to get mail every day. It was a real pioneering venture to get the required number of farmers to agree to put a box on a post.

After her father's death, Adeline decided that she would try for his job. She was a young woman, slight of build, but long on determination and persuasiveness. She passed the examination, she received the necessary recommendations, and she was appointed mail carrier. What is more, she soon up and married Kenneth Staley, one of the young men on her route.

Her description of 30 years as a mail carrier is a classic.

She saw more than the mud, and rain or snow or sleet. She saw the valley and the hills in all their grandeur, as the seasons rolled by. She saw the toll the depression exacted, when many farms were not quite paid for. Yet she saw many of those same families beat their way back in better times in the forties.

She knew intimately the problems of families along the way as they shared their joys and sorrows, their aches and pains, their fears and accomplishments. She welcomed new babies and she held the hand of one soon to be claimed by death.

When Social Security came along, it was a friend, the mail carrier, who helped older patrons assemble all the data the government required in order to qualify for payments.

True to her oath of office, Adeline kept all confidences to herself. She did a neighborly deed here and there as her judgment directed.

The title of her autobiography might well be, "Tell Me What the Mail Brings, and I Will Tell you the History, the Character and the Dreams of the Household."

10-4-60

Chronicles of The Farm Woman

THE FARM WOMAN

The old alarm refused to keep time longer on the shelf. It had been replaced by a more slender model, in keeping with those stream-lined times.

One of the delights of my childhood was for my mother to tell of the annual visit of the clock tinkerer. His was a visit looked forward to by the children, in fact by the entire family. He came in his old horse and buggy, usually in mid-morning. He would sit and visit until after dinner. Then he would casually ask if there were any clocks or watches that needed fixing. Likely he would commence on grandfather's watch, cleaning it and looking it over carefully. He brought news of the outside world and frequently he would lay down his tools to tell a particularly good yarn. Early next morning he would start on the big clock that sat on the mantel. All those little pieces were spread out on the dining table. The children wondered if he could ever get them all back again. When he eventually did it proved that he was a smart man, almost as smart as the president.

The clock tinkerer was never in any hurry. He might tinker three or four days or a week. His stock of news and stories seemed inexhaustible. And grandmother's cooking came in for its full share of praise. One morning he would announce at the breakfast table that he must be getting on. The boys would hitch up the nag who had munched corn and hay during her stay. Grandfather would ask how much he owed, draw out his huge wallet and pay the small charge. Then the old tinkerer would be off and away to the neighbors down the creek, never missing a meal.

If anything happened to a clock or watch it was laid away to await the next visit of the tinkerer. It could not be taken to town for repair, for only two trips were made to town each year.

The clock tinkerer would not fit in today's bustling household routine with dollar alarm clocks. He belonged distinctly to the era in which he lived. Yet his memory is one of the colorful events of pioneer life. 5-12-39

THE FARM WOMAN

The kitchen is the center of interest in the farm home. The once musty parlor is now the living room. True, it is used oftener than formerly when the blinds were raised only for weddings, funerals or annual visits of the preacher. Shutters have given way to screens and window shades and the latter are not drawn as of yore. Still the family and visitors gravitate to the kitchen. Joys and sorrows, the weather, fears for democracy, all are discussed around the glowing range. The cook frets sometimes and complains about folks under her feet. But she would not have it otherwise. These dissertations go on while the bread is being mixed, potatoes peeled or the dinner dishes washed. If the participants retired to the living room the cook would miss out on all this or the beans would scorch.

There in the kitchen sits the old black range. Along side it a modern new sister in gleaming white. The range sits close to the floor on short squat legs. The electric stove with its smooth table top stands boldly several inches taller on long, straight legs. It somehow reminds one of a Victorian grandmother and her granddaughter of today, clear-eyed, buoyant, and athletic.

How proud grandmother was of that range. In her childhood her mother had cooked on an open fireplace with black iron pots. In turn she had a sheet iron stove but she never could bake well until she procured the black range - a wonder stove indeed. Grandma's cooking was famous the country round. Now, at the turn of a button, granddaughter has heat. Controlled heat in the surface units or in the oven. No wood to carry in or ashes to carry out. No scouring of pots and pans. Another wonder stove.

One does not have to be the skilled artisan to get a delectable meal on the new stove as grandmother or great-grandmother did. Yet no doubt the feasts that great-grandmother spread for her guests were as appetizing as those of today. After all, there is a bit of the personality of the cook in every creation served.

Soon the old black stove will pass out of the picture and the new one reign supreme. 5-1-37

Chronicles of
The Farm Woman

THE FARM WOMAN

The fresh turned mound of earth around a hard maple sapling on the Statehouse grounds marks the spot where the memorial tree was planted last Friday. The occasion commemorates the 75th anniversary of the founding of the University of Kansas. Out of the ashes of Quantrill's raid and bloody border struggles the old North College rose on the tip of Mount Oread.

Some 25 years after its founding a country girl up in Doniphan County set her head and her heart on attending school there. She drove an old white mule to a 1-horse cart while she taught the district school earning money for her higher education. When the news got around that Kate was planning to go to the university the local Methodist preacher felt it his duty to pay a call upon her family, admonishing against it. Those were the days of brimstone and hell fire and the parson told her parents he would as soon see Katie in hell as enrolled in the university. Chancellor Snow, Canfield and Carruth were leading lights at this time.

Probably because her paternal grandmother was the widow of a Methodist minister, Kate's father told her the next day, with a twinkle in his eye, that if she still wanted to go to the university, she had his consent. She went. And she came to call Snow and Canfield, Carruth and Miller friends. No heart ever beat with greater zeal or loyalty for her alma mater. The annual pilgrim-

age to commencement exercises was one of the few indulgences she allowed herself. Her zeal was so great that it has carried on to the second generation of her descendants who are marking time a bit impatiently until they are old enough to enroll there.

Down through the years it has been the spirit of the faculty and alumni that has made the school great. The plant-ing of the young maple reminds us of that heritage. It's growth will challenge those who follow to carry on.

As a postscript it might be added that Kate's family did not lose their religion. They are still Methodists.

4-4-41

And, wouldn't Kate and Mary be proud of the tradition they set for the remainder of their generation?

Kansas University Jayhawks

1st Generation

Kate Blair Evans	1893

2nd Generation

Mary Frances Evans McKinney	1924
James Clifford McKinney	1924

3rd Generation

James Thomas McKinney	1948
Zara Zoellner McKinney	1951
Esther McKinney Stockebrand	1951
Walter Ralph Stockebrand	1950
Kathleen McKinney Whitmer	1951

4th Generation

Larry Scott Whitmer	1975
Sue Gile Whitmer	1976-1977
Thomas Evans Stockebrand	1983
James Frederick McKinney	1985
Bridgette Wren McKinney	1986

5th Generation

Kirk Andrew Whitmer	2010

Chronicles of
The Farm Woman

THE FARM WOMAN

Farm extension service throughout the United States is celebrating its 25th birthday. For a quarter century the Smith Lever Act has been functioning to bring more practical, more abundant life to farm people.

It must have been 25 years or more ago that Frances L. Brown came to Hartford to conduct a cooking school. It was more of a shock to the hired man than to my father when mother calmly announced that she was going to town all day every day for a week, to attend cooking school. The hired man was accustomed to meals served to him regularly. It was such a shock that he called for his time and moved on, a thing father could not do, had he been so inclined. He was constantly adopting improved methods with his registered Hackneys and Herefords, so why couldn't women learn something about homemaking. Thus he reasoned.

Promptly at 8:15 every morning the team and buggy was at the step. A good team could make the four miles in half an hour, allowing 15 minutes to tie the horses and get to class at 9 o'clock. I can see her yet as she drove off down the road toward new horizons.

The school was held in the basement of the Christian church. Women in town loaned their oil stoves and the drayman hauled them down. Tables were probably improvised on saw horses. Each one enrolled was required to take certain equipment. A spatula was on the list. I had never had a spatula before.

In those classes, homemakers learned for the first time to use level measurements and to sift flour before measuring. They learned something of the principles of cooking eggs, - to prepare hard cooked eggs without boiling, to combine an angel food cake with confidence. Many more essentials were learned in that week. These are the principles a farm girl gleaned second which have remained with her to this day.

From this pioneer field home economics in extension has progressed to the point where we have four hundred farm women regularly enrolled in Farm Bureau units in this county. The bases of it all is a live-at-home program for the farm. Extension continues to bring new horizons to farm women.

6-2-39

Chronicles of
The Farm Woman

THE FARM WOMAN

No matter what college she attended the old grad is lost when he or she returns to the alma mater today. She is lost, that is, until she comes upon a few landmarks that still remain. Even these landmarks seem small - much smaller than she has remembered them all through the years.

In this case the old grad returned to the University of Kansas at Lawrence. All was confusion until she neared Fraser Hall. There Fraser stands with twin turrets gleaming in the sun, with the flag pole atop it as in days of yore. The law school building, the art museum, the natural history museum, all look much smaller than they did when they dominated the campus. And Potter Lake glistens like a jewel in its wooded setting. This old grad used to think that Potter Lake was quite a large body of water.

Dormitories, classrooms, the field house, all were imposing. Yet, the most interesting sight was the students scurrying about the campus. There were a great number of youngsters who did not look to be old enough for college. She chatted with two of these girls and learned that they were high school students. They will be high school seniors this coming year.

Eight hundred to a thousand high school boys and girls from over the state have been on the campus for several weeks in summer camps - music, art, science, mathematics. They were as much at home on the University campus as at any high school in the state, whether it be large or small. They are housed in dormitories, they have a counselor (these girls adored their counselor), they eat their meals at the cafeteria, they swim in the pool. They are busy, interested, happy.

An exhibit of work done by students in the art camp was on display in the Student Union.

These high school students said they were recommended by their teachers. One of them needed a scholarship and was fortunate to receive a full scholarship. The other girl was sent by her parents because they were glad for her to have such an opportunity.

The old grad has now returned to her desk in the big city. She is forever grateful to her alma mater, the University which gave her basic training in Chemistry and home economics. She is gratified to see many changes in a changing world. Most of all she is proud of the fact that someone dreamed up the idea of bringing nearly one thousand high school students, giving them a challenge and inside look at the college of today.

If any reader of this column is critical of today's teenagers, and thinks that this generation is going to the dogs, let him hie himself to the campus in Lawrence.

7-27-59

Chronicles of
The Farm Woman

THE FARM WOMAN

This community was stunned and saddened by the tragic accident and death of George Suggs. For George Suggs was an institution in this area - one of those people who did what he saw to be done without asking or being asked.

He carried mail for more than 30 years and knew three and four generations of his patrons. Children raced to the mailbox to meet him. Often they had their first assignment of trust and responsibility when George showed them how to hold the mail tight and carry it to the house to mother. If children revealed family secrets, those secrets were forgotten before he came to the next mailbox.

Just one year ago he retired. What a party his patrons gave him, including a watch to mark the seconds tick by as he sat in a rocking chair. Alas! There was no rocking chair for George. His garden was the best in all the country round, his lawn and roadside ditch clipped the shortest. He helped in painting the church parsonage and tending the lodge hall. He fell from a new ladder in a heavy laden pear tree.

As an orphan in Missouri, George made up his mind that he was going to leave that part of the country. Some folk were visiting there from Hartford, Kansas. Hartford meant only a place out of Missouri at that time and he returned here with them. Fifty years ago a single hand could always find a job. He worked for one farmer and another.

In some way, he met the Milner family. Mrs. Milner impressed upon him the need and desirability of a high school education. She offered to take him into the family. Mrs. Milner may have done most of the talking but Mr. Milner heartily concurred. George became one of the family and lived with them until he married. He finished high school in three years, obtained a teachers certificate and taught school two years before becoming a mail carrier. He walked from Hartford to Emporia when he went to take the Civil Service examination and did not feel sorry for himself in doing it.

George Suggs, the friend of children, a good neighbor, a volunteer, has gone to his reward.

11-3-58

One of the Games we played at the One Room Schoolhouse was 'Andy, Andy Over'

"One needs a building over which a "soft" ball (not a softball) can easily be thrown and sufficient space on either side to make good playing territory. Any number may play. Choose two teams and place one team on each side of the building.

A player starts the game by throwing the ball over the building, shouting, "Andy, Andy, Over!" The team on the opposite side tries to catch the ball. If anyone does, all run around to the opposite side of the building. The one with the ball tries to tag as many of the other players as possible, but all on the other team try to escape to the other side of the building without being hit with the ball. Those who are caught become players for the side catching them.

If the ball is not caught, the side missing it must return it across the building, calling out, "Andy, Andy, Over!" as the signal to the other side. The ball must be caught on the fly and not on a rebound.

The game ends when one team has captured all the members of the opposing team."

Chapter 13

This is an article reprinted from the Hutchinson News on Sunday October 19, 1975.

J.C McKinney squints into the sun of a crisp fall morning and points calmly toward a small spot of open water in the marshy swamp.

"There's a wood duck," he says. A casual observer would have trouble seeing the duck, but McKinney has spotted it with ease. "And there's a young heron. It's a young one, immature." The heron is high in the sky, a speck against the bright blue.

It is McKinney's birthday and his 75-year-old eyes are as sharp as a young hunter's.

He and his wife are standing at the edge of what Emporia State College biologists refer to as the McKinney Marsh. It's a natural marshland, a paradise for biologists - faculty and students- who are making use of the area for study, research, and practical learning experiences.

McKinney talks softly and fondly about the area, pointing to a Great Blue Heron stalking stately through shallow water, to an area where a colony of beaver live, and to a bevy of dragonflies and damselflies darting through the air.

The McKinney Marsh, a few miles northwest of Hartford in East Central Kansas, borders the Flint Hills National Wildlife Preserve. The Neosho River flows nearby and the shores of John Redmond Reservoir are not far away.

"It's hard to believe it's Kansas." And that's what makes this particular area so special to Emporia State biologists who gratefully make use of McKinney's land.

"It's a different type of environment than we have in the Flint Hills," said Carl Prophet, an aquatic ecologist in Emporia State's Division of Biological Sciences.

"It's practically unique to this area, and our faculty and students are doing some interesting studies there. We are also able to observe species of plants and animals that, for the most part, are not found in either of the college's two natural areas, Reading Woods and Ross Natural History Reservation."

McKinney wants to keep the area in its natural state and was happy to make it available for use by the college in the 1950's when Clarence Gladfelter, now retired from the E-State biology faculty, suggested it would be helpful to the college.

Prophet said almost all of the college's field biology courses make use of the marsh in some way. Limnology classes as well as students studying aquatic invertebrates, plant taxonomy, ornithology, and other subjects find the marsh a teaching aid.

"We have students who are doing master's theses on several aspects of the ecology of the marsh," said Prophet. Birds and water fowl, vegetation, the ecology of dragonflies and other topics are under study here.

Mrs. McKinney, who was born in the house where they live not far from the marsh, points out that a type of water lily grows there that is found also in certain places along the Mississippi River.

"We think there are more than 300 species of plants and animals over there." McKinney said. Emporia State faculty and students have found at least that many.

McKinney is interested in preserving and protecting the area. His interest in preservation, though, is not new. When the government began to encourage conservation years ago, the McKinney's were "number one in the county" in conservation farming.

Much of the area around the marsh has never been touched with a plow. McKinney has burned it off a few times, but not in the last few years.

"It is the original marsh," he said. During the drought in the 1930's, some duck hunters dug a well to provide water for the area and hit pure gravel about six feet down.

A small gravel operation worked part of the area for a few years, leaving several gravel pit lakes, but since then the area has remained untouched.

J.C. 'Mac' & Mary Frances McKinney
At their home in Hartford in October, 1975

Chapter 14

Life as it Should Be!

Take note of thy departure?
All that breathe will share thy destiny.
from William Cullen Bryant's *Thanatopsis*

Esther, when asked to write something for the book, she chose not to write about her mother's activist activities in the community, the county, the state and the nation. Instead she chose to write about her as "Mother".

"My first clear memory of Mother is standing on the front porch of our farm house waving goodbye to Mother and Daddy. It was September 1936 and Mother was going to campaign for Alf Landon. Mother gave talks in rural schoolhouses in Indiana, Illinois and Wisconsin. They were

gone a month or more. When they returned in October they had purchased a Halloween mask for every child in our country school. Alf Landon carried every precinct in which Mother talked.

We lived across the road from the one-room country school. The teacher boarded at our house. Every day at noon Mother had a tray for each of us - Jim, Kathleen and I - and a tray for the teacher sitting on the kitchen table each filled with a good hot lunch. A student was appointed each week to get the teacher's tray. Mother went to all this work so that we could eat with the other children. I could run, jump a hedge and two ditches balancing my tray. Even when Mother was gone at noon the trays would be set out and lunch would be in the oven.

The one activity that Mother insisted on and which really was a great idea was that when Jim, Kathleen and I would have an argument, one of us or maybe both of the guilty parties had to go outside and run around the house three times. I can remember pounding along and counting, and never once doubted that this had to be done. Perhaps I had to run more than Jim or Kathleen. Of course, after three rounds the reason for the spat had been forgotten and peace could return. Mother lost her only sibling, a little brother when she was five and he was three. She said she 'yearned so' for a brother or sister that she could not understand why, those of us who were fortunate enough to have a brother or sister, would argue with each other. Anyway now that running has become such a fitness icon, I think that perhaps that's why I'm so healthy. I spent much time in my childhood running around the house.

Mother baked all the bread we ate. I did think it was very good. Sometimes she made cinnamon rolls. We took wheat to a mill on the banks of the Cottonwood River in Emporia and brought home flour. But, if Sunday noon came and the bread box was empty, we would stop on the way home from church at a little bakery in Hartford and get a loaf of that food of the God's - `bought'n bread'! I remember sitting in the back seat and eating a slice of bread on the way home. It was as good as angel food cake to me.

Mother made all the clothes, including coats, that she, Kathleen and I wore. Our family subscribed to the Kansas City Star and Times. Mother would see a dress in the store ads and then copy that dress for us. She made shirts for Daddy. He was too big for shirts off the rack. She learned to tailor through Extension from Kansas State. During World War II when fabric was scarce, she took an old wool suit of Daddy's apart and made a suit for herself. I did not have a coat from a store until I was a junior in college I did love that coat.

One year Mother gave aptitude tests to the high school students at Hartford High. Perhaps just the seniors. The students would come to our house, one at a time and sit at a table in the living room. They had to punch their answers with a thumb tack. The hole made by the thumb tack went through more than the layer of the test. That table had a 'holey' surface thereafter.

Mother's mother died when Mother was 16 years old. I've often thought what a remarkable person Grandmother Evans must have been to have passed so many outstanding personality traits to our mother. We were truly blessed with a wonderful and unusual Mother.

Her son, Jim, remembers his mother as being very even tempered and practical. She never raised her voice, but he did remember some of her looks and tone of voice. She never complained about what life had brought her. When they moved to the farm, running water was out of the picture. Instead they had a cistern for all their water needs.

She was quick to complement. When he was in the army she wrote to him with regularity, and he could count on getting a box of cookies fairly often.

She dearly loved being involved in Republican politics, and her two main accomplishments were a county library tax and mental health financing.

In what naturally is part of life, along with taxes, comes death. All things have a season. And we are born, not to live on forever, but to do what comes naturally.

Earth, that nourished thee, shall claim Thy growth, to be resolv'd to earth again.

Thanatopsis

It was fortunate that Mac and Mary were healthy and they passed their health on to their children. Mac had been gassed in World War I in Europe. Each year after World War II he had to check in at the Veterans Administration in Wichita to keep their records up-to-date, because he received a small stipend.

It was appropriate & fitting that he should die on July 4th. He was a very patriotic person. By his chair was always a framed picture with Lady Liberty, along with his discharge paper. He belonged to the American Legion, and he always bought a poppy on Memorial Day. The ever fervent patriot.

In his last illness he was only in the hospital a short time. He died in Newman Hospital in Emporia. The year was 1985. He had been on the board of the hospital for over 20 years and had seen it's expansion into a top regional hospital.

It was during their Christmas visit with her mother that Kathleen realized her mother was not well. She was living in the Presbyterian manor in Emporia, where she moved from the farm in December of 1985, after Mac's death.

"When Larry & I got there about 11 a.m., she was still in her nightgown and robe. She asked us to take her to see her Dr. as she wasn't feeling too well. She visited the Dr. and was put in the hospital. We didn't know it then, but this was the beginning of the end - six weeks later she was gone.

She never recovered, but she was cognizant of where she was up to her last breath. She never wanted to last a long time as `a vegetable' as she put it. About 15 minutes before she died, she looked up and said `something is drastically wrong.'

A former pastor, Rev. Pittman, said a prayer with us. She didn't struggle, she just quit breathing at 3pm on a cold winter day."

Mary died February 6th 1990 at age 89 of emphysema. She never smoked but attended a lot of smoke filled conventions.

The McKinney's are interred at the National Cemetery in Leavenworth, Kansas.

Mary's Legacy

by Margaret Sherman 1990

When I taught country school in 1932-33, I was fresh out of a teacher's college two-year course. I had a life certificate and all the confidence of a 19-year-old - but few skills.

One of my third graders, Jim Tom, lived across the road. His parents had just settled down in the family home to try to make a living for themselves and three children. Mac had lost his drugstore in northern Kansas due to the depression. Mary McKinney accepted the hard work and became active in the church and school where she had grown up.

One week that winter I stayed with Mary and Mac as there was too much snow to drive to town. I began to notice that this was no ordinary farm home. Jim Tom was a star in my schoolroom, learning more from the civics and geography lessons than the 8th grader. Due to Jim Tom's home environment, he comprehended far above his grade level. Everyone in the home was expected to do his share - even the two and four-year-old girls could set the little table where they ate. There was lots of work, but always time for reading and discussing the news.

One summer when I was visiting at the farm, Mary invited the governor of Kansas to come eat dinner with the family and hired hands. We're talking noon dinner, of course. I don't recall that we dusted, but we may have swept the floor. We didn't "put on the dog" - only put another potato in the pot and made extra gravy. There was never any pretense with Mary. She was the same person with all. She was well read, had thought through her ideas, but didn't expect others to agree with her.

For years, she wrote a weekly column for William Allen White's newspaper. It was called *Farm Woman Down on the Neosho.*

She worked long and hard to establish a Mental Health Center in Emporia. Home, church, school and community all benefited from her time and mind.

Her sense of the needs of others was well known. She always had time to listen, but did not judge. Many times I have poured out my problems to her. She helped me sort them out so I could solve them.

How can I put her loving spirit and her wise influence down on a piece of paper? I had to try, for I just found out that she died February 6th, a vibrant force in many lives - right up to the last.

Margaret was a long time family friend. She was Margaret Turner when single.

Editorials

Mary

By Barbara White Walker

I CANNOT not write something about Mary McKinney, for she was the kind of person who gets in your head and stays there.

But I did not know her well, as I would have liked to; and yet she is there in my mind - her smile, her shine, her cute little top knot that sat like a coronet on her intelligent head.

She always looked so gentle that I was sometimes surprised by her quick wit and firm admonishments - but I was always thankful for them.

Just before she died she had one last word for me - told to a daughter, repeated to a friend and passed on to me.

Her advice was that, although local news is important, it is also imperative to keep Emporia in touch with the nation and the world. "When you go places - when you meet people from other parts of the world and the country - share them with your readers," paraphrased the friend for Mary McKinney.

We will do our best, Mary - but we will miss you and your guidance, your encouragement and your ability to tell it to us straight. It takes a special person to risk that.

Emporia will miss you. 2-15-90

With her keen detail and fervent insight we have seen her life unfold. The pen is so very powerful. She made time stand still and showed us the way the farm family endured, grew and enjoyed. As her articles graced the pages of *The Emporia Gazette,* it probably never felt like 30 years. She was telling us about life, as it happened to her, and we are grateful for this treasure.

This is her life's work in vivid detail, left behind for her family to cherish forever. An accomplishment beyond compare. Rarely do we leave behind a detailed life prospectus, a time capsule of our life. Mary Frances McKinney did, and how truly gratifying.

THE FARM WOMAN

After a series of long dreary cloudy days, the telephone rang. A neighbor was calling to see if we were watching the sunset. We weren't. There was a lilt in her voice and a sense of urgency as she told us to look quick. We hurried to the back door.

There, for all to see was a vibrant prairie sunset. Waves of color surged across the heavens - flame and mauve, scarlet and warm charcoal. The canvas was stretched cross the late afternoon sky. A palette held at the rim of the horizon gave forth moving, pulsating colors with each sweep of the ethereal brush. In that moment our spirits were snatched out toward the infinite.

Because a neighbor called another, both could feast on the glories of a winter sunset. Each one felt cheered and lifted up. And as the story was told to others who had not seen it, they too, were lifted momentarily from the cares at hand.

With all the blood and thunder on television westerns, with disquieting news in the headlines, with the irritations of the day's routine, it is well to !ook out at the sunset and thrill at its infinite beauty.

This morning the robin is singing in notes loud and clear and cheery that spring is coming. These are great days on the farm.

3-11-59

Each day brings a new dawn on the farm.
Sunsets, pale salmon, rich red orange and warm violet all beautifully blended, all harmonious…crown the day's efforts.
Mary Frances McKinney, The Farm Woman

Jean McKay lives with her husband of 44 years at **Elm Creek Farms** in Medicine Lodge, Kansas, where she has a thriving soap business. They raised three sons in San Diego, California where Jean was a travel counselor, for 23 years and owned a travel agency. They have traveled extensively and realized they loved the pastoral life. It was fitting and natural for them to purchase a farm in rural Kansas some 10 years ago. Their six grandchildren love to come to the farm.

Jean's first book *Tillie's Bridge* is also about a farm woman from Kansas in the early 1900's.